Jacob Chapman

Leonard Weeks, of Greenland, N. H. and Descendants, 1639-1888

With early records of families connected, including the following names: Bailey.

Bartlett. Brackett. Burley. Chapman. Chesley. Clark. Eastman. Folsom. Fowler.

French. Frost. Haines. Hilton etc.

Jacob Chapman

Leonard Weeks, of Greenland, N. H. and Descendants, 1639-1888
With early records of families connected, including the following names: Bailey. Bartlett. Brackett. Burley. Chapman. Chesley. Clark. Eastman. Folsom. Fowler. French. Frost. Haines. Hilton etc.

ISBN/EAN: 9783337317409

Printed in Europe, USA, Canada, Australia, Japan

Cover: Foto ©ninafisch / pixelio.de

More available books at **www.hansebooks.com**

LEONARD WEEKS

OF GREENLAND, N. H.

AND DESCENDANTS, 1639-1888.

WITH EARLY RECORDS OF FAMILIES CONNECTED, INCLU-
DING THE FOLLOWING NAMES

BAILEY, BARTLETT, BRACKETT, BURLEY, CHAPMAN, CHESLEY, CLARK, EASTMAN,
FOLSOM, FOWLER, FRENCH, FROST, HAINES, HILTON, HOME, LANE,
MARCH, MEAD, MOODY, MOORE, PHILBROOK, PICKERING, PER-
KINS, ROLLINS, SANBORN, SCAMMON, THOMPSON,
WIGGIN AND WINGATE.

By Rev. JACOB CHAPMAN,
Exeter, N. H.

ALBANY, N. Y.:
JOEL MUNSELL'S SONS, PUBLISHERS.
1889.

PREFACE.

It is said that few persons read a preface; but it is sometimes a relief to an author, to open his heart and say a few words to the few who are interested in the subject to which he has given so much anxious thought and protracted labor.

If we naturally prefer to receive, ourselves, the credit for any supposed preëminence we have attained, still I presume we all feel some pride of birth; and most of us are willing to admit that for this preëminence we are in some measure indebted to those who have gone before us. We cannot deny that physical health as well as disease is often hereditary, and mental and moral traits seem to be inherited. Still it is sad to see that so many seem willing to forget their progenitors as soon as they are put under ground. They will not be willing to hear it said that their forefathers were mean men, and their foremothers worthless women. They may contribute to erect over their ashes marble slabs or granite columns, containing the brief inscriptions that will be seen and read by few of the relatives, but will grudge a single dollar needed to prepare printed records that will be preserved on hundreds of pages, and be read by thousands of the friends and relatives, and be easily consulted for centuries to come.

Does not every man like to have us believe that he comes of good blood, of a stock, in some respects, above the av-

erage of humanity? And yet, when this is true, how
many are willing to spend the time and means necessary
to *prove* this fact, and perpetuate the memory of it?

Whatever attainments we have made by our own energy and industry, it will be hard to prove that we are indebted to none of our predecessors for the energy and the
opportunities which have enabled us to make these acqui-
sitions. Thousands have died in obscurity who, had they
inherited the health, the mental vigor, and the opportunities for improvement which we have enjoyed, might have
surpassed us.

It is not strictly true that "circumstances make the
man ;" but it must be admitted that they must afford him
the means to make himself or he will never become a man.

When we are tempted to despise the wisdom of the past,
and to imagine that we, alone, are to be credited with the
rich results of "advanced thought" it will be well to remember the words of the apostle who died 1800 years ago.
"Who maketh thee to differ? and what hast thou that thou
didst not receive? But if thou didst receive it, why dost
thou glory as if thou hadst not received it?" (1 COR.
4 : 7, *Revised version.*)

By birth we inherit not only brains, and a natural incli-
nation to use them, but many advantages of social surround-
ings which ought to enable us to rise above those from
whom we have inherited these possessions. If we stand
on the shoulders of other men, ought we not to see farther
than they? If we do not, we must have become very short-
sighted.

It is reasonable that we should feel some pleasure in the
thought that much of what men see in us worthy of com-
mendation may be inherited from worthy ancestors. And
if we have no interest in preserving the records and per-
petuating the memory of our worthy ancestors, may not

others suspect that our reputation will suffer in comparison with the reputation of those from whom we are descended?

If some families degenerate and die out, and others leave to their offspring no precepts nor examples to kindle aspirations for pure principles and noble characters, still the descendants of the unworthy and unfortunate do sometimes learn to avoid those habits and control those passions which tend to degrade our better nature, and to shun the paths which led their fathers astray.

The true man will not fail to profit by knowing the history of his ancestors. If any of them have been swept away from the right course, and been shipwrecked, he will receive an impressive lesson, teaching him to avoid the shoals and the rocks upon which they were driven. If, on the other hand, they have been persons of intelligence and true worth, shining as lights in a dark world, he will find the path of duty brighter and more pleasant when illumined by the light of their principles and their practice.

J. CHAPMAN, *Exeter, N. H.*

EXPLANATIONS.*

1. The name of the state is not given with the names of towns in New Hampshire.

2. When several children are born in one place the name of the town is given with the first, and not repeated with the name of each child.

3. Dates, before 1752 are in Old Style; and when double dates are given, from January 1 to March 25, I use the last figure to indicate the historical, in preference to the civil and ecclesiastical year, which began March 25. When during, that period, I find only one date, the year is uncertain, and we may find in different records that a different year is named.

4. Abbreviations: abt., about; æ., aged; b., born; bapt., baptized; ch., children; d., died; dau., daughter; m., married; unm., unmarried; rem., removed; res., residence or resided; s., son; w., wife; *s. p. (sine prole)* without issue.

5. The small index figure, at the right of a name denotes the generation of the person, dating from Leonard Weeks the emigrant from England.

6. The families are numbered in order, and large figures, at the left of a name, refer to the number of that person's family on following pages.

7. The children of a family are numbered by Roman numerals i, ii, iii, etc. These numbers are not always in the same order as their births. The grandchildren are numbered by Arabic figures, 1, 2, 3, etc. The great grandchildren by figures, in parentheses, as (1), (2), (3), etc. The great great grandchildren by letters in parentheses as (*a*), (*b*), (*c*), etc.

8. The names of children that died young are often omitted in the index.

9. Passages, enclosed in brackets followed by an interrogation point [ ]? are doubtful.

10. In spelling I usually follow the briefest and latest form, spelling those names among the earlier generations as I suppose they wrote their own names.

11. Many families would have received more extended notice if I had received their records in season. After completing the main body of the work, one cannot introduce much new material without disarranging what he has carefully put in its place.

---

* These explanations refer mainly to the body of the work.

(vi)

THE WEEKS FAMILY IN ENGLAND.

FEW of the families of early settlers in New England are able to trace back their pedigrees, with much confidence, into the period before their ancestors left Europe. The tradition, among the descendants of Leonard Weeks, has been that he emigrated from Wells, in Somersetshire, England; and of course that he was born not far from Wells. Though tradition has often proved to be unreliable, it seems that in this case it deserves much credit.

If Leonard Weeks knew the name of the place from which he started, when he left the old world, for America, his children could not be ignorant of it; and there is no good reason why it should have been concealed from his grandchildren, born in the place where he lived over fifty years.

His grandson Dr. John Weeks, of Greenland, visited England to complete his education, and different members of John's family visited England at different times. Is it reasonable to suppose they knew nothing of the place from which their ancestors came, only one hundred years before? Dr. John Weeks, whose father was one of Leonard Weeks' favorite sons, was the grandfather of Hon. John Wingate Weeks and of my mother. It is hard to believe that he left his children ignorant of his grandfather's birth-place.

There was a large family of the name Weeks, in Devonshire, England, and quite a number of them emigrated to

(vii)

America; but we are unable to find any evidence that they were nearly related to Leonard Weeks. It seems probable that Leonard's father died in England and that he had in this country no brothers nor sisters, unless William Weeks of Kittery, Maine, a few years older than Leonard, was his brother.

Note.—I am very confident that Hon. John W. Weeks, was correct in the statement that Leonard, his ancestor, came from Wells, Somerset County, England, for he was born near the homestead which still remains in possession of Leonard's descendants, and Leonard died less than seventy-five years before his birth. I knew this man, and his father Captain John Weeks, who lived several years, near his grandfather, Captain Joshua, a son of Leonard; and I do not see how they could have been deceived.

I have been earnestly requested to furnish for this volume, the coat of arms of our family, and would gladly do so, if any body would help me *find* it. My inquiries in America, and in England, have all been very unsatisfactory. Mr. Paynton gives me the arms of one family, named Wykes, as follows:

"Argent a chevron gules between 3 crosses fleurine sable." But I doubt if it belonged to our family.

A genealogist, Mr. T. C. Noble, Dalston, London S. W., England, says, in a letter dated, April 11, 1887, "The Weeks' family in the west of England was a very large one, in its various branches, with various forms of spelling, in Somerset, Gloucester, Wiltshire and Devon." "Respecting the Weeks of Devon, a lively controversy occurred, a short time ago, between Joseph Foster, editor of the Peerage, a Mr. Ellis and Burke. Ellis compiled a genealogy of the Weeks of county Sussex who he declared were descended from the Weeks of Devon, and bore the same arms. But Foster denied that the family were so descended, and certainly not entitled to the shield. The dispute is not yet settled."

Inquiries at other sources in London have met with no better success.

Examining the Parish Register of Wells, Chew Magna, Compton Martin and vicinity, Somerset County, England, from 1573 to 1680, more than fifty entries are found of baptisms, marriages and burials, of members of the Weeks' family. The Christian names are often the same as we find in the families of Leonard the emigrant, and his sons, in Greenland. The surnames of the same persons are spelled differently in different entries, viz. : Week, Weeks, Wick, Wyke, Wickse, Weekse, etc.

Sometimes we find two names, one an *alias, e. g.* : In 1619 is a record of the burial of "Thomas Weeks, *alias* Collins," who is supposed to have been a son of William and An (Weeks) Collins, married in 1500, who took the name of his mother in preference to that of his father.

So the father of John Folsom born in Hingham, England, once signed his name "Adam Foulsam, *alias* Smith."

By the kindness of A. M. Haines, Esq. of Galena, Ill. I have the following letter :

"*Kelston, Eng.,* 16 *Oct.,* 1886.

DEAR MR. HAINES :
I write expressly for the purpose of sending you the following entry, from Compton Martin Register, with which I think you will be highly pleased, and perhaps many more in the U. S. A.
"Baptized, — 1639 Aug. 7, Leonard, son of John and Anne Wyke of Moreton." [Moreton is in the parish of Compton Martin.]
"Sincerely yours,
FRANCIS J. PAYNTON."

[Moreton and Chew Magua are on the little river, Chew, which comes from the Mendip Hills, Somerset County, and enters the Avon, at Keynesham, seven and one-half miles from Bath. The Avon rises in Wiltshire and enters Bristol Channel.]
A. M. H.

B

RECORDS FROM THE PARISH REGISTER OF CHEW MAGNA, IN SOMERSETSHIRE, ENGLAND.

COPIED BY REV. F. J. PAYNTON OF KELSTON.

BAPTISMS.

CHN. YEAR.

1573. Roger Weeks of Sutton* bapt. ix^d March.
1591. Anne, dau. of John Weekes ye xxix August.
1592. Richard s. of John Weeks bapt. the 24th of Dec'r.
1593. Marie dr. "   "   " same xxii April.
1594. Saraie "   "   " same xxx June.
1595. Thomas son   "   " same xxiv Sept.
1596. Bridget ye dr. of "   " same viii August.
1597. Elizabeth ye dau. of Ralph Weeke ye 29 Sept.
1598. Agnes ye dau. of John Weekes xvii Maie.
N. B. 1598. John the sonne of Leonarde [eldeste son of Henry Wyke of Stanton Wyke] Weeke, ye xxiiij June.
1599. John the son of John Weeks† xxx Sept.
1599. Willm son of Jo. Weekse (? day or mo.).
1602. Francis s. of John Weeke.
1603. Judith dau. Jn. Weeke.
1604. Ralphe Weekse s. of John W. bapt. xxiv Aug.
1607. John s. of Ralphe Week.
1609. Mary, dau. of John Weeks, xvi April.
1610. John, s. of John Wickse, bapt. viii August.
{ 1610. Thomas, s. of Ralph Wickse ix Dec'r.
{ 1615. John, s. of Ralph Wickse the x Feb.
1618. Frances the dau. of John Wick, 10th May.
1621. Thomas s. of John Weekes xxviii Dec'r·
1625. Henrie s. Jn. Weekse xxx Nov.
1633. John s. Jn. Weekse, 22 April.
1652. John s. of Francis Weekes 22 Jan'y.
1654. Henry s. of Francis Weekes 2 Feb.
1655. Mary dau. of Francis Weekes 5 April.
1659. Elizabeth dau. of Francis Weekes.
1661. Joane dau. John Weekes.

[Searched to 1682 but no more Weekes.]

WEDDINGS OF WEEKES AT CHEW MAGNA, SOMERSET.

1560. Wm. Collins & An (*sic*) Weekes viii Feb.
1596. Ralphe Weekes & Joan Nattwage, ye xix of Januarie.
1606. Walter Blinman & Bridget Weeks were m—d.
1624. Henrie Weeke & Marie halle xxviii June.
1628. Ralph Weekse & Judith halle the 9th daie of June.
1629. John Wickse & Mary Wight,—6th daie of July.

[I read to 1672, but saw no more marriages of male Weekses.—F. J. P.]

---

* Sutton is a district of Chew Magna in the direction of Harptree.
† Brother of Leonard.

BURIALS OF WEEKSES FROM CHEW MAGNA, SOMERSET.

1565. Richard Weeks xxi Male.
1589. Marie dau. Jn. Weeke xix August.
1593. An Weeks v Sept.
1609. William s. John Week 2ⁿᵈ of August.
1611. Joane Weeke xxviii Feb.
1619. Thomas Weeks,— alias *Collins*.*
1620. Margaret Weeks, alias Collins.
1622. Joane Weeks Wed. xxx Nov.
1636. Frances dau. John Weeks the 21 Januarie.
1638. Mary wife John Weeks bur'd 20 March.

[I searched to 1640.—F. J. P.].

RECORDS FROM ENGLAND.

Copied by Rev. F. J. Paynton of Kelston, Somerset Co., and obtained by A. M. Haines, Esq., Galena, Ill.
Entries from Compton Martin,† commencing 1559.

BAPTISMS.

(*Wyke, Wykes, Weekes, etc.*)

1562. Johan [Joan] Weekes was baptized xliiijᵗʰ day of Maye.‡
1567. Agnes Wikes was baptized the xv day of June.§
1569. Alice Weeks, dau. of Michael Weeks, bapt. the xviij day of Dec'r.‖
1572. John Weekes, the son of Michael Weeks was bapt. the xxiiij day of Sept.¶
1573. Agnes Weekse, dau. of John Weekes, bapt. xix Julye.
1574. Roger Weeks, son of Michael Weekes was bapt. xxiii March.**
1587. Michael Weekes son of John Weekes, bapt. x̄i June.
1588-9. William Weekes son of John Weekes, xii day of Januarye.
1590-1. Alice Weekes, dau. John Weekes, 31 Januarye.
1598. Agnes Wickes, dau. of John Weekes, minor, bapt. 17 Maye.
1599. Agnes Wickes, dau. of John Wickes, 17 Oct.
1599. Sarah Weicke, dau. of Leonard Weyke (*sic*) 25 Nov.††
1601. Peter Weeke, the sonne of Leonard Weeke, the 30 day of Auguste.
1603. Elizabeth Weike, the daughter of Leonard Weike, was baptized the 12ᵗʰ day of June.

---

* See Mar. Weeks & An Collins, 1560.
† Compton Martin is between Wells, in Somerset and Bristol, on the road over the Mendip hills, eight miles north of Wells, and about four miles south of Chew Magna. Moreton is in the Parish of Compton Martin.
‡ See marriages 1585.—F. J. P. § These were doubtless daughters of Michael Weekes. See marriages in 1592. ‖ See marriages 1592. ¶ See marriages 1597.
** See his marriage 1601. †† This Weicke, I consider represents Wyke.—F. J. P.

1603. John Week, the sonne of Roger Weeke, was bapt. 12th day of Sept.

1605. Johan dau'r. of Roger Weeke, bapt. xv̄ daye of April.*

1605. Leonard, sonne of Leonard, bapt. the xxix daye of Julie, 1605.

1607. Benjamin, the sonne of Richard† was bapt. the third day of May, being Sonndaye.

1607. Henry the sonne of Leonard Weekes was Xtened the xiii daye of Dec'r being Sonndaye.

1612. Francis, sonne of Leonard Weeks, was bapt. xvii daye of Maye.

1614. Christian, the dau'r of Roger Weeks was bapt. the īx daye of October.

1616–17. Roger Weekes the sonne of Roger Weekes, was bapt. ix day of Feb'y being Sonnday.

1621. Mary, dau. of the same 25 March.

1624. Thomas the sonne of Roger Weekes, bapt. the 11th day of April.

1628. Elizabeth Weeks, the daur. of John Weeke, bapt. 2 day of Nov.

1630. Sara Weeks, the daur. of Same, bapt. 5th day of Sept.

1632. Ann the daughter of Raffe Weeke of Moreton bapt. 30 May [in Compten].‡

1633. Roger the sonne of John Weekes, the son of Roger, dec'd bapt. 5 April.

1634–5. Martin§ Weeks son of Jn. Week (*sic*) was bapt. the 8th of Jan'y.

1637. William the son of John Weekes & Agnes, his wife, bapt. the 10th day of Sept.

1637. Henry the son of Rafe Weekes & Judith his wife, bapt. 8th day of November.

1639. *Leonard, sone of John & Anne Wyke* of Moreton was bapt. Aug. 7.

MARRIAGES.   COMPTEN MARTIN, SOMERSET.

Ao. 1585. William Davys married Johan Weekes, of this parish, the 11th day of November.

1592. Benjamin Cannard was married unto Alice Weekes, the xvij th day of Auguste.

1597. John Wikes, sonn of Michaell Weekes of this parish, was married to Johan Payson the 8th day of Aprile.

1597. John Bates was married to Agnes Wikes, daughter of Michaell Weekes, the 29th day of May.

1601. "Roger Weeke of this parish was married to Eddith Hotkins, dau. of Wm. Hotkins‖ of this parish, the 23d day of Aprile were married."

(N. B. Leonard Weeks' servant was married this year.)

1613. Thomas James of this parish was married unto Margaret Weekse of the same parish, the last day of Januarie.

---

* See marriage 1628.
† I should judge Richard a clerical error for Roger.—F. J. P.
‡ See marriage of Ralfe Weeks and Judith Hale at Chew Magna 9 June, 1628.—
F. J. P.   § Or Marlow,—indistinct.   ‖ Hodgkins?

1621. Henry Millard & Als Wickes* the XVI of Aprile.
1628. John Cooke & Joane Weekes was married the 21st day of
Aprile.

BURIALS OF THE WEEKS, AT COMPTEN MARTEN, SOMERSET CO.

Ao. 1559. John Weeks, was buried the 8th day of March.
1565-6. Johan Weekes widow, the 26th day of January.
1568-9. Alice Weekes, widow, XVI day of February.
1572. Ambrose Weekes, 23d day of ffebruarie.
1598. Agnes Wikes, dau. Jn. Wikes was buried the 6th day of
June.
1605. Margaret Ardin† servant of Leonard Weeke,‡ was buried
the 29th of Julie.
1612. Jane Weeks was buried the 27th day of Aprile.
1613-14. Jane Weekes was buried the 4th Februarie.
1618. Michael Weeke of High Hall, was buried, the 27th daye of
Maye, being Wenysedaye.
1618. Harrye, the soune of Leonard Weeke was buried the 6th
day of October, being Wensedaye.§
1619-20. Annis Weekes, dau. of Jonne (!) Weeke was buried the
17th day of Februarie, being Thursdaye
1625. Thomas the son of Roger Weeks,— the 7th day Aprile.
Ano 1625-7. Leonard Weeks of Moreton was buried 27 Feb ‖
1628-9. Roger Weeks of Moreton was buried the 17th day of Feb.
1631. The XI day of auguste was Agnes Weeke buried.
1639. Christian Harding, servant to John Wyke¶ of Moreton.
[buried.]

PROBATE RECORDS IN WELLS, ENG.

In May, 1887, by request, Mr. Paynton examined the
Records of the Probate Court, in Wells, and found that
all the wills from 1626 to 1660 (the date of the Restora-
tion) are missing removed, it is supposed, in the Com-
monwealth times and ultimately lost. If we had the wills
made during this period, they might probably throw much
light upon the question respecting the ancestry of Leonard
Weeks of Greenland, N. H.

---

*Or Hickes?   †For Arding?
‡ This Leonard was doubtless, the grandfather, through John Weekes of Leon-
ard of Greenland.—F. J. P.
§ Uncle of Leonard, the emigrant.
‖ This was grandfather of Leonard the emigrant, I take it. His son, Leonard,
died in 1618, in the Vita Patris.—F. J. P.
¶ "This John Wyke is the father of Leonard the emigrant.—F. J. P.

I copy a few abstracts from wills dated later than 1660, which may perhaps aid others, inquiring for their ancestry in England, if they do not substantiate our opinions about the origin of Leonard Weeks.

FROM WILLS, IN THE PROBATE OFFICE, WELLS, ENGLAND.

COPIED BY REV. F. J. PAYNTON, OF KELSTON, ENG., MAY, 1887.

The Will of Ann Weaks of Morton, in p'ish of Compton Martin, Single Woman (sic) dated 20 Feb., 1662. "I give and bequth unto my bro'r henry Weakes £40 wh. my fathr gave me" [& other small things]. "To my sistr Elizabeth one shilling. Item, I give to Richard Grayle 1ˢ I give to Ez-ill Grayle 1ˢ All the rest of my goods to my sister Ester, make her my holl & Solle Ex'or." Signed X.

Proved at Wells 25 Feb'y, 1662.

II.

Francis Weak of K—— in Chew Magna dated 2 Nov., 1665. [Religious preface]. "To Frances, my wife 'her thirds,' of all my laud
To my daur. Ann, £100.
"   "   " Elizab. £.100
To my Sonne, henrie, my ground at Kingson, for life. Residue to——
J. John, he sole Ex'or." Signed with + No date of proving, but valuation of inventory 21 Nov., 1665, £ 94-6-8.

III.

Will of Henry Weeks of Morton, in Compton M., date 2 Nov., 1676. [Religious Preface]. "Unto my Neve" [cler. error for niece] "Judith Graile £5. My Neve" [local pronunciation of nephew] "Richard Grauile £ 5.—my niece Edith Graule—my neve John King £ 5. To my dear love, Mary Badman, the some of £150, — all the rest of my goods to my sister Esthr, she sole Ex'or. To be overseers, John Fisher, the younger, & Leonard Weeks of Morton each to have 20ˢ" Signed with mark. Valuation £2112, 12s-8. Taken 6 Dec., 1676.
Witnesses, Thomas Weeks.
     John Weeks.
     Leonard Weeks.

Proved probably in opening of next year; indexed 1677.

IV.

Will of Petter (Peter) Weeke Parish of Wrington date 5 June, 1685.

"To John Wecke & his wife each 10ˢ· To Henry W. my sonne, my wearing apparell. To Henry Weeke, Elizabeth, Martha" [Hester or Peter]? "my grandchildren each 10ˢ· to be paid out of land at Kingson. To my dau. Idith Weeke 45 £. & dau. Mary Weeke 45 £.

If my son Henry shall refuse these sommes, Then Sarah, Idith & Mary Wceke to hold and enjoy the land at Kingson.

My wife Judith Sole Ex'or." No date to Inventory, signed by Thomas Weckes, John Joues, Leonard Weeks. No proof of will.

V.

Will of Roger Weeks of Compton Martin, date 8 March, 1692.
Names testator's "sister, Mary Bush" for his "2 best cows," etc.
Names "cousin Wm. Bush | a Lease called Ridelings : but the *profits* to go to sd. Mary Bush.

My cousin, Mary Bush   5 £. ⎞ Thes. sums to be pd. after Mary, the
   "   "   Cxt Bush £. 10 ⎬ sister's death.
   "   "   Ann Bush £. 50 ⎠

Residue to the above Wm. Bush, & he be sole Ex'or."
Proved by sd. Wm. B. 2nd Nov. 1695. Val. Inv. £95–12ˢ–9.

VI.

Will of Leonard Weeks of Moreton, dated 5th Mch., 1698.
[Rel. Preface.]
"Imprimis | I give to my son John, all my lands of inheritance, whatsoever.

To my son William £. 140, in lew of my grounds, called 'Wrastling Closes,' provided he suffer my soun John quietly to hold them.

To my son Henry Weeks £. 50.

To my wife Ann £. 15 [besides other such things] a bedstead at Priston in the chamber over the entry.

               "My copyhold estate at Priston."

"To my dau'r Elizabeth, one hundred & four score pounds, & an old peece of gould, of six shilling value, to be pd. hr at 23 yrs. or her day of marriage . . . " He gives small sums to people of the same parish e. g., Richard & Sarah Fyler, and the Poor of Compton Martin, of Moreton & Priston [Priston near Marksbury?—F. P.].

"To Elizab. Weeks dau. of my John . . and the rest of his children 5ˢ· a piece. To my son William's 20ˢ· a piece. To my son, Henry's children a claim on mortgage. Residue to son John . . . . to be sole Ex'or."

                      Signed, *Leonard Weeks.*

Witness John Athay
       John King
       Hannah Gray[as a marksman].
Proved at Wells 7 May, 1698.

Mr. Paynton has visited Wells again, and examined wills, made previous to those which were lost, viz. : the will of "John Weeks of West Harptree (about three miles from Compton Martin), Somersetshire, made 3 Jan., 1624. It was all in giblets & all to pieces; it dropped away in decay. But I made out" names of "Wife Alse, daughter Alice & sons, Wm. & John. He left his temporal goods to wife."

Will of Roger Weeks of Moreton, Compton Marten, husbandman, 4th Charles (1629). He mentions:
" Elizabeth Weeks daūr. of John Weeks my son, daūr. Jane, wife of

John Dock of Pylton.   Residue to son John, Ex'or.   John King &
Peter Weeks to be overseers. . . ." Witnesses, Jno. Ringe, Peter
Weeks & Thos. Pope.
    Will of Ambrose Weeks of Compten Martin, 17 Feb., 1571, mentions
" brother Michall Weeks, Brother Richard hypsley " (sic) [probably
sister's husband]. "Residue To brothers John Weeke & Michell Weeks,
they to be Ex'rs."
    Witnesses,
        Leonard Stephens, parson of Compton Marten, John Smith, Wm.
Smith, Richard Hipsley.

It was supposed that the will of John Weeks, father of
Leonard might be found in London, where are forty-six
wills made by persons named, Weeks, Wick, Wyke, etc.,
between 1635 and 1652, and Mr. Noble was requested to
search for the will of John and Anne, etc.

He says, "I have made an exhaustive search among the
wills, and administrations of the Principal Registry in London . . . and of those described of the district about
Somerset, and such others of the χtian names, John and
Anne, down to A. D. 1670, and I am compelled to conclude
that there is no will or administration in the P. C. Court
by which we can identify the John and Anne [Weeks]."

PEDIGREE OF LEONARD WEEKS FROM ENGLAND.

By Rev. F. J. Paynton, Kelston, Somerset Co.. Eng., 11-8-'86.

Founded on visitation of Essex Ao., 1634.

Hart. So. Edit. Part I, p. 535.

The Parish Registers of Chew Magna and Compton Martin, both Co. Somerset.

Henry Wyke, of Stanton Wyke [in Stanton Drew, Co. Somerset] a younger brother's son, of Henry Wyke, of Hanham Wyke, Co. Gloucester. = Willett one of 20 daus. of Thos. Willet of Batcomb [near Urington, Co. Somerset] sister of Mr. Willet of Lincoln's Inn.

Jn. eldest s. of Henry Wyke of Stanton Wyke = Bridget (dr. of Edmund) West of [Harptree, Co. Somerset.

(1) Blanche Nightingale = Peter = (2) Frances | Leonard Wyke | Jn. Wyke of Chew Magna by visitation, Co. Essex, in 1634.

sister of Sir Geoffrey N., the father of Sir Thomas N., Baronet, seat at Newport pond, Co. Essex.

Wyke of Newport, Co. Essex; Gent. of the Middle Temple, living 1614-1634.

dau. Wm. Elsington of Hormead, Co. Hertford, 2d wife.

of Compton Martin, 1599, appear by name in visitation, Co. Essex; but was not living there, buried as of Moreton in Compton Martin, 27 Feb., 1625-6.

Jn. Wyke, bap. = Agnes See baptisms of children | Sarah bapt. 12 June, 1599 | Elizabeth bapt. 12 June, 1603. | Leonard | Henry bap. Dec. 13, 1607. d. Oct. 1618. | Francis bap. 17 May, 1612.

Chew Magna, 24 June, 1598, res. Compton, when his servant Xntain Hardin was buried, 1639. Bapt. at Compton.

bapt. Compton, 29 July, 1605, buried 23 Dec., 1618, his father still living.

1 Roger, 1633 | 2 Martin, 1634-5 | William, 1637 | Leonard bapt. Compton. 7 Aug., 1639. = m. 1667 in America, Mary, (dau. of Sam'l) Haines of Portsmouth, N. H.

C   (xvii)

NOTE. According to their testimony, in court, William was a few years older than Leonard. William is supposed to have been the father of Nicholas and Joseph Weeks, the families among the early settlers of Kittery in Maine.

If this is correct, it will be seen that Leonard Weeks named his first son John, after his own father, and his second son Samuel after the father of his wife. Two of his daughters, Sarah and Margaret were named, one for his aunt and the other for a relative in New England.

NOTE.

Hon. John Wingate Weeks of Lancaster, born in Greenland, 1781, spent much time investigating the history of the origin of his father's family, corresponding with others who remained on the ground originally occupied by Leonard the emigrant.

He left a manuscript in the form of a family tree which contains some of the valuable results of his studies. If I could have had access to this work ten years earlier, it would have saved me a great amount of hard work. As it is, it now confirms the records which I had collected by my own independent researches.

It is a document too valuable to be omitted in a history of this branch of the Weeks family, and I have therefore copied it in a more compact form, making some slight corrections and additions which the author failed to obtain, or, perhaps, which he had not room to include in his plan.

Robert D. Weeks of Newark, N. J., has, at great expense of labor and money, prepared a genealogy of the family of George Weeks of Dorchester, Mass., including notices of Thomas of Huntington, L. I., and of Nathaniel of Falmouth and Hardwick, Mass.; but we have not learned that Leonard was related to any of them, or any others who emigrated from England, unless William of Kittery was a relative.

LEONARD WEEKS AND FAMILY.

THE name Weeks* is said to have been a Devonshire name of Saxon origin ; but it was also common in parts of Somersetshire.† Tradition says that Leonard came from Wells, in that county. The parish records of Compton Martin contain the name of Leonard Wyke, bapt. 1639, and his brother William about two years earlier, sons of John Wyke of Moreton, which is in that parish.‡

We know nothing more of the father of Leonard, nor of the time when Leonard landed in America. His name appears first as witness to a bond in York County, Me., 6 Dec. 1655, and next in the Portsmouth Records, 29 June, 1656, when he received a grant of eight acres of land, in Portsmouth. ["When he first went to the part of Portsmouth now called Greenland, he lived one year on a farm owned by Capt. Champernoon."—A. M. H.]. July 5, 1660, he received grants, of 44 acres, of 34 acres and 10 acres of

---

* In the old records the name is spelled in many different ways, as Wick, Wicks, Wyke, Weicke, Weaks, Weekse, Weekes, etc.

† Wells, Somerset County, England, fifteen miles southwest of Bath, is an ancient city, beautifully situated at the foot of the Mendip hills with extensive and fertile meadows on the south, east and west. It is said to have received its name from a remarkable spring, called St. Andrews' well. Its cathedral, a stately pile, 381 feet long by 131 feet wide, with a tower 178 feet high, is a beautiful edifice, commenced in A. D. 704 and enlarged in 1138. The bishop's palace, founded in 1088, is surrounded by a wall and a moat, abundantly supplied with water from St. Andrews' well. The city is small, neat and clean, with water flowing through its principal streets. The population in 1872 was 4,518.

There must have been a great contrast between this city and the forests of Greenland, where Leonard Weeks toiled so hard and endured so much to secure comfortable homes for himself and his descendants.

‡ Moreton and Chew Magna are on the little river Chew which comes from the Mendip Hills, Somerset County, and enters the Avon, at Keynsham, seven and one-half miles from Bath. The Avon rises in Wiltshire, and flows into Bristol Channel.
—A. M. HAINES.

(1)

land. In February 1660–61, he had settled at Winnicut river, now in Greenland, where he spent the remainder of his life, dying in 1707.

In June, 1682, Leonard Weeks testified that "20 yrs. ago, he put his horse into his father Redman's pasture, by leave & license of sd. father Redman," "which pasture joineth to the east end of ye planting of lot of John Redman Jr." John Redman, sen., is named, about the same time. From this it seems that he may have married, first, a daughter of John Redman, sen., or more probably his widowed mother may have married John Redman, sen., who is said to have come from the same vicinity, and settled in Hampton, not far from the place occupied by Leonard Weeks.

In 1667, he had married Mary, daughter of Deacon Samuel Haines of Portsmouth, his neighbor. She was the mother of six children.

During the political contest in 1665 respecting the separation of New Hampshire from Massachusetts, "Leonard Weeks stood for Massachusetts rather than for the crown." We find in the court records, 1660, 4th mo. 26. "Leonard Weeks, for swearing by God and calling John Hall of Greenland, ould dog, & ould slave, & that he would knock him in ye head," fined "10 shillings for swearing, & to have an admonition for his reviling and threatening speeches, & fees of court, 3 shillings."

In the year following, he was elected one of the selectmen of Portsmouth. He was afterwards constable and for several years sheriff.

In 1669, he "was on a committee" with men from Dover and Hampton, "to lay out the highway between Greenland & Bloody Poynt."

His seat in the church, at Portsmouth, was No. 4 in front of the pulpit.

After quietly occupying for more than twenty years the lands he had purchased, he was called into court to resist the claims of some heirs who hoped to eject him on the ground of a defective title.

I find records of four deeds, made on 23 April, 1706, and acknowledged 15 May, 1706, probably instead of a will, in which he conveys to his four younger sons, Samuel, Joseph, Joshua and Jonathan, his lands, retaining possession himself during life and making also some provision for the elder son John, and for his now wife Elizabeth and three daughters, Mary, Margaret and Sarah (see Appendix, Note i). He died before March 1707–8 (see Appendix, Note ii); but much of the land he owned in Greenland has remained in the possession of his descendants till the present day. It seems reasonable that his descendants should feel an interest in the history of the persons from whom they have inherited not only their names and their blood, but many of them their homes and a portion of their personal property.

1

Leonard Weeks of Greenland in Portsmouth and his wife Mary (Haines) had born in Greenland*

Children :

(2) i John,² b. 14 June, 1668, who d. before Feb.,1711–12. He is supposed to have had three or more children.

(3) ii Capt. Samuel,² b. 14 Dec., 1670, a farmer residing on the homestead. He m. Elinor, dau. of Samuel Haines, jr.,† of Greenland, b. 23 Aug., 1675, who had seven children, and d. 19 Nov., 1736. He was a man of intelligence, wealth, energy and influence, in the church and in the town. He is said to have built about 1710, the brick house which gave name to

---

* Greenland, a part of Portsmouth, was incorporated in 1703. In 1705, there were three hundred and twenty inhabitants. The church was organized in 1706, and Rev. William Allen, their first pastor ordained in 1707, from whose records, printed in N. E. Hist. Geneal. Register, I have obtained much aid in preparing this volume. They were found and printed by Wm. P. Haines, Biddeford, Me.

† See Appendix, Haines Family.

his branch of the family called "The Brick House Family"
as distinguished from the "Bay Side Family," which descended from his brother Joshua. The same house is now
occupied by Robert B. Weeks, one of his descendants. He
d. 26 March, 1746, æ. 75.

In his will, proved 30 April, 1746, he left his house to his
son, Walter, and a bequest to his daughter, Mary, wife of
Paul Chapman (see Appendix, Note III; also "The Chapman Family " in Appendix).

(4) iii Joseph Weeks,[2] b. 11 March, 1672; was a cordwainer in
Greenland. He m. Hannah ——— and had four or more
children. He joined the church in 1723, and died 27 Nov.,
1735. His son Jedediah was appointed administrator and
Samuel Chapman was, with others, appointed to appraise
the estate.

(5) iv Capt. Joshua,[2] b. 30 June, 1674; d. 13 June, 1758, æ. 84. He
m., in Boston, Nov., 1699, Comfort (sister of Thomas)
Hubbard. Her brother was treasurer of Harvard College
and a wealthy Christian merchant of Boston. They resided at the Bay Side, and had ten children born on the
place, now occupied by their descendants, the heirs of the
late Deacon Wm. Weeks. She died 20 March, 1756. He
joined the church in May, 1735, at the same time with
Joshua Weeks, tertius; but he was offended when his son,
Dr. John, became a follower of Whitfield. It appears
from his will that he did not, however, lose confidence in
the Doctor's ability and honesty (see Appendix, Note IV).

v Mary,[2] b. 19 July, 1676; m. Lieut. Joshua Bracket[3] (Thomas,[2]
Anthony[1]), b. 1672; d. 1749; and in 1712 had had eight children baptized in Greenland:

1 John[3] (Brackett).
2 Joshua.[3]
3 Thomas[3]
4 Samuel.[3]
5 Anthony.[3]
6 Mary.[3]
7 Abigail.[3]
8 Elinor.[3]
9 James,[3] b. 3 Jan., 1714; bapt. 1714.
10 Mary,[3] bapt. 1716.
11 Keziah,[3] b. 1718.
12 Margaret,[3] b. 1720.
13 Nathaniel,[3] b. 1722.

(See Brackett Family, in Appendix).

vi Jonathan,[2] m. Eliz. Cate; d. s. p., "an old man," 27 June,
1748. It is said that his nephew Jonathan, son of John,
cared for him in his old age and was to receive a part of
his estate, in return for his service. The uncle delayed
making the change in his will till his last sickness, and
then his wife gave him a dose that so affected him that he
died without completing the change. The two younger children of Leonard are said to have been twins and daughters
of the second wife Elizabeth.

vii Margaret,[2] b. 4 June, 1679, is supposed to have m. Tobias Lear,
grandfather of Tobias Lear who in 1785 was private secre-

tary to General Washington, and the husband of his niece.
He was b. in Portsmouth, abt. 1760. In 1805 was ambassador to Algiers and negotiated a treaty with Tripoli. He
was auditor of the Treasury department; but in 1816 shot
himself.

viii Sarah[2] is said to have m. [Tobias Langdon of Portsmouth, the
grandfather of Gov. John Langdon who was b. in Portsmouth, 1739]?

2

John Weeks[2] (*Leon.*[1]), born 1668, died [1710?], of
Greenland, probably had

i   Walter,[3] b.—; called, 18 April, 1758, "Walter Weeks, jr., of
Greenland, deceased." His widow, Mary* (dau. of Joseph
Jewett,) b. 1733, was administratrix; and in her account of
the estate, 26 Sept., 1759, names his three sons,

     1 *William*[4] [in 1778 Wm. Weaks of Portsmouth, cordwainer,
bot. of Thos. Moses ½ ho. & lot in Portsmouth]. He d.
1806.

     2 *John.*[4]

(6)   3 *Walter*,[4] b. 22 Feb., 1757, who m., 1st, 3 May, 1791, Nancy
Jewett of Stratham, b. 1766 and had four children, b. in
Stratham. He died 1825, æ. 68.

ii   Joshua,[3] supposed to have taken a letter to the church in Portland, Me., in 1732 and d. there in 1756, *s. p.*

(7) iii   Jonathan,[3] b. 1707, "owned ye cov't in 1724;" d. 20 Nov., 1794.
He lived with his uncle Jonathan till his death and had six
children, bapt. in Greenland.

3

Capt. Samuel Weeks[2](*Leon.*[1]) born 1670, died 1746,
farmer in Greenland, and his wife Elinor (Haines), had
born in Greenland

Children :

(8) i   Lt. Samuel,[3] bapt. 1712; was a tanner; m. abt. 1725, Mehitable, dau. of Thos. Pickering of Portsmouth. Both joined
the church in 1728. They had seven children. His will,
made in 1762, was proved 8 Nov., 1763 (see Appendix,
Pickering Family.)

(9) ii   John,[3] bapt. 1712, cordwainer in Greenland; m., 1st, Hannah
———, joined the church in 1728, and had eight children
bapt. before 1744. In 1758 he was of Epping, and in 1762
had a second wife, Abigail.

---

*She m., 2d, 15 Oct., 1760. Andrew (s. of Bradstreet) Wiggin; had seven children
and d. 24 Jan., 1834, æ. 100 years and 4 mos., leaving 156 descendants.

6 LEONARD WEEKS AND FAMILY.

(10) lii Walter,[3] bapt. 1712, farmer on the homestead, resided in the brick house; joined the church, 1727; m., about 1726, his cousin, Comfort, dau. of Joshua Weeks, at the Bay Side. In 1755 he was selectman in Greenland. They had nine children. He d. in 1774. She d. in Dec., 1786; a woman of talent and energy.

(11) iv Matthias,[3] b. 1708; m. about 1735, widow Sarah Ford, dau. of John Sanborn of North Hampton, and had nine children. In 1766 he sold the land inherited from his father, on the Great Bay, and in 1773, with his children, removed to Gilmanton, where he d. before Oct., 1777. His widow, Sarah, d. there 7 Dec., 1799, æ. 86.

v Mary,[3] bapt. 1712; m., about 1744, Paul Chapman of Greenland (Samuel,[3] Samuel,[2] Edward[1]) b. 4 Nov., 1704, who d. 18 Oct., 1754, æ. 50. They had b. in Greenland, on the Chapman homestead, one-half mile south of the Parade, four children. She d. in 1762, leaving two minor sons.

1 Samuel[4] (Chapman), b. 6 Jan., 1745; m. ——, settled in Wakefield, had Betsey and Lydia who m. two brothers, Wm. Goodwin and Samuel Goodwin and had large families.

(12) 2 Job,[4] b. 1 Nov., 1747, farmer on the homestead; m. by Mr. Fogg of Kensington, 8 Jan., 1771, Penelope,[6] dau. of Benj.[5] Philbrook of Hampton (Elias,[4] John,[3] John,[2] Thomas). She was b. in 1751. In twenty-two years they had six sons and a daughter born here. After ten years in Deerfield they all settled in Tamworth, where he d. 26 Mar., 1837, and his widow, Penelope, d. 10 May, 1838 (see Appendix. Chapman Family).

3 Paul,[4] b. May, 1749.

4 John,[4] b. July, 1751. Both he and Paul d. in Sept., 1753, of throat disease, supposed to have been diphtheria.

vi Elinor,[3] bapt. 1714, who, after the death of her sister, Mary Chapman, took charge of the two orphan sons, and closed her long unmarried life in the family of Job, the younger, in Deerfield.

vii William,[3] bapt. 1717. I suppose d. young.

4

Joseph Weeks[2] (*Leon.*[1]), born 1662, died 1735, of Greenland, and his wife Hannah ——, had born in Greenland

Children :

(13) i Jedediah,[3] b. about 1710, farmer; m. Eleanor, dau. of Nath'l and Sarah Haines Huggins of Greenland; both joined the church 11 May, 1735, and had seven children bapt. Removed to Epping. He made a will 12 Dec., 1760, and d. 28 Jan., 1761. His widow had returned to Greenland in 1776.

ii Joshua,[3] bapt. 1725; [m. in Rye, 1760, Sarah Marston]?

iii　Joseph,[3] bapt. 1725; [supposed to have settled in Falmouth, Mass., with two sons who d. early, and three daughters. One m. —— Bartlett, another —— Bates, and third —— —— Kennedy.] One son was Capt. Jas. Weeks, mariner.

(14) iv　Leonard,[3] bapt. 1725; joined the church in May, 1742; m. Margaret ——, had three children bapt. in Greenland, where he was a farmer, in 1753, and where he d. Aug. 1761.

5

Capt. Joshua Weeks[2] (*Leon.*[1]) born 1674, died 1758, farmer, at the Bayside, and his wife Comfort (Hubbard), had born in Greenland

Children :

i　Martha,[3] b. 1704; m., 1st, 9 Jan., 1723, Chase Wiggin (see Appendix, Wiggin Family). He died in 1733 and she m., 2nd, 9 Dec., 1736, Col. Winthrop Hilton of Newfields in Newmarket, posthumous son of Colonel Winthrop (*Hilton,*[3] *Edward,*[2] *Edward*[1]). His father, while at work upon timber in Epping, was killed by the Indians in 1710 (see Appendix, Hilton Family).

Children of Martha (Weeks) and Chase Wiggin :

　1　*Bradstreet*[4] (Wiggin), b. Nov., 1724; m. Mary Coker and d. Oct., 1757; had six children.

　2　*Comfort,*[4] b. ——, 1727; m. B. Gilman of Epping; had five children.

　3　*Chase,*[4] b. 12 July, 1730; m. Mary Perkins and had five children.

　4　*Joshua,*[4] b. July —, 1733; m. Eliz. Lyford of Epping; had seven children.

Children of Martha (Weeks) and Col. Winthrop Hilton :

　5　*Winthrop*[4] (Hilton), b. 7 Oct., 1737.

　6　*Ichabod,*[4] b. 1740.

　7　*Ann,*[4] b. 1745, who m. Lt. John Burley and d. 26 Oct., 1769, leaving a dau. Martha (Burley), wife of Col. Eben Thompson. Mrs. Hilton d. 31 Mar., 1769, æt. 65. Col. W. Hilton d. 26 Dec., 1781, æt. 71.

ii　Joshua,[3]* bapt. Hampton 19 Nov., 1706; farmer; m., 24 Oct., 1734, Sarah (dau. of Richard) Jenness of Rye. He d. 10 Feb., 1736, a little more than fifteen months after his marriage. About four months afterward his posthumous son 1 *Joshua*[4] was born in Rye (Note iv in Appendix).

iii　Comfort,[3] b. ab. 1708; m. Walter (s. of Capt. Sam'l Weeks); had nine children b. in the brick house; d. Dec. 1786 (see No. 10).

---

*In Hampton church records I find " Bapt. 19 Nov., 1706, Joshua son of Capt. Joshua *Wingate.*" evidently a clerical error for Capt. Joshua *Weeks.* Joshua Wingate had a son Joshua born about four years *after* this date; but no son *near* this date.

iv   Mary,[3] b. 1710(?); m. Capt. Jonathan Chesley of Durham, who d. there July, 1765; he gave, in his will, in May, 1765, to one "son Jonathan, two-thirds of all lands in Durham, when he is 21 years old; second son, Samuel, one-third lands and house in Durham; third son, Ebenezer, lands in Nottingham." His sister Mary (Chesley) m. 10 Oct., 1751, Col. Benj. Chadbourne of Berwick, Me., and had (1) Jonathan, b. 1752; (2) Mary; (3) Benj., b. Nov., 1756. Benj. Chadbourne, with the widow Mary, was executor. To his daus. Comfort and Lydia (Chesley) Jonathan gave £300 each, to be paid when they became 18 years of age.

v   Ichabod[3], bapt. 1713, a young man of promise, who joined the church in 1735; and d. of throat disease, 3 Nov., 1736.

(15) vi   Dr. John[3], b. 1716, a physician; completed his studies in England; joined the church in 1737. He m., 1st, 10 Nov., 1737, Martha (dau. of Maj. Joshua) Wingate of Hampton; b. 30 March, 1718. She had ten children; and d. of "violent fever" March 9, 1758, æ. 40. He m., 2nd, Elizabeth ——; and d. of consumption, 20 Oct., 1763, æ. 47. Dr. John Weeks practised ten years in Greenland and vicinity, then removed to Hampton, where he d. leaving a widow and nine children, most of them young. He was an energetic business man, had an extensive practice, owned much land, held the offices of justice of the peace, and colonel of a regiment, etc. He was a prominent member of the church, a warm friend to the cause of education, and to the improvement of society.

Hampton sustained a select school, taught by a graduate of Harvard, and afforded the young superior advantages for intellectual and moral improvement.

In 1886, his great-grandson erected a marble slab over his grave where the stones had decayed in the old cemetery of Hampton.

vii   Thankful,[3] bapt. 1720; m. 17 April, 1740, Geo. Marshall of Portsmouth, and had ch :

    1   *Geo.*[4] (Marshall).

    2   *John.*[4]

    3   *Comfort.*[4]

    4   *Margaret*,[4] who m. (as 2nd. w.) Rev. Samuel Haven, D.D. (H. Col. 1749) and had six children, bapt. in Portsmouth; he d. in 1806.

(16) viii   Major William,[3] b. 28 July, 1723, who d. in Greenland, 17 Sept., 1798, æ. 75. He m. 20 March, 1748, Elinor (dau. of Colonel Clement) March, b. 1 Nov., 1730, who d. 1 Nov. 1807, æ. 77. They lived at the Bay Side; had thirteen children; expended much for their education, having as private tutor, for a time, Dr. J. Belknap, afterward pastor of the church in Dover. and the historian of New Hampshire. Two of his sons graduated at Harvard College, and several of his daughters completed their education in Boston.

ix   Richard,[3] bapt. 1727 [d. early]?

x   Margaret,[3] bapt. April, 1728, "m., 1st, Dea. Eben Smith, & lived at the garrison," in Durham; m., 2d, in 1774, Hon. George Frost of Little Harbor, New Castle, b. 26 April, 1720, who rem. to Durham.

The children of Margaret and Dea. Eben Smith were :

1 *John*[4] (Smith), m. Mary Jewett.
2 *Comfort*,[4] m. Joseph Chesley of Durham.
3 *Hon. Eben*,[4] b. 13 Mar., 1758, forty years a lawyer in Durham; m. Mehitable Sheafe of Portsmouth, and had:
  (1) Mehitable, w. of Eben Coe of Northwood, (2) Alfred,
  (3) Eben, (4) Charles and a dau. (5) Mary, the excellent
  wife of Rev. John K. Young, D.D., of Laconia.
4 *Margaret*,[4] w. of John Blydenburg, trader in Durham.

The children of Margaret and Hon. Geo. Frost were:

5 *George*[4] (Frost), b. —— who m. Peggy (Margaret), dau.
  of John Burley, who d. 20 March, 1846, æ. 71.
6 *Mary*,[4] w. of Jere. Mead, of Newmarket, whose dau. Margaret m. Hon. Wm. (son of Gov. Wm.) Plumer of Epping.
7 *Martha Wentworth*,[4] 2nd w. of Henry Mellen of Dover, a
  lawyer.
8 *John*,[4] b. 1776; m. —— Salter of Portsmouth and d. there
  15 Feb., 1847, æ. 71, *s. p.* (see Appendix, Frost Family).

6

Walter Weeks[4] [*Walter*,[3] *John*,[2] *Leon.*[1]] ?, born 1757,
died 1825, of Stratham, and his wife Nancy (Jewett), had
born in Stratham
Children :

i   Nancy,[5] b. 1792; d. 1792.
ii Sukey Ann,[5] b. Feb., 1795; m. —— Taylor.
iii Ira,[5] b. Jan. 26, 1800; m. Nov., 1822, Mehitable C. (dau. of
    Benj.) Norris of Stratham, b. 12 Oct., 1804, and had three
    children.
    1 *Martha*,[6] d. unm.
    2 *Rosilla Octavia*,[6] b. ——; m. N. B. Treadwell and d. *s. p.*
    3 *Walter*,[6] m. Lucina, dau. of Hiram Wiggin, who d. 1887.

7

Jonathan Weeks[3] [*Jn.*,[2] *Leon.*[1]] ?, born 1707, died
1794, farmer of Greenland, and his wife, had
Children :

i   Ester,[4] bapt. 1736.
ii Hannah,[4] b. 12 Aug., 1738; m. in Greenland, 12 July, 1756,
    Symonds Fowler, b. Ipswich, Mass., 20 Aug., 1734; resided
    at Newmarket and at Epsom, where she died 9 Dec., 1807.
    They had eleven children :
    1 *Hannah*[5] (Fowler), b. 1757.
    2 *Susanna*,[5] b. 1760; m. Jn. Jenness.
    3 *Symonds*,[5] d. early.
    4 *Hannah*,[5] b. 1764; m., 1st, D. Robinson; 2nd, J. Phelps.
    5 *Abigail*,[5] b. Apr., 1767; m. Nathan Libbey.
    6 *Benj.*,[5] b. 10 June, 1769; m. Mehitable Ladd.

2

7 *Sally*,[5] b. 1771; m. Zebadiah Lovejoy.

8 *Samuel*,[5] b. 1775; m. Betsey Davis.

9 *Polly*,[5] b. 1777; m. Sam'l Learned.

10 *Esther*,[5] b. May, 1780; m., 1803, Rev. Asa Merrill of Stratham and had twelve children of whom Phinehas Merrill of Stratham is the fifth.

11 *Winthrop*,[5] b. Apr., 1788; m. Abigail Davis.

iii Jonathan,[4] bapt. 1740 [d. 1744]?

iv Sarah,[4] bapt. 1742 [d. 1744]?

(17) v David,[4] b. 3 Jan., 1744–5; joiner in Greenland, 1767; m. 12 March, 1770, Ruth Page, b. 27 March, 1752; in 1783, res. in Bath; had four children; d. 22 Jan., 1827. His wife Ruth d. 9 March, 1829.

vi Abigail,[4] bapt. 3 July, 1748.

(18) vii Jonathan,[4] bapt. 7 April, 1751; m. Margaret (dau. of Nath'l) Caverly of Portsmouth, gr. dau. of Eliz. Banfill, from whom she inherited rights, sold in 1782. They had four children.

8

Lt. Samuel Weeks[3] (*Sam.*,[2] *Leon.*[1]), born 1700, died 1763, tanner, and his wife Mehitable (Pickering), had born in Greenland

Children :

i Eleanor,[4] bapt. 1728.

ii Joseph,[4] bapt. 1730 [d. early]?

(19) iii Elizabeth,[4] bapt. 1732; m. Sept., 1753, Richard[4] (son of Wm.[3] and Rachel[2]) Scammon,* farmer of Stratham, b. 17 Nov., 1722; d. 26 Aug., 1806. She removed with her sons to western New York, and died there. " An able, active, upright woman."

iv Joshua,[4] bapt. 1736; m. Comfort ——; no issue in 1762; was living in 1767.

v Samuel,[4] jr., bapt. 1738; res. in 1767 in Greenland.

vi Mehitable,[4] bapt. 1742; m. —— Pickering.

vii Mary[4], bapt. 1745; [d. early]? (see Appendix, Pickering Family).

9

John Weeks[3] (*Sam.*,[2] *Leon.*[1]), born 1702, died ——, cordwainer of Greenland and of Epping, and his wife Hannah, had born in Greenland

Children :

i Thomas,[4] bapt. 1728; m. Abigail ——; res. in 1757 in Greenland, removed about 1760 to Epping. His son Joseph,[5] bapt. in Epping, 11 Feb., 1760.

---

* Rachel (Thurber) mother of Richard Scammon is said to have been the first Baptist in N. H. and to have been active in establishing that denomination in Stratham.

ii   Mary,[4] bapt. 1730.

iii   Abigail,[4] bapt. 1732; d. 4 July, 1743, of throat disease.

(20)iv   John,[4] jr., b. 1732-3, bapt. 1734, farmer in Greenland; m. 1753-4, Abigail, dau. of Sam'l Piper of Stratham, res. in Epping in 1760, was surety for a sheriff, and lost his property,—sold his land, and about 1769, went with his wife and six children to Damariscotta, Me. Enclosed, for himself and six sons, 500 acres of land in what is now Jefferson, Lincoln Co., Me., for which he afterward paid the government. Many descendants of his nine children now live in that vicinity. He d. 20 March, 1804, æ. 72; but his widow lived to be more than 90 years old, retaining her sight, etc., till the close of her life.

v   Joseph[4] or Joshua, bapt. 1736; [d. 14 July, 1743, of throat disease]?

(21) vi   Cole,[4] b. 1737, bapt. 1738; joiner; m. Hannah[5] (dau. of John[4]) Chapman of Epping, about 1767, an early settler in Sanbornton, and a very active and useful citizen, where he d. 5 April, 1801, æ. 64. His wife d. 10 Feb., 1815, æ. 78. They had nine children who " were said to have averaged, in weight, 218 pounds apiece; what the girls fell short of those figures the boys made up." John Chapman[4] of Epping was son (Jn.,[3] Sam.,[2] Edw.[1]) of the family that came from Ipswich to Hampton, in 1700.

(22) vii   Benjamin,[4] b. 26 April, 1742; in 1760, bought of his father twenty acres, in Epping; m., abt. 1761, Marion Hanniford, b. 29 Feb., 1741, and had ten children. In 1764, he was a laborer in Epping, afterward resided in Deerfield, then in Wentworth, and finally [settled, a farmer, in Piermont]?

viii Ellnor,[4] bapt. 1744 [d. early]?

10

Walter Weeks[3] (*Sam.,*[2] *Leon.*[1]), born 1706, died 1774, farmer, and his wife Comfort (Weeks), had born in Greenland

Children :

(23) i   Sarah,[4] bapt. 1727; m. in Hampton, 27 July, 1746, Abner Haines, b. 1724, d. abt. 1798. In 1772, he sold his homestead, on Winnicut river and the Great Bay, and in 1773 settled in Canterbury where they died. They had six children b. in Greenland.

ii   Samuel,[4] bapt. 1728. In 1765 sold lands in Greenland; had son Sam'l,[5] b. in Greenland 4 Nov., 1768, who d. in Danville, Vt., 7 May, 1834, leaving a son Peaslee[6] (Weeks) b. 15 Feb., 1791. In Nov., 1774, Sam'l[4] Weeks of Canterbury sold lands in Newmarket from the estate of his father, Walter Weeks.

iii   Walter,[4] bapt. 1730.

iv   Richard,[4] bapt. 1732; d. 1736.

v   Comfort,[4] bapt. 1734; d.——.

(24) vi   Dr. Ichabod,[4] b. 16 Sept., 1738; studied medicine with his uncle, Dr. John Weeks of Hampton, res. Greenland; d.

1807. He m., 1st, 30 Oct., 1760, Sarah Cotta (dau. of Rev. Ward) Cotton, b. in Hampton, 19 Oct., 1739, who d. 24 July, 1770, *s. p.*; m., 2nd, in Rye, 1 Nov., 1770, Comfort Johnson, of Greenland, b. 13 May, 1750, who d. 26 Oct., 1775; had two children. He m., 3rd, 24 Sept., 1776, Abigail (dau. of Clement) March of Greenland, who was b. 10 Feb., 1741, and d. 26 Nov., 1814.

   vii Comfort,[4] 2nd, bapt. 1741; m., between 1773–1781,——Mariner.

(25) viii William,[4] bapt. 1743; m. Eliz. Hubbard of Seabrook; res. in the brick house; farmer, with seven children; d. 1813.

    x Martha,[4] b. 1744; bapt. 1745; m. Joseph Doe, b. in Newmarket, a joiner, trader and farmer, who d. 7 Nov., 1817, æ. 80. She d. 29 Oct., 1812, æ. 68. They had seven children, b. on the homestead, near Newmarket Junction. Joseph Doe and his w. Martha (Weeks) Doe, had b. in Newmarket:

     1 *Patty* (Doe),[5] b.——; m. Jn. Allen, and had (1) Jn. K Allen, (2) Joseph D.

     2 *Polly*,[5] b. 1773; m. Joshua Pickering, and d. 17 Oct., 1803, æ. 30, leaving two children : Clarissa and Augustus (Pickering).

     3 *Walter*,[5] b. 1774; d. 25 April, 1843, æ. 69; was a trader in Wilton, N. Y., where his six children were born: (1) Marietta V., (2) Harriet Olivia, (3) Caroline A., (4) Walter P., (5) Sarah E., (6) Hannah E.

     4 *Joseph*,[5] b. 15 Nov., 1778; d. 28 Feb., 1860; a trader and farmer. He m. Mary Bodwell Ricker, b. 7 May, 1787, who d. 31 Dec., 1869. Their children, except Charles, b. in the part of Somersworth, now Rollinsford, were: (1) Mary Elizabeth Doe, b. 30 Aug., 1812, m. Wm. Pickering Weeks[6] (s. of Brackett Weeks[5]) a lawyer in Canaan, N. H., and had ten children (see Nos. 24–iii). (2) Martha (Weeks), b. 7 Dec. 1813, and d. 12 Oct., 1835, unm. (3) Ebenezer Ricker, b. 29 Nov., 1815, d. 11 Dec., 1864, a merchant in N. Y. city and Janesville, Wis. (4) Joseph Bodwell, b. 20 April, 1817, a merchant and bank cashier in N. Y. city, res. now in Janesville, Wis. (5) Thos. Bartlett, b. 12 Feb. 1819, d. 8 Sept., 1883, merch. and farmer in N. Y. city and Danville, Va. (6) Charles, b. in Derry, 11 April, 1830, D. Coll. 1849, read law with Hon. D. M. Christie of Dover and Harvard law school, was Judge in 1859, res. in Salmon Falls, in 1876, Chief Justice of Supreme Court of N. H.

     5 *Sally*,[5] b. ——; m. Joseph Doe of Parsonsfield, Me.

     6 *Comfort*,[5] b. 1783; d. 2 July, 1802, æ. 19.

     7 *Nicholas Bartlett*,[5] d. 1856; was a lawyer in Saratoga, N. Y.

    x Thankful,[4] bapt. 27 Nov., 1748, m., as 2d w., Capt. Benj. Randall, who sailed the next day, and was lost at sea.

   xi Elinor,[4] m. (probably) Joseph[4] (*Enoch*,[3] *Henry*[2]) Clarke of Greenland, b. 1 Jan., 1731–2 and d. 4 Dec., 1761, by whom she had five children. Before 7 Dec., 1773, Mrs. Elinor (Weeks) Clarke had m. Mr. Mason; but I find no record of any more children.

Children of Elinor (Weeks) and Joseph Clarke were:

    1 *Hannah*[5] (Clarke), who m. —— Lunt of Newbury, Mass.

2 *Mary.*⁵ m. —— Langdon.
3 *John,*⁵ b. 1756, a soldier in the Revolution; m. 1791, Mehitable Corliss Hutchins; had eight children and d. in
Haverhill, N. H., 14 Oct., 1811.
4 *Comfort,*⁵ m. 25 Nov., 1783, John Weeks of Greenland, who
rem. to Bartlett; d. 1825 and had ten children (see No.
13-vii).
5 *Eleanor.*⁵

11

Matthias Weeks³ (*Sam.*², *Leon.*¹), born 1708, died
1777, of Greenland, and his wife Sarah (Sanborn) (Ford)
Weeks, had nine children born in Greenland. Late in life
he followed his children to Gilmanton.

Children :

(26) l John,⁴ bapt. 1736; m. Dorothy ——; in 1773, rem. to Gilmanton; settled in district No. 2, near his brother Benjamin
and Orlando Weed. In 1787, he was paid £6 for killing two
wolves; d. Feb. 1815, in Gilford. æ. 84, and his wid. Dorothy
administratrix, 2 Mar., 1815. It has been difficult to find
the names of his children : [Nath'l, b. ——; John Lang,
b. in Greenland, 1763; Noah, b. 1771, m. Sarah Morrill and
d. in Alton, 1804]?
ii Olive,⁴ bapt. 1738; m. in Hampton, 26 Aug., 1755, John Haines
a joiner of Greenland, b. 1731, who rem. to Epsom, and d.
1809. They had seven children b. in Greenland, and three
in Epsom.
1 *Elinor*⁵ (Haines), m. Bennet Libbey of Strafford, Vt. Eight
children; all joined the Shakers in Canterbury.
2 *Jeremiah,*⁵ a soldier in the Revolutionary War; m. Mary
Dearborn and had two children.
3 *Lydia,*⁵ d. unm.; made a will Dec., 1811.
4 *Elisha,*⁵ b. 1762; served in the Revolutionary War; m. 1784
or 1785, Betsey, dau. John Bartlett of Pembroke, b.
1763, d. in 1812. Eight children. He m., 2nd, in 1816 or
1817, wid. Mary Johnson, and d. in Concord, 1834.
5 *Olive,*⁵ m , 1st, Thos. Bickford, had seven children; m.,
2nd, Francis Locke.
6 *Jennie,*⁵ m. John Dearborn, and d. in Canterbury, *s. p.*
7 *Sarah,*⁵ m., 1st, Nathaniel Wiggin; had six children; m.,
2nd, John Robinson, d. in Epsom, 1811.
8 *John,*⁵ b. June, 1775; m. 1797, Betsey Merrill of Stratham,
b. Oct. 1775, d. 1850. He rem. in 1800 to Norridgewock,
Me.; had eight children; d. 27 June, 1850.
9 *Levi,*⁵ b. Apr., 1779; m. 23 July, 1803, Polly Dolbeer, and
d. in Epsom. Aug., 1856.
10 *Matthias,*⁵ b. 1781; m. 8 July, 1807, Sarah R. Smith. b. 1781,
d. 1861. In 1827 he settled in Glover, Vt., where he d.
10 Jan., 1856.
(27) iii Matthias,⁴ jr., b. 5 June, 1740; m. in Exeter, 21 Nov., 1760,
Judith (dau. of Dudley) Leavitt of Exeter, b. 23 Aug.,1741,

where he was a tanner. In May or June, 1778, he rem.
to Gilmanton, where she d. 23 April, 1810. He d. 20 Mar.,
1821, æ. near 81. They had fourteen children.

iv Elinor,[4] bapt. 1742; living Dec., 1778.

v Mary,[4] bapt. 1744.

(28) vi Rev. Samuel,[4] b. 21 Nov., 1746; m., 1st, Mercy Randlet of
Stratham, b. 22 Jan., 1748. He was a joiner; rem. to Gilmanton in 1773. In 1777 he was clerk of the Baptist
Church; was licensed to preach, and on the 25 June, 1780,
was ordained. He soon left the Baptist Church, and in
Feb., 1783, went to Parsonsfield, Me., and was the first
pastor of the Freewill Baptist Church of that town. He
m., 2nd, Sarah (Barnes), widow of S. Guptail. He had
thirteen children and d. 19 June, 1832, æ. 85 yrs. and 5
mos. (see Note v, Appendix).

vii Joanna,[4] bapt. 14 July, 1751.

(29) viii Benjamin[4] (called Esquire), b. 28 Feb., 1749; rem. in 1772
to Gilmanton, lower parish, rem. in 1787 to what is now
Gilford; lived two or three years in Burton, returning in
1792; m. 26 May, 1774, Sarah Weed of Sandwich, b. 28
Oct., 1755; had seven children; d. in Guilford, 1829; a man
who had the confidence of his neighbors and often acted
as a peacemaker in cases of arbitration left to his deci-
sion.

He was also a large landholder, dealing extensively in
lands. He was much interested in the education of his
children.

(30) ix Dea. Noah,[4] b. 12 July, 1754; m. by his brother Samuel in
Gilmanton, 28 Feb., 1782, to Betsey Meed, who was b. 11
Apr., 1759, and d. in Guilford, 12 Mar., 1825, æ. 71. He
had nine children; "a worthy family marked for their piety
& honesty."

x Josiah,[4] b. about 1756; a shipwright; m. in Exeter, 31 Oct.,
1776, Abigail (dau. of Dudley) James; both of Exeter.
Nov. 8, 1779, he sold in Exeter and in 1781 rem. to Gilmanton, "near the upper parish Meeting House," where
he d. in 1802. His widow Abigail on the 14 March, 1812,
made a will bequeathing her estate to her two sons:

(30a) 1 *Dudley J.*,[5] b. 1788; m. Lucy Sampson, b. 1791; was a
cooper and a soldier in 1812. Five children.

(30b) 2 *John*,[5] m. (Sarah Abbot)? and administered on his mother's estate.

12

Job[4] (son of Paul and Mary Weeks) Chapman, born
1747, died 1837, farmer, and his wife Penelope (Philbrook) had born in Greenland

Children :

i Benjamin,[5] b. 1773; m. 10 Sept., 1795, Sarah Wedgewood of
Deerfield. He settled in Tamworth on a farm; d. 16 July,
1826, æ. 53, *s. p.*

ii   Job,[5] b. 1776; a cabinet-maker; unm.; d. 9 June, 1822.

iii Eliphalet,[5] b. 1778; m. in Deerfield, 10 Mar., 1803, Peggy Kennison, who d. in Tamworth 8 Aug., 1826. He d. in Newton, Mass., June, 1863. Their children were:

1 *Penelope*,[6] b. 1804; d. 1826.
2 *Andrew*,[6] b. 1806.
3 *Eliphalet*,[6] b. 1808; d. 1874.
4 *Benjamin F.*,[6] b. 1810; m. and went west.
5 *Lucinda*,[6] b. 1812.
6 *Elona*,[6] b. 1815.
7 *Joseph*,[6] b. 1817.
8 *Timothy*,[6] b. 1821.
9 *John*,[6] b. Sept., 1825; d. 1852.

iv Samuel,[5] b. 11 May, 1781; m., 1st, in Tamworth, 10 Feb., 1808, Elizabeth (Betsey) S. Folsom (dau. of Levi and Joanna Weeks) Folsom, b. 29 Mar., 1783, who d. 5 Aug., 1821. He m., 2nd, Mary Hoit; and 3rd, Mrs. Betsey(Morse) Gilman; d. in Tamworth, 30 Oct., 1857, æ. 76. He had six children b. in Tamworth (see No. 40–III.)

By his second wife he had Joanna Weeks, who m., 11 July, 1871, Jere E. Chadwick in Deerfield. They settled in Brazil, Ind.; rem. to Waldo, Fla., where he d. 11 May, 1883, æ. 54.

v   Mary[5] (Polly), b. 1784; m., 1st, 5 June, 1806, Bradbury (son of Mark) Jewell, a farmer in Tamworth; m., 2nd, in June, 1845, Phineas Wentworth of Barrington; d. in 1862, æ. 78.

Children of Mary (Weeks) and Bradbury Jewell were:

1 *Bradbury*,[6] jr., b. 1807; m. in Tamworth, 27 Jan., 1833, Lucinda (dau. of Eliphalet) Chapman; d. in Newmarket, 1843, leaving: (1) Mary[7] (Jewell), wife of S. H. Potter of Suncook; (2) Col. David (Jewell), agent of cotton mills, Suncook, N. H.
2 *David*,[6] b. 1808; d. æ. about 21.

vi John,[5] b. 1788; d. 21 June, 1812, æ. 24; m. 22 Oct., 1809, Mercy Ballard, and had b. in Tamworth, Lucy, b. 1811, who m. Henry Luce of Industry, Me., and d. at the West, 9 March, 1886.

vii Joseph,[5] b. 1791, farmer and cooper in Tamworth; m., 1st, in 1813, Huldah Howard, who d. 7 May, 1826; m., 2nd, in 1827, Julia Atkinson of Hollis, Me., who d. 12 May, 1884, *s. p.*; he d. 15 Sept., 1869, æ. 78.

Children of Joseph and Huldah (Howard) Weeks were:

1 *Rebecca*,[6] b. 1817, who m. Enoch Perkins of Great Falls, where she d. Apr., 1859.
2 *Simeon*,[6] b. 1824; living unm. on the homestead, in 1888.

13

Jedediah Weeks[3] (*Jos.*,[2] *Leon.*[1]) born 1710, died 1761, of Greenland, and his wife Eleanor (Huggins), had born in Greenland

Children :

    i   Bridget,[4] bapt. 1735.
   ii   Margaret,[4] bapt. 1735; [d. 17 Nov., 1735]?
  iii   Joseph,[4] b. 1738; was living in 1761. (In 1765 a Joseph
        Weeks res. in Newmarket.)
   iv   Thankful,[4] bapt. 1740; m. Daniel Hoit of Northwood.
    v   Josiah,[4] bapt. 1743; d. early.
   vi   Nath'l,[4] bapt. 2 June, 1745; m. Elizabeth (dau. of Wm. and
        Olive) Burley of Stratham, b. 27 Apr., 1752; in 1779 was
        a farmer in Loudon, dealing in lands. He d. *s. p.*
  vii   Joshua,[4] bapt. abt. 1747; d. before 3 Apr., 1776 [supposed
        to have]? m. Polly Perkins and had children :
       1 *Polly,*[5] b. —— ; m. Miles Thompson of Bartlett, who had
          eight children : (1) Joseph, (2) Miles, (3) Abigail, (4)
          Betsey, (5) Solomon, (6) Sally, (7) Lovey.
       2 *Thankful,*[5] m. —— Melcher, res. in Portsmouth, who d.
          at sea. She d. of yellow fever, and her two children,
          Edward (Melcher), who m. —— Rogers of Bartlett, and
          Mary were taken to the home of her sister Polly, in
          Bartlett. Mary returned and m. —— Marden of Ports-
          mouth.
(31)   3 *John,*[5] [b. 1763]? m. 25 Nov., 1783, Comfort (dau. of Joseph
          and Eleanor) Weeks Clarke,* of Greenland, rem. to Bart-
          lett, and d. Oct., 1825. He was thrown from his horse
          by a yoke of wild steers, and d. from the fall. They had
          ten children.
(32) viii   Josiah,[4] 2d, b. 17 Feb., 1749; was eighteen months in the Rev-
        olutionary war; settled in Bartlett; m. Polly (dau. of Jas.)
        Emery, b. 5 Sept., 1775; seven children.
   ix   Sarah,[4] bapt. in Epping, 8 Nov., 1761, presented by wid. Elea-
        nor Weeks; m. James Bean of Nottingham and had ten
        children :
       1 *Joshua*[5] (Bean), m. —— ; ch : (1) Henry, (2) Jn., (3)
          Joshua.
       2 *Samuel,*[5] b. 1775, settled in Deerfield, 1803; m., 1st, Miss
          Deborah Avery, b. 1777; had : (1) Dea. Jas. of Deerfield,
          b. 18 Apr., 1815, who m. Lydia O. Furber, and had seven
          children; (2) Lucinda, (3) Sally, (4) Polly.
       3 *Jedediah,*[5] m. McDaniel; had : (1) David, (2) John, (3)
          Sam'l, (4) Harris, and three daughters.
       4 *James,*[5] had three sons.
       5 *John,*[5] left when young, and was lost.
       6 *Hannah,*[5] m. —— Ford, and res. in Lowell, with sons.
       7 *Sarah,*[5] m. S. Tuttle, res. in Lowell.
       8 *Thankful,*[5] m. Nathan Burnham.
       9 *A dau.,*[5] m. Leavitt and
      10 *Eleanor,*[5] m. Samuel Gile; both in Effingham. Their dau.
          Sarah (Gile), m. in 1820, Winthrop M. Burley of Effing-
          ham.†

---

*See Appendix, "Clarke Family."
†See Appendix, Buleigh Family.

(33) x Jedediah,[4] bapt. in Epping, 8 Nov., 1761; lived in the family
of Major Wm. Weeks of Greenland, was a soldier in the
Revolutionary war; then settled as a farmer in Northwood;
m. Lydia Knowlton, and had three children.
    xi Thomas,[4] bapt. 5 June, 1763.

14

Leonard Weeks,[3] (*Joseph,[2] Leon.[1]*), born 1725, died
1761, farmer, and his wife Margaret, had baptized in
Greenland

Children :

(34) l Phineas,[4] bapt. 1745; cooper, removed to Loudon; had seven
children.
(35) ii John,[4] b. 10 May, 1747; d. in Wakefield, Jan. 1832, æ. 85. He
m. Deborah Allen, who d. about March, 1831, æ. 79. He is
called John Weeks,[3] of Greenland, farmer, in Dec. 5, 1772,
when he bought land lot 13, in 2d division of Easttown,
now Wakefield, where he settled and had eight children.
   iii Margaret[4], bapt. 28 May, 1749.
     In 1771, March 29, Wm. Walles, sold to Josiah, Phineas,
John and Joshua Weeks of Greenland, land " which belonged to the Weeks grant, except 5 acres he bot. of Joseph
Weeks, dec'd," which seems to indicate that these four men
may have been brothers.

15

Dr. John Weeks[3] (*Joshua[2], Leon.[1]*), born 1716, died
1763, of Greenland and Hampton, and his wife Martha
Wingate), had born in Greenland

Children :

(36) l Rev. Joshua Wingate,[4] b. 1738, graduated at Harvard College, 1758, studied divinity; in 1763 was ordained by the
Episcopal bishop in London, England; took charge of St.
Michael's church, Marblehead, Mass. He had m., about
1762, Miss Sarah Treadwell of Ipswich, Mass. [or of
Portsmouth]. When ordained, he took the oath of allegiance to the King of England; and at the Declaration
of Independence, " his piety was stronger than his pa-
triotism " and he refused to violate his oath. In 1775 he
was driven from his parish for his political principles, and
took refuge with Rev. Jacob Bailey of Pownalboro (now
Dresden), Me., whose wife was his sister. In 1778, he
asked permission to leave the country with his wife and
eight children, which was refused. He escaped to a British vessel, was taken to England,— appointed chaplain at
Halifax, N. S., where he died in 1806, æ. 68.

3

(37) ii   Comfort,[4] b. 10 Jan., 1740 (or '41); m. 13 March, 1760, Dr.
Coffin Moore of Stratham, b. 25 Feb., 1739 (son of *Wm.
Moore*,[3] *Wm.*,[2] *Col. Jonathan*[1]). He is said to have been
a man of fine personal appearance, learned and skilful in
his profession, but intemperate. He practised in Brentwood, removed early in 1765 and settled in Georgetown,
Me., afterward in Candia, where he d., 30 Oct., 1784, æ. 45.
They had seven children. " She was a woman of superior
understanding," and well educated. It is said, that when
she felt obliged to reprove her husband in the presence of
the children, she sometimes used the French language.
She m., 2d, Simon French of Candia, and d. 1 Nov., 1814.
(See Appendix, Moore Family).

iii   Martha,[4] b. 1742; m. Capt. Benj. Randall, but d. of consumption, two years after, leaving a son, William (Randall) who
d. in the West Indies of yellow fever, æ. 18. Captain Randall m., 2d, Thankful (dau. of Walter) Weeks. (See No.
10-x).

iv   Mary,[4] b. 22 Feb., 1745; m.,1st, Adino Nye of Hingham, Mass.;
res. in Georgetown, Me. She m., 2d, in 1770, Joseph (s. of
Jas.) Brackett of Greenland, b. 1740; res. in Newmarket.

Children of Mary (Weeks) and Adino Nye were:

1 *Elizabeth*[5] (Nye), b. 1765; m. Lt. Meuce, a British officer
who d. in India. She d. soon after in England.

2 *Mary Weeks*,[5] b. 1768; m. Nov., 1787, Nath'l Goss and had
six children; d. in Lancaster, about 1852. She had:
(1) Mary, m. Whidden; (2) Sarah, m. Spaulding; (3)
Eliza, m. Stebbins; (4), Martha, m. Dr. Stickney; (5)
Lydia, m. W. J. Brown; (6) Nathaniel.

Children of Mary (Weeks) and Joseph Brackett were:

3 *A dau.*,[5] b. 1771; d. early.

4 *John Weeks*[5] (Brackett), b. 3 Sept., 1773.

5 *Joseph Warren*,[5] b. 10 Aug., 1775.

6 *Adino Nye*,[5] b. 1 Nov., 1777; clerk Coos Co. Court. (See
No. 38-vii).

7 *Martha Weeks*,[5] b. Oct., 1779; m. Hon. Jn. W. Weeks of
Lancaster, and d. *s. p.*

8 *James*,[5] b. 3 March, 1782; of Cherry Valley, Otsego Co.,
N. Y.

In 1789 Joseph Brackett and wife removed to Lancaster,
N. H., a new settlement, where she d. 15 Jan., 1814, "an
excellent woman, spoken of in terms of unqualified praise."

v   Sarah[4] (Sally), b. 1747; m. Aug., 1762, Rev. Jacob Bailey[5]
(*David*,[4] *Nath'l*,[3] *Jn.*,[2] *Jas.*[1]), A.B., of Harvard College,
1755; b. in Rowley, Mass. 1731.

He was classmate with Pres. John Adams, and governor
John Wentworth. In 1763 he visited England to be ordained, and was appointed rector of an Episcopal church at
Pownalboro (now Dresden), Me. Fifteen years afterward,
he was obliged to flee from the opposition incurred by his
attachment to the English cause, leaving his wife and six
children in destitute circumstances.*

---

*See Note VI, Appendix.

From 1783 till his death, 26 July 1808, he was rector of
St. Luke's church, Annapolis, Nova Scotia. In twenty-six
years, he was absent from service but one Sunday. His life,
written by Wm. S. Bartlett with the title "The Frontier
Missionary," was published in Boston, 1833. His widow
d. at Annapolis, 22 March, 1818, æ. 70. "He was poor, yet
hospitable and kind, always retaining the personal regard
of all who knew him." He had six children :
1 *Charles Percy*[5] (Bailey), b. Pownalboro, Me. ;* killed in the
battle at Chippewa, 5 July, 1814.
2 *Rebecca Lavinia*,[5] d. at Annapolis.
3 *Charlotte Maria*,[5] living in 1857.
4 *Thomas Henry*,[5] a British officer; d. early, leaving a wife
and three daughters.
5 *Wm. Gilbert*,[5] a lawyer, did much business ; d. early, leaving a small family.
6 *Elizabeth Anne*,[5] m. Jas. Whitman. For many years she
corresponded with her mother's relatives and informed
them respecting her mother's family, and furnished most
of the information we have respecting them. (See Appendix, Bailey Family.)
(38) vi† Capt. John,[4] b. Hampton, 17 Feb., 1749; d. 10 Sept., 1818; m.
27 Dec., 1770, Deborah(dau. of Jas.) Brackett of Greenland,
b. 25 Dec., 1749, who d. in Lancaster, 5 July, 1831. In
1783, he left Greenland, spent some years in Lee, and in
May, 1787, was settled in the new town, Lancaster, Coos
Co. He was a zealous patriot, "was Lieut. in the Revolutionary Army, a member of the convention that adopted
the Constitution of New Hampshire, several years representative in the Legislature of N. H., and an influential citizen, wherever he resided."
On his way from Lancaster to Greenland, in 1818, he visited his sister and her children in Tamworth, seeming very
cheerful, and happy ; but the next morning after he left my
father's house, as he was about to get into his carriage,
at Wakefield, he suddenly fell and died from disease of the
head. His age was sixty-nine years, seven months. He had
eight children. [See Appendix, Note VIII.]
(39) vii William,[4] b. Hampton, 20 May, 1751, m. Susannah[5] (dau. of
Dea. Wm.[4]) Haines of Greenland (*Wm.*,[3] *Sam.*,[2] *Sam'l*[1]), b.
28 July, 1752, who d. at Auburn, 31 May, 1845, æ. 94. Being
left an orphan, at the age of eight years, his friends were
anxious that he should study medicine and engage in the
profession his father had followed. But he declined, saying, "I could not bear to go from one sick bed to another,
and spend my days in visiting such scenes of distress as the
doctor is called to witness." So he learned the carpenters'
trade, lived in Portsmouth, in No. Hampton; and in May
1778, he bought of P. Car, a farm in Chester, west of the
road to Candia where he d. Sept. 1821, æ. 70. He had five
children.

---

*See Note VII, Appendix.   †Appendix, No. VIII. Sketch of Capt. John Weeks.

20 LEONARD WEEKS AND FAMILY.

viii Ward Cotton,⁴ bapt. 15 July, 1753, m. Mary (dau. of Jonah)
Barber, of Exeter, where he was. in 1778, a clothier, in company with Jonah Barber. He was, afterwards, a sea captain,
and d. of yellow fever, before August 1789, leaving one son
(39a)   1 *John Wingate* (Weeks), under seven years of age, who lived
in Wakefield, where his father owned land. He m. ——
Durgin, and removed to Cornville, Me., and had a large
family. Eight children.
ix Abigail,⁴ d. an infant.
(40)x Joanna,⁴ b. Hampton, 31 Dec., 1755. At the age of three yrs.
she was motherless, and fatherless at eight years of age;
brought up by her sisters; m. in Newmarket 4 Dec., 1777,
Levi (s. of Col. Jere.) Folsom of Newmarket. Before she
was of age, her father's large estate was mostly spent in
providing for eight older children, and she was left with
little but her education. In eighteen months after marriage
they removed to the new town of Tamworth, where by
much toil and self-denial they brought up nine children to
become useful members of society. She died 17 July, 1826,
æ. 70 yrs. and 6 mos. She was fond of books, and was a
very intelligent and influential Christian woman, much respected by her neighbors.

16
Maj. William Weeks³ (*Joshua,²Leon.¹*) born 1723, died 1798, farmer, at the Bayside, Greenland, and his wife Elinor (March), had b. in Greenland
Children :

i Joshua,⁴ b. 6 Dec., 1748. farmer in Greenland (Bay Side); m.
1787, wid. Martha M. Rust (dau. of Chase Wiggin) and both
died of scarlet fever, 28 June, 1817, and were buried in one
grave. She was widow of Dr. Richard Rust of Stratham.
Their children were:
1 *Geo. Washington*,⁵ d. unm. in Florida, æ. abt. 50.
2 *Mary Ann*,⁵ m. Thos. Pickering, and had four children :
(1) William (Pickering), m. Josephine (dau. of Rev.
Edwin) Holt and had (*a*) Mary E. not m. ; (*b*) Josephine
H., w. of Frank Scammon of Stratham; (*c*) Katie Tit-
comb, unm. ; (*d*) Edwin Holt. (2) Susan Walker, d.
unm. (3) Martha Abigail, d. unm. (4) Georgiana
Toseau, d. unm. (5) Thos. Edwin, d. unm.
3 *Martha*,⁵ m. before 20 June, 1817, Sam'l Pickering and had
(1) Martha Ann Weeks (Pickering) who resides in Greenland.
ii Clement⁴, b. 24 Dec., 1750 (A.B., H. Coll., 1772) ; was a
teacher, unm., spent the last of his days with his brother
George and unm. sisters; d. 4 Jan., 1829, æ. 79.
iii Elinor,⁴ b. 1 Jan., 1753; d. unm. 7 Jan., 1829, æ. 77; was buried in one grave with Clement in the old cemetery, at the
Bay Side.
(41)iv Capt. William,⁴ b. 28 Apr., 1755 (A.B., H. Coll., 1775) ; m., 1st,
5 Oct., 1780, Nabby Rogers, b. 1760, a descendant of Rev.

Nath'l Rogers, who emigrated to Ipswich, Mass. in 1636. She d. 8 May, in 1783, leaving two sons. He m., 2nd, Sarah Cotton (dau. of Dr. Ichabod) Weeks of Greenland, and settled in Hopkinton. He was on the staff of Gen'l Washington. He d. in Greenland, 1843, æ. 90; and his widow Sarah C. in 1845, æ. 74. His children were thirteen.

v   Dea. John,[4] b. 1 Apr., 1757, farmer at the Bay Side; m. Mary Coffin, had four children, and was accidentally killed, 11 Apr., 1821, by an insane man. His children were :

   1   *George*,[5]* m. Caroline Avery and d. 2 Aug., 1869, æ. 59.
   2   *Ellen*,[5] d. 1823.
   3   *Joshua Clement*.[5]
   4   *Mary*,[5] d. 1883.

vi   Col. George,[4] b. 11 April, 1760; d., unm., on the homestead in 1830.

vii   Comfort,[4] b. 26 Mar., 1762; m. Nov., 1781, Benj. Chadbourne of Berwick, Me., and d. Feb., 1784, *s. p.*   He was a lawyer in Eastport, Me.

viii   Jacob,[4] b. May, 1764; d., unm., in Charleston, S. C., in 1800.

ix   Martha,[4] b. 10 Aug., 1766; m., 1st, Feb. 1789, Daniel (s. of Ichabod) Rollins of Somersworth, who d. 4 June, 1795, æ. 36. (See Appendix, Rollins Family.) She m., 2nd, Samuel Hale of Barrington, and d. Sept., 1840, æ. 74.

   Children of Martha and Daniel Rollins were :

   1   *Ichabod*[5] (Rollins), b. 1790.
   2   *Hon. Wm. W.*,[5] b. 1794; m. Eliz., dau. of George Frost of Durham.
   3   *Ann W.*,[5] m. 19 Mar., 1822, Samuel C. Hale of Rollingsford (s. of Hon. Samuel Hale of Barrington), and had :
     (1) Samuel (Hale), (2) Francis W., (3) Ann W.

x   Mary,[4] b. 8 May, 1770; m. 4 May, 1797 (as 2nd wife) Col. Eben. Thompson[3] of Portsmouth (son of Judge Ebenezer,[2] Robert[1] of Durham) and had children :

   1   *Ebenezer*[5] (Thompson), b. Durham, 5 Feb., 1798; m. Ann Mary (dau. of Benj.) Thompson. He was master of a vessel, and called Capt. Eben Thompson. He was an active man, useful and influential in the Congregational church. He d. in Durham, Jan., 1853, and his widow d. about one hour afterward.
   2   *Martha W.*,[5] b. 25 Nov., 1799; m. Sept., 1827, Benj. Odiorne and d. in Barrington, 1 Feb., 1855; left a daughter Mary, unm.; res. in Dover.
   3   *Jacob W.*,[5] b. 2 Jan., 1802; m. 3 Nov. 1829, Artemisia Rindge of Portsmouth, res. there until his death, 7 July, 1864. He was master of a vessel and known as "Capt. Jacob Thompson."
   4   *Benjamin*,[5] b. in Portsmouth, 31 March, 1804; m. in Barrington, 23 Dec., 1833, Lucinda J. Drew of Barrington, and d. there 23 Apr., 1875.
   5   *George Weeks*,[5] b. in Portsmouth, 29 Mar., 1807; m. 18 Apr., 1833; graduated Gilmanton Theological Seminary,

---

*George (son of Dea. John) Weeks[4] of Greenland was a quiet farmer, but highly respected, and honored by his fellow-citizens with various offices. His death was much lamented.

1839, was ordained 29 Apr., 1840, at Kingston, N. H.;
preached afterward at Dracut and at Carlisle, Mass., re-
tiring after thirteen years to his estate in Stratham. His
wife was Mary (dau. of Den. John) Wingate of Stratham,
b. 2 Nov., 1810, and granddaughter of Hon. Paine Wingate, judge of the Superior Court, etc.

6 *Hannah Eleanor W.,*[5] twin sister of George W., b. 1807;
m. 13 Aug., 1827, Dr. Josiah Bartlett, b. 1803, who d. 13
May, 1853. He was grandson of Hon. Josiah Bartlett of
Kingston, governor of N. H., etc. Their children were:
(1) Mary (Bartlett), b. in Stratham; m. George Frost
Rollins of Dover, and had (a) Rev. Daniel (Rollins) of
Pittsfield and (b) Hannah B. (2) Josiah (Bartlett), m.
Frances (dau. of Jeremiah) Robinson of Exeter. (3)
Ezra, m. in Boston, and d. in Stratham, 1880, *s. p.* (4)
George, res. in Boston, unm. (5) Ariana Antoinette, d.
unm., in Boston, 1886. (6) Hannah Ann Laurette, d. in
Boston, 1886, unm.

xi Nancy Ann,[4] b. 25 Sept., 1774; d. unm., 4 Jan., 1864.
xii Hannah,[4] b. 13 Feb., 1778; m. Hon. Josiah Bartlett, M.D., of
Stratham, and d. there 25 Aug., 1865, *s. p.*

17

David Weeks[4] [*Jona.,*[3] *Jn.,*[2] *Leon.*[1]]? born 1745, died 1827, joiner, and his wife Ruth (Page), had born in Greenland

Children :

i   Ruth,[5] b. 1772; m. James Smith, farmer in Bath. She d. 18
Nov., 1861, æ. 89 yrs. and 10 mos.
(41a) ii David,[5] jr., b. 14 July, 1774; m. Matilda Child, b. 8 Aug.,
1778; had eleven children. He d. 13 June, 1842, æ. 68. She
d. 3 Oct., 1847.
iii Jonathan,[5] b. 1777; d. 11 Apr., 1785, æ. 8.
iv Mary,[5] b. 1778; m. Dudley Child, farmer in Bath, and d. 29
July, 1831, æ. 53.

18

Jonathan Weeks[4] [*Jona.,*[3] *Jn.,*[2] *Leon.*[1]]? baptized 1751, died —— , and his wife Margaret (Caverly), had born in Portsmouth

Children :

(41b)i Joseph,[5] b. abt. 1780; shipwright in Dover; m. abt. 1801,
Charity D. (dau. of Jacob) Hurd of Somersworth, and had
nine children. He was a soldier in the War of 1812.
ii Hannah,[5] m. —— Wiggin of Portsmouth and had one dau.,
who d.
iii Comfort B.,[5] m., in Portsmouth, Micajah Parshley of Bath,
Me., and d. leaving one dau.; res. Boston.

LEONARD WEEKS AND FAMILY.   23

iv Edward Q.,⁵ m.; rem. to Provincetown, Mass.; [d. 1882]? Ch.:
    1 *Edward*,⁶ jr., father of Rev. Joseph H., of Walpole, Mass.
    2 *John.*⁶
    3 *Joseph.*⁶
    4 *Mary Jane.*⁶
    5 *Hannah.*⁶
    6 *Abigail.*⁶

19

Richard Scammon of Stratham, a farmer, born
1722, died 1806, and his wife Elizabeth (Weeks), had
born in Stratham
Children:

  i Rachel, b. 12 Oct., 1754; m. about 1778, Walter Neal; res. W.
     Newmarket and had three children:
     1 *Sophia.*
     2 *Harriet.*
     3 *George A.*
 ii William, b. 31 March, 1756; m. Dec., 1780, Sarah Robinson,
     and had five children. He d. 19 Jan., 1836, in Ledyard,
     N. Y. Children:
     1 *Edward*, b. 1782.
     2 *Richard*, b. 1784; d. 1867.
     3 *Elizabeth*, b. 1788; d. 1836.
     4 *Samuel.*
     5 *Mary C.*
iii Elizabeth, b. 1757.
 iv Samuel, b. 1759; d. early.
  v Mary, b. 24 Sept., 1760; d. 1 Aug., 1846; m., 1st, abt. 1782,
     Edward Burleigh, a sea captain. He was lost at sea, be-
     fore Oct., 1801, and in March, 1803, she had m., 2nd, ——
     Stiles; rem. to western N. Y. Children of Mary and Ed-
     ward Burleigh were:
     1 *Jas.*, b. 1783.
     2 *Richard*, lost with his father.
     3 *Sarah.*
     4 *Jn. M.*, b. 1793.
 vi Richard, b. 31 May, 1762; m. Eliz. Chase; d. in N. Y., abt.
     1848. He res. in western New York. His son, Hon. Elia-
     kim (Scammon), b. 1785; res. E. Pittston, Me.; d. Nov.,
     1870.
vii Samuel, b. 10 June, 1764; d., unm., Feb., 1789.
viii Elizabeth, b. 9 May, 1768; m. 179-, Kingsley Lyford of Exe-
     ter; d. 7 June, 1808.
 ix James, b. 26 Apr., 1771; m. Apr., 1796, Lydia (Parker) Wig-
     gin, b. 15 Feb., 1777; d. 15 Oct., 1840. He res. in Strat-
     ham; d. 6 Apr., 1859. Children:
     1 *Judge John*, b. 22 Aug., 1797; m. 11 Oct., 1824, Mary G.
       Barker of Exeter, and had four children: (1) Lydia P.,
       (2) Jn. James, (3) Susan D., (4) Mary Ellen.
     2 *Lydia*, b. 1800; w. of Benj. Barber of Exeter.

3 *Ira Jas.*, b. 1803; m. Ann Lyford; d. in Stratham, 1852.
4 *Stephen*, b. 1805; m. Monah Gordon; d. 1883.
5 *Richard*, b. 24 Oct., 1809; m. 9 Feb., 1842, Abigail Philbrick Batchelder of No. Hampton; d. in Stratham 6 Sept.,
1873. Their children were: (1) Hezekiah, b. 31 Jan.,
1843; m., 1866, Mary E. Jewell, res. in Exeter. (2) Hon.
Jas., b. 10 June, 1844; grad. Brown Univ., 1868, is a lawyer in Kansas City, Mo.; m. 4 Mar., 1876, Laura Ever-
ingham. (3) Sarah C., b. 16 Dec., 1848, res. in Stratham,
unm. (4) Richard M., who has aided in this work, b. 6
Dec., 1859; res. in Stratham, unm.
6 Elizabeth Susan, b. 10 May, 1812; m., in 1839, Michael Dalton of No. Hampton; had four children; d. Mar., 1874.
x　Hezekiah, b. 26 March, 1773; farmer and cabinet maker in
Stratham; m. Leah Stockbridge; d. 9 Apr., 1817. Three
children.
xi　Jonathan, b. 1775; d. in infancy.

20

John Weeks[4] (*Jn.*,[3] *Sam.*,[2] *Leon.*[1]), born 1732, died
1804, farmer, etc., in Jefferson, Me., and his wife Abigail (Piper), had born in Greenland

Children :

(42) i　Joseph,[5] b. 1755; m. Margaret Hussey of Newcastle, Me.,
had nine children b. in Jefferson, Me., where he d. 28 Nov.
1847, æ. 92.
ii　Abigail,[5] b. 1757; m. Col. Jonathan Jones of Whitfield, Me.
Children :
1 *Jonathan*[6] (Jones).
2 *Simon.*[6]
3 *Elsey,*[6] m. Edmund Murphy.
4 *Comfort,*[6] m. Briggs Turner.
5 *George*[6].
6 *Maria,*[6] m. Rufus Choat.
(43) iii　Thomas,[5] b. 1762; m. Ruth (dau. of Joseph) Taylor of Jefferson, Me., b. 3 Feb., 1764, d. 3 Feb. 1857, æ. 93. He d.
11 Jan., 1846, æ. 84. Had ten children.
(44) iv　Mary,[5] b. 1764; m. 4 Feb., 1790, Maj. Daniel (s. of Samuel)
Waters of Newcastle, Me., b. 8 Mar., 1768. He was a man
of intelligence and integrity, was a surveyor, Justice of
the Peace, etc. He d. 18 Aug., 1856. She d. in Jefferson,
Me., æ. 96. They had ten children.
(45) v　Mark,[5] b. 1766, m. Sally Moody of Nobleboro, Me., b. 18
Aug., 1764, who d. May, 1840; he d. 26 Feb., 1850, æ. 84.
They had seven children.
(46) vi　John,[5] b. abt. 1768, farmer; m. Rachel Avery of Jefferson;
had six children b. in Jefferson.
(47) vii　Winthrop,[5] b. in Jefferson, Me., 12 Feb., 1770; m. Hannah
(dau. of David) Hopkins of Jefferson, b. 1771, who d. there
15 Dec., 1848; nine children. He was a farmer and lumberman, d. in Jefferson 12 Nov., 1856, æ. 86. David Hopkins

and his wife Jane (Simpson) came from Scotland. He was
a ship builder.

(48) viii Dea. Daniel,[5] b. in Jefferson, 25 Nov., 1774; m. 1798, Martha
(dau. of Joseph) Taylor of Newcastle, Me., b. there 25 June,
1776, who d. 10 Nov., 1858; he d. 7 Oct., 1854, æ. 80. They
had nine children.

  ix Jane,[5] b. abt. 1776; m. Col. Joseph Rust of Washington Mills,
and had :
   1 *Mary*[6] (Rust), m. Timothy Cunningham and had six children.
   2 *James*,[6] m. —— Gilpatrick.
   3 *Lot*,[6] m. —— Jones.
   4 *Emily*,[6] m. R. E. Rider.
   5 *Jane*,[6] m. Abiel Erskine.
   6 *John*,[6] m. —— Patrick.
   7 A *dau*.,[6] m. Geo. Myers.*

21

Cole Weeks[4] (*Jn.*,[3] *Sam.*,[2] *Leon.*[1]) born 1737, died
1801, joiner of Epping and of Sanbornton, and his wife
Hannah (Chapman), had born in Epping :

  i Eleanor,[5] b. 1755; m. (as 2nd w.) Josiah Calley; and d. 1829,
æ. 74. She had a dau.
   1 *Ann*[6] (Calley), b. 17 Oct., 1795, who m. Wm. Tilton.
  ii Dorothy[5] (Dolly), b. [1758]? bapt. in Epping, 1760; m. 1784,
Josiah (s. of Jona.) Shaw; and d. 29 Nov., 1819. She
had :
   1 *Sherburn*[6] (Shaw), of No. Hampton.
   2 *Polly*,[6] b. 1788; m. Moses Kimball.
   3 *Dolly*,[6] b. 1793; m. (as 2d wife) Moses Kimball.
   4 *Asa*,[6] b. 1795; d. 1801.
(49) iii Chase,[5] b. 30 Jan., 1762, a farmer; m., 1st, 8 June, 1784, Patty
Cawley, b. 16 Jan., 1764, who d. 31 May, 1813, æ. 49. She
had twelve children. He m., 2nd, in Nov. 1813, Mrs. Elizabeth Moore (wid. of James) Sanborn, who d. 3 Feb., 1841,
æ. 74. He m., 3d, Mrs. Lydia Whitcher and d. 15 Dec., 1847,
æ. 85.
(50) iv William,[5] b. 24 Oct., 1764; was Justice of the Peace in Sanbornton; m., 1st, Sally Calley, who d. 24 June, 1827, æ. 61.
He m., 2nd, Mrs. Molly Dustin (wid. of John) Shaw, who d.
1837. He m., 3d, Mrs. Dolly (wid. of Wm.) Sanborn, and
d. 10 Sept., 1839, æ. 74. He had eight children.
  v Polly,[5] b. 1766; m. 3 May, 1787, Joseph (s. of Jas.) Wadleigh
of Sanbornton, and d. 18 Aug., 1823, æ. 57. She had :
   1 *Eunice*[6] (Wadleigh), b. 1788; m. R. Caverly.
   2 *Huldah*,[6] b. 1790; m., 1st, Thos. Cawley; 2nd, A. S. Jud-
kins.
   3 *James* D.,[6] b. 1792.

---

* "This family of John Weeks[4] were tall, large, with full black eyes, and the
nine averaged ninety-one years of age."

4

4 *Molly*,⁶ b. 1797; m. N. Buswell.
5 *Newell*,⁶ b. 1799.
6 *Joseph*,⁶ b. 1802.
7 *Chase W.*,⁶ b. 1805.
8 *Simeon H.*,⁶ b. 1809.
(51) vi John,⁵ b. 1769; m. —— Calley; moved to Jefferson, Me.,
        near his uncle John,⁴ and his cousins. He had five sons
        and several daughters.
(52) vii Joseph,⁵ b. 27 April, 1773, a farmer in Sanbornton; m. Apr.,
        1791, Huldah (dau. of Edmund) Chapman, and d. 28 May,
        1840. His widow d. 18 Jan., 1847. They had six children.
(53) viii Jonathan,⁵ b. 19 July, 1776; "the strongest man in Sanborn-
        ton;" m., 1796, Polly (dau. of John) Call, and had six chil-
        dren. On the 28 Jan., 1850, he was found in the morning
        dead in his bed, æ. 74.
(54) ix Capt. Cole,⁵ jr., b. 2 Mar., 1778; m., 1st, 14 Jan., 1802, Eliza
        Elkins, who d. 1840. In Jan., 1841, he m., 2nd, Abigail E.
        (dau. of Benj.) Smith, and d. 17 June, 1854. He was captain
        in the militia; selectman of Sanbornton; eight children.

22

Benjamin Weeks⁴ (*Jn.*,³ *Sam.*,² *Leon.*¹) born 1742,
farmer, and his wife Marion (Hanniford), had born [in
Epping]?

Children:

(55) i   John,⁶ b. 26 Oct., 1762; m. Esther (dau. of Hubbard and
        Eunice) Spencer, b. 17 Sept., 1769, who d. 6 Dec., 1833.
        He was a farmer, with nine children, in Piermont, where
        he d. 3 Jan., 1841, æ. 79. He gave the town, Piermont,
        land for a public cemetery.
ii   Abigail,⁶ m. Samuel Aiken.
iii Anna,⁵ owned the covenant and was bapt. in Deerfield, 4
        Sept., 1781. She m. John Aiken.
iv   Marion,⁵ m. Richard Pillsbury, dealer in stoves and tin ware,
        Bradford, Vt.; and d. 7 Aug., 1846.
v   Eleanor,⁵ m. Jonathan Fellows.
vi   Polly,⁵ m. David Smith of Warner.
vii Benjamin,⁵ b. 11 Aug., 1775; m. Polly Gibson; was farmer
        in Piermont.
viii Betsey⁵ (twin sister of Benjamin), b. 11 Aug., 1775; m. Thos.
        Pillsbury, farmer, b. 27 Nov., 1771; res. in Warren; and d.
        there — Jan., 1835. She d. in Bradford, Vt., 7 April, 1851.
        Children:
    1 *Joseph*,⁶ m. his cousin Ruth Pillsbury, and had: (1) Dan-
        iel.⁷ All d. in Bradford, Vt.
    2 *Thomas*,⁶ who m. Mary Osborne, and had eight children:
        (1) Betsey. wife of M. D. Farr of Bradford, Vt.; (2)
        Esther, m. Hartwell Farr; (3) Ezra. m. Olive Davis; (4)
        Hartwell H., m. Sarah Keller; and four others that d.
        young.
    3 *Richard*,⁶ d. unm.

4 *Ester,*[6] m. Timothy Ladd of Piermont, N. H., and had : (1)
a dau., Mrs. John Hartwell of Warren, N. H.; (2) Samuel (Ladd).

ix Edna,[5] b. 30 Jan., 1782; m. Stephen Lund; and d. 1 Feb.,
1838.

(56a) x Joseph,[5] m. Lucy Lund; and d. in Piermont, 3 Apr., 1841.
She d. in Edenville, Iowa, 1871.

23

Abner Haines, born 1724, died 1798, of Greenland and Canterbury, etc., and his wife Sarah (dau. of Walter) Weeks, had born in Greenland

Children :

i   Samuel (Haines), b. in the old brick house, 26 Aug., 1747; he
m. 9 July, 1772, Hannah Johnson, b. 22 Dec., 1749, who d.
in Canterbury, 13 Feb., 1813. He was a soldier in the Revolutionary War. He outlived all his brothers and his own
sons, and died 29 Oct., 1838, æ. 91.

ii Richard, bapt. 27 Nov., 1748, a cooper; m. Prudence, b. 20
May, 1753, and d. 6 Nov., 1798; had eight children. His
widow m., 2nd, 21 Nov., 1799, Col. Josiah Sanborn of Sanbornton, and d. 1843, æ. 90.

iii Matthias, bapt. 5 Aug., 1750; a blacksmith; d. Portland, Me.,
1796. He m., in Portland, Me., 21 Sept., 1775, Molly Cammet, b. 1751, d. Portland, 1841. During the War of the
Revolution, he made wrought iron balls for cannon used
in defence of Portland.

iv Walter Weeks, b. 1754; served in the Revolutionary War; m.
Rachel Knowles of Chester, a native of Rye, and died in
Poplin, 16 May, 1808.

v   Stephen, b. 23 May, 1759; m. Hannah Carter, b. in Northfield,
1759. He served in the Revolutionary War, and d. 3 Feb.,
1807.

vi Josiah.

24

Dr. Ichabod Weeks[4] (*Walter,*[3] *Sam.,*[2] *Leon.*[1]) born 1738, died 1807, of Greenland, had no children by first wife, Sarah C. Cotton. By second wife, Comfort Johnson, he had :

i   Sarah Cotton,[5] b. 29 Nov., 1771; m. Capt. Wm. Weeks of
Hopkinton, and had eleven children; and d. in 1845, æ. 74
(see No. 16-iv, and No. 41).

ii Comfort J.,[5] b. 26 Nov., 1773; m. Joseph (s. of Greenleaf)
Clark of Greenland; res. in Wolfboro, and had :
1 *Ichabod* (Clark),[6] b. 1793; d. 3 April, 1825.
2 *Mary M.,*[6] b. Aug., 1795; d. 6 Mar., 1876.
3 *Comfort,*[6] b. 17 Aug., 1797; m. Benj. Hubbard Weeks; and
res. in Concord (see No. 25, v).

4 *Sarah*,[6] b. Mar., 1800; m., 1820, Lewis Hayes of Milton;
d. 1883; had six children.

5 *Enoch M.*,[6] b. 12 Apr., 1802; d. 7 Aug., 1863.

6 *Greenleaf*,[6] b. Mar., 1806; d. 2 Mar., 1874.

7 *Brackett Weeks*,[6] b. 2 Nov., 1809; d. 1 Jan., 1885.

8 *Alfred Metcalf*,[6] b. 17 Oct., 1812; d. 18 Aug., 1855.

iii   Brackett,[5] b. 18 Oct., 1775; d. 26 Oct., 1832; m. Sarah Pickering, b. 29 Sept., 1780, and had :

1 *Eliz. Pickering*,[6] b. 29 Sept., 1801; m. Gordon (son of
Thos.) Burley, b. 25 Aug., 1795, who d. in Middleton,
Ont., 17 Jan., 1864. He was a lumber man. She d. in
Ticonderoga, N. Y., 14 Mar., 1872. Their son (1) Henry
G. Burley,[7] b. in Canaan, N. H., 1832, was, in 1884, mem-
ber of Congress from the seventeenth district, New York.

2 *Wm. P.*,[6] b. 22 Feb., 1803; A.B., Dart. Coll., 1826; was a
lawyer in Canaan from 1829 till his death in 1870. He m.,
20 July, 1833, Mary Eliz. Doe of Derry. and had born in
Canaan : (1) Joseph Doe,[7] b. 27 Oct., 1837, D. Coll., 1861.
(2) Wm. Brackett, b. 14 May, 1839, D. Coll., 1861; m.
(3) Marshall Hill, b. 13 Oct., 1841; m.   (4) Mary E , b. 24
Dec., 1844. (5) Susan H., b. 18 Mar., 1853; d. 1881.

3 *Mary P.*,[6] b. 18 Nov., 1804; m. Sam'l Wright; res. and d.
in Dorchester.

4 *Sam'l P.*,[6] b. 3 Aug., 1806; d. in Lyme.

5 *Clement Storer*,[6] b. 1 Jan., 1809; m. Nancy Piper; d. in
Dorchester; farmer.

6 *Richard P.*,[6] b. 14 May, 1811; cabinet-maker; m. Olive
Walker; res. and d. in Woburn, Mass.

7 *James E. P.*, b. 21 Nov., 1813; a lawyer; m. Eliza A.
Webb; and d. in San Francisco, Cal.

8 *Stephen H. P.*, b. 22 Jan., 1816; merchant in Boston; m.
Mary Lord ; and d. in Newtonville, Mass.

9 *Thompson*,[6] b. 19 Mar., 1817; d., unm., in Boston.

10 *Sarah A.*, b. 7 July, 1821; m. —— Bryan; and res. in
San Francisco, Cal.

By third wife, Abigail March, he had :

iv   Elizabeth[5] (Betsey) March, b. 23 July, 1777; m. 2 Apr., 1797,
John (s. of Joseph) Greenough, b. 20 May, 1768, hatter in
Newburyport, who d. in Sandwich, Mass., 23 June, 1839.
She d. there 23 Nov., 1857. Their children were :

1 *Sarah B.*[6] (Greenough), b. 23 May, 1798; m., 1st, in Green-
land, 10 Apr., 1824, Rev. Joshua Eveleth of Princeton,
Mass.; 2nd, in Eastport, Me., 10 Jan., 1835, Hon. Samuel
Morse of Machias. Me.; and d. 10 Nov., 1873.

2 *Mehitable F.*,[6] b. 1 Jan., 1800; m., 6 Aug., 1826, Theodore
T. Abbot of Concord, N. H.; d. in Lunenburgh, Mass.,
10 March, 1887. He invented and made cotton machinery,
was a member of the Legislature and mayor of Manchester, N. H.

3 *Joseph*,[6] b. 2 June, 1802; m., 1st, 8 Sept., 1834, Eliza Kelley
of Hopkinton ; 2nd, 12 May, 1838, Susan Williams of Hopkinton ; 3rd, Betsey Wilcox of Newport, N. H., 16 Oct.,
1841; d. in Hopkinton, 11 Feb., 1884. He was a stone
mason and farmer.

4 *Stephen W.*,[6] b. 15 Feb., 1804, shoe manufacturer; m. in
Philadelphia, 26 Feb., 1836, Ellen M. McPherson; d.
there 13 Mar., 1848.
5 *John G.*.[6] b. 20 Dec., 1806; m. in Milford, N. H., 25 Dec.,
1830, Maria J. Putnam. He was a contractor and builder;
d. 20 Nov., 1883.
6 *Susan J.*,[6] b. 10 Jan., 1810; m. in Greenland, 15 June, 1832,
Ezra Dillingham of Sandwich, Mass.; d. there 30 Aug.,
1860.
7 *Eliza A. B.*,[6] b. 10 Sept., 1812; m. in Greenland, 18 Apr.,
1833, William Coombs of Bangor, Me.; d. there 16 Jan.,
1885.
8 *Ephraim A.*,[6] b. in Greenland, 4 July, 1818; m., 1st, 6 Apr.,
1843, Maria L. A. Sanborn of Canterbury, N. H.; 2nd,
Nancy B. Towne of Manchester, N. H. He is a farmer;
res. Falls Church, Virginia.

v   Susan,[5] b. 23 Oct., 1780; d. 7 Nov., 1857. She m. Ephraim
Pickering, b. 28 Sept., 1779, who d. 5 July, 1809. They had,
b. in Newington:
1 *John*[6] (Pickering), b. 1804; m. Sarah Wheeler; d. 1 Dec.,
1848; she d. 1845. They had: (1) Ephraim, who d. 1865.
2 *Theodore*,[6] b. Mar. 1806; m., in 1830, Mary Hart of Newington, who d. in 1832. They had (1) Henry, who d. Aug.,
1849. æ. 17.
3 *Ephraim.*[6] (twin), b. 1806; d . unm., 16 Apr., 1850.
4 *Abigail March*,[6] b. 10 Nov., 1808; m., 1st, 17 May, 1832, E.
W. Toppan, who d. 17 May, 1845. On the 20 Sept., 1872,
Mrs. Abigail P. Toppan, m., 2nd, Col. Peter Sanborn, a
prominent citizen of Concord. They res. in 1888, in
Hampton. Children: (1) Sarah P. (Toppan), b. 12 Feb.,
1833; m. 4 Apr., 1860, Charles N. Healey of Stratham and
had (a) Chas. W. (Healey), b. 29 Dec., 1860; (b) Anna T.,
d. 1 July, 1865; (c) Alice Grafton, b. 28 Dec., 1867. (2)
Christopher Grafton, b. 16 Feb., 1835; m. 1st, Jennie Dudley; 2nd, Annie Bean of Deerfield, who has three children:
(a) Christopher, (b) Abigail M., and (c) Mary C. (3)
Ann Eliz. S., b. 10 Mar., 1837; m. 10 Oct., 1857, George
Thompson of Portsmouth, and d. 9 Sept., 1859, *s. p.*
(56) vi   Stephen March,[5] b. 23 Nov., 1781; m., abt. 1807, Mary Shack-
ford Gookin, a descendant of Dr. John Cotton. He was a
farmer in Greenland, and had six children. He d. 25 Dec.,
1859.
vii Thomas March,[5] b. 20 Jan., 1784; d. 6 June, 1797.

25

William Weeks[4] (*Walter*,[3] *Sam.*,[2] *Leon.*[1]) born
1743, died 1813, farmer, and his wife Elizabeth (Hubbard), had born in the Brick House, Greenland

Children :

(57) i   Walter,[5] b. 20 Dec., 1769; d. 28 Dec., 1851; m., 1st, 1794, Sarah
Tarleton of Greenland, who had five children and d. Aug.,
1848. He m., 2nd, Nancy Presby, and lived on the Chapman

place, one-half mile south of Greenland Parade; a shoemaker.

ii   Joseph,[5] m. Hannah Johnson, and d. *s. p.*
iii William,[5] b. 14 Nov., 1779; m. Jan., 1814, Harriet (dau. of
     Philip) Barker, of Greenland; b. 27 May, 1785, lived in the
     Brick house on the old homestead, and d. 7 May, 1849. She
     d. 3 Jan , 1864.   Children :
   1 *William H.*,[6] b. 20 Mar., 1815; m. 31 Aug., 1841, Mehitable
     S. (dau. of Rev. John) Brodhead, of South Newmarket b.
     11 Nov., 1811, and had b. in Greenland : (1) Gertrude,[7] b.
     17 Dec., 1842; d. 1 Jan., 1843; (2) Julia A., b. 27 May,
     1844; m. June, 1877, Geo. A. Francis, and has : (*a*) Josie
     H.[8] (Francis), b. 5 Oct., 1878; res. Greenland. (3) Josie
     B., b. 7 May, 1846; m. Apr., 1876. Rev. Charles E. Hall;
     res. in 1887, Titusville, Penn.; they had one daughter.
     (4) John W.. b. 24 Oct., 1848; m. in Great Falls, 23 Apr.,
     1874, Sarah E. (dau. of Jn. O.) Lord. He is postmaster
     in Greenland and keeps a grocery. His children were :
     (*a*) Charlie H., b. 12 Sept., 1875, d. 14 March, 1887; (*b*)
     Thornton Norris, b. 21 May, 1882.
   2 *Robert Barker*,[6] b. 18 Dec., 1818; m. Dec., 1862, Annie B.
     Jewell, b. 19 Feb., 1815; res. Brick House; *s. p.*
   3 *Josiah Bartlett*,[6] b. 9 Feb., 1821; m. Nancy Bates (dau. of
     Stephen) Tozier, b. 27 Apr., 1827, of Waterville, Me.
     They had b. in Greenland : (1) Hattie Bates,[7] b. 12 Dec.,
     1855; m. 21 Jan., 1880, Charles Austin Jenness of Rye,
     b. 30 Dec., 1842, and has : (*a*) Fannie Austin[8] (Jenness),
     b. 28 Mar., 1885; (*b*) Herbert Leon, b. 25 June, 1887. (2)
     Fannie Maria, b. 12 Jan., 1858; d. 27 May, 1880.
   4 *Mary Moody*,[6] b. 24 May, 1824; m. Thos. T. Milton of N.Y.;
     had one dau., and d. 1884.
(58) iv Joshua,[5] m. Ann (Nancy) (dau. of Nicholas[5]) Rollins of
     Stratham, b. 15 May, 1782, and d. 7 June, 1848. He was a
     blacksmith and had five children.
   v   Benj. Hubbard,[5] m. Comfort (dau. of Joseph) Clark of Green-
     land, b. 17 Aug., 1797; res. in Concord, where both died.
     Their children were :
   1 *Ichabod*,[6] d.
   2 *Elizabeth*,[6] b. 1819; m. Oliver Towle of Hampton, lived in
     Westfield, Mass. She d. 20 Feb., 1884, æ. 65.
   3 *Ellen*,[6] m. John Lane of Concord, N. H.
   vi Elizabeth.[5] m. Brackett Weeks of Greenland; d. *s. p.*
   vii Comfort,[5] d. young.

26

John Weeks[4] (*Matt.*,[3] *Sam.*,[2] *Leon.*[1]) born 1736,
died 1815, of Greenland and of Gilmanton, and his wife
Dorothy, had, besides others, born in Greenland
Children :

(59) i Nathaniel[5] (I suppose), b. abt. 1758, shoemaker and tanner,
     rem. 1773 to Gilmanton; m. Huldah Pottle (probably from
     Stratham). Had Samuel P., b. in Gilmanton, 1784. He

m., 2nd, in Exeter, 6 May, 1787, Polly Pottle both of Exeter, and had ten or more children. Between Sept., 1788, and April, 1789, he removed to Stratham,— returned to Gilmanton and d. before 21 July, 1815. His widow, Polly, afterward lived with her children in Exeter.

(60) ii John Lang Weeks,[5] b. in Greenland, 3 Aug., 1763. When he was ten years of age, his father rem. to Gilmanton. He settled in Tamworth; m. in Burton, Mar. 4, 1800, by Orlando Weed, Esq. (his father's neighbor), to Judith Plummer, b. in Wakefield, 11 Nov., 1780; had sixteen children; d. in Tamworth.

(60a) iii Noah (Weeks),[5] b. 1771 in Greenland; m., in Gilmanton, 12 Mar., 1793, Sarah Morrill and had b. in Gilmanton four children.

27

Matthias Weeks,[4] jr. (*Matt.*,[3] *Sam.*,[2] *Leon.*[1]) born 1740, died 1821, tanner and farmer, of Exeter and Gilmanton, and his wife Judith (Leavitt), had born in Exeter Children :

(61) i John,[5] b. 8 Sept., 1762, farmer; m. 10 Oct., 1786, Hannah Moody of Gilmanton; rem. about 1801 to Canaan, Vt., where he d. Sept., 1852. Had children b. in Gilmanton.

ii Elizabeth,[5] b. 16 Jan., 1764; m. in Gilmanton, 9 Oct., 1786, John Moody, jr., b. 1766, d. in Tunbridge, Vt., 28 Nov., 1840. Their children were:
1 *Betsey*[6] (Moody), b. 28 July, 1787; m. Aretas Haskell and d. 21 Feb., 1816. Children: (1) Eliza, b. 1808; m. Geo. W. Adams, and d. 1885. (2) Jn. W., b. 1810; m. M. A. Williams, and d. 1885. (3) David M., b. 1813; d. 1837.
2 *Sally*,[6] b. 1789; m. Joseph (son of Joseph and Sarah (Weeks) Badger, and d. 29 Aug., 1868. Children: (1) Sarah Eliz., (2) Joseph P. W., (3) Martha.
3 *John*,[6] b. 1791; m. Sally Smith and had: (1) Stephen, (2) Betsey, (3) Mary, (4 and 5) Comfort and Edith (twins), (6) Ann, (7) Sarah, (8) Lucina, (9) Judith, (10) Malvina.
4 *Abigail*,[6] b. 1793; m. John Noyes, and had seven children: (1) Eliz., (2) Mahala, (3) Ju., (4) Cyrus, (5) Joshua, (6) Washington, (7) Abigail.
5 *David*,[6] b. 23 Apr., 1795; m., 1st, Martha Smith, who d. 10 Jan., 1842. He m., 2nd, Mary Tucker, and d. 26 Oct., 1886. Children: (1) Ruth, m. E. Wills; (2) Judith A., m. C. Avery; (3) Clarissa Jane, (4) Helen, m. 1st, Wm. Jones, 2nd, Da. Reed; (5) Dudley F., m. Mary Cram; (6) Harriet, m. Fred. Buzzell.
6 *Dudley*,[6] b. 9 Feb., 1797; m. Clarissa Hunt, and d. 12 April, 1876.
7 *Washington*,[6] b. 1799; m. Sally Hall and had five children :

(1) Nath'l, (2) Olive, (3) George W., (4) Wm., (5)
Thirza.

8 *Thirza*,[6] b. 11 Dec., 1801; m. John L. Hall, and d. 18 Dec.
1868. Children: (1) George, (2) Harriet, (3) Ellen, (4)
A son.

9 *Mahala*,[6] m. Burnham Hunt.

10 *Judith*,[6] m. Hazen Little, and had had four children: (1) Frank,
(2) Fanny, (3) Ellen, (4) Arabel.

iii Sarah,[5] b. 15 Sept., 1765; m. 8 June, 1786, Joseph Badger,
3rd (son of Hon. Joseph B., jr.) and had:

1 *Joseph*[6] (Badger), b. 1787; m. Sally (dau. of Jn.) Moody,
b. 1789. Three children.

2 *Judith*,[6] b. 20 Sept., 1788; "an energetic woman;" m. Josiah Parsons, Esq., b. 26 Sept., 1781, and d. 10 Dec.,
1842; she d. 28 Mar., 1879. He was of the Society of
Friends; was twelve years postmaster and twenty-six
years town clerk of Gilmanton. One of their daughters
m. Rev. Chas. Tenney and d. *s. p.* Another m. Rev. E. N.
Hidden, and is, in 1888, a widow, having lost her children.

3 *Nathaniel*,[6] m. Susan Eveleth; and d.

4 *Eliz.*,[6] d. unm.

5 *Parish*,[6] m. Nancy Osgood of Loudon; and had nine children.

6 *Sally*,[6] m. ——— Williams of Tunbridge. Vt. Three children.

7 *Polly*,[6] m. Parker Leavitt of Dover; and had (1) Mary F.,
(2) Joseph.

8 *Hiram*[6], m. Margaret Christian; res. in New York City.
Children: (1) Chas., (2) Wm., (3) Constantine, and (4)
Jocelyn.

(62) iv Matthias[5], b. 13 Apr., 1767; m. 26 May, 1794, Mary (dau. of
Jn.) Bennet of Gilmanton; and d. there "of spotted
fever," 10 Apr., 1815. She d. 24 Aug., 1825. They had
seven children.

v Mary,[5] b. 14 Feb., 1769; d. in Tunbridge, Vt., 22 June, 1853.
She m. in Gilmanton, 14 Apr., 1791, David Folsom[6]
(*Dan'l*,[5] *Dan'l*,[4] *Abi.*,[3] *Jn.*[2]), b. May, 1770; settled in
Tunbridge, Vt., where he d. 4 Jan., 1815. Their children
were:

1 *Matthias*[6] (Folsom), b. 1791; a farmer in Worcester, Vt.;
m. Eliza Stevens; and d. Jan., 1864. Children: (1)
Rhoda, m. H. Templeton; res. in Worcester, Vt. (2)
Mary, m. Sewell Copp. (3) David, m. ——— Seaver. (4)
Sarah, m. Joseph Ford.

2 *Anna*,[6] b. 1793; m., 1816, Aretas Haskell, farmer; and d.
June, 1878. Eight children: (1) Harrison S., m.; and d.
s. p. (2) Mary A., m. D. Noyes; and d. Oct., 1880.
(3) Sarah W., b. 1821; m. L. Wright; and d. *s. p.* (4)
Olive F., m. E. R. Williams; had (*a*) Dora and (*b*) Fred.
A. (5) Betsey Ann, b. 1825; m. 1882, D. Noyes. (6)
Frank A., killed at Cold Harbor, 3 June, 1864, æ. 36. (7)
Harvey M., b. 1831; m. M. Mills. (8) Alma S., m. G.
W. Moody; and d. Apr., 1868.

3 *Daniel*,[6] b. 1 Sept., 1795; m. 22 Jan., 1832, Philinda Ord-

way of Stafford, Vt. Children: (1) Betsey J., m. Geo.
Martin, 1861, s. p. (2) Mary A., m. Wallace Fuller; and
has (a) Lizzie ——. (3) Frank, b. 1838. (4) Susan, b.
1840; m. M. Sargent; and d. 1821. (5) Sarah, unm.
4 *Joshua*,⁶ b. 1797; farmer; m. 1833, Lucy Andrews of Tunbridge, Vt., and d. 1852. Children: (1) Sylvia, b. 1835;
m. F. Dearborn. (2) Leruah, m. M. Myers. (3) Lucy,
b. 1840; m. —— Speare. (4) Lamila, m. A. Stegeman,
s. p.
5 *David*,⁶ b. 1799; farmer; m. Mehitable Fellows; d. in New
York, 1852. They had eight children.
6 *Olive*,⁶ b. 1803; m. Jn. Hale; seven children; d. in Minneapolis, Minn , Nov., 1876.
(62a) vi Samuel,⁵ b. 2 Dec., 1770; m. Abigail Moody of Gilmanton;
and d. in Canaan, Vt., 1 Sept., 1854. She d. in Canaan, Vt.
(63) vii Dea. William,⁵ b. in Exeter, 18 Sept., 1772; a tanner; m., 1st,
about 1794, Mary (dau. of Thos.) Beede of Poplin, b. 30
Nov., 1773, who d. 25 Dec., 1831. He moved to Gilmanton in 1797 and had nine children.   He m., 2nd, Abigail
Towle, b. 2 June, 1788, sister to his son James' wife. She
d. in Loudon, 18 Nov., 1886.
      He was an original member and afterward deacon of the
Third Free Will Church in Gilmanton, where he d. 14
March, 1852.
vii Joshua,⁵ b. in Gilmanton, 30 Mar., 1774; m. Mary Fellows
of Tunbridge, Vt.; and d. there 16 Sept., 1818. Children:
1 *Mary*,⁶ m. Gilman Bennett.
2 *Judith*⁶, m. Elijah Stoddard.
ix Judith,⁵ b. 28 Aug., 1776; m. Nov., 1796, Smith Kimball, carpenter, b. in Exeter, Feb., 1777, of Gilmanton; d. there,
16 May, 1834. He died in Gilmanton, 12 Feb., 1842. Children born in Gilmanton:
1 *John* (Kimball) b. 22 Mar., 1797; m., 1st, 29 Dec., 1822,
Abigail (dau. of Moses) French of Loudon; and settled in
what is now Belmont. She d. 15 Oct., 1870. He m., 2nd,
16 June, 1872, Mrs. Louise (Cate) Sanborn; and d. 21
July, 1883. Children: (1) Jas. French, b. 1823.   (2)
Romduta G., b. 1825; d. 1826. (3) Elvira Jane, b. 1828.
(4) Amoshetta, b. 1834; d. 1842.
2 *Matthias*, b. 8 July, 1800; m. 16 July, 1824, Eunice (dau.
of Nicholas) Buswell; res. in Belmont.   He d. 8 Feb.,
1881. She d. 16 April, 1882. Children: (1) Ezekiel F.,
b. 1826; d. 1869. (2) Jeremiah S , b. 1828. (3) Francis
B., b. 1830; d. 1869.   (4) Jane F., b. 1832; m. J. M.
Lee. (5) Hannah, b. 1834; d. 1835. (6) Narcissa S , b. 15
Apr., 1839; m. J. S. Plummer. They res. in Belmont
and had (a) Myrtie Jane, and (b) Flora E. (Plummer).
3 *Nancy*, b. 7 Nov., 1807; m. Jan., 1826, Isaiah Clough; and
d. 1879. He d. Aug., 1863. Children: (1) Lucinda H.
and (2) Geo. Franklin.
4 *Stephen S.*, b. Nov., 1820; m. 20 Nov., 1841, Mary French
of Loudon; and d. Nov., 1843. Children: (1) Stephen
S., b. in Loudon, 17 Aug., 1843; m. Mary E. Odell.
x   Olive,⁵ b. 21 Oct., 1778; d., unm., 20 Nov., 1825.
xi Dorothy,⁵ b. 10 July, 1780; m. in Gilmanton, 24 Jan., 1816,
5

Jonathan Jenness of G.; and d. in Meredith, 24 Mar.,
1861. Children:
1 *Orrin* (Jenness), m. Sally (dau. of Wm.) Jenness; and
had three children.
2 *Czarina*, b. about 1820; d. since 1860.
3 *Jonathan P.*, m. Mary J. (dau. of Cephas) Smith, b.
1821. By the fall of the town house in Meredith he was
made a cripple for life.
xii Dudley,[5] b. 2 Mar., 1782; m. 15 Jan., 1811, Polly French;
and d. in Gilmanton, 15 Nov., 1854. Children b. in Gilmanton:
1 *Sam'l French*,[6] stone-cutter; d. of fever at Quincy, Mass.
2 *Adeline*,[6] m. Simon (son of Leavitt) Knowles; res. in
Belmont; d. 18 Dec., 1881. Children: (1) Chas.[7]
(Knowles), b. 1849; d. 1851. (2) Geo. S., b. 1851; m.
Nettie Hall; and had (a) Adeline[8] and (b) Charles. (3)
Samuel, m. Lizzie Eastman; and have (a) Inez and (b)
Emma.
3 *Lyman*,[6] d.
xiii Anna (Nancy),[5] 22 Mar., 1784; m. Jonathan Sargent. Her
husband left home and never returned. They had:
1 *Judith Ann*, b. 1815; and d. 17 Mar., 1859; m. Jn. P. Osgood; and had three children, who all d. before Mar.,
1859.
(64) xiv Stephen,[5] b. 5 June, 1785; m. 29 Dec., 1808, Betsey (dau. of
Dan'l) Weed, b. in Poplin, 2 June, 1791, who d. in Sanbornton, 3 July, 1880; had six children.
"He was a prominent citizen of Gilmanton and was
called Master Weeks." He d. there 4 April, 1862.

28

Rev. Samuel Weeks[4] (*Matt.*,[3] *Sam.*,[2] *Leon.*,[1]) born
1746, died 1832, of Greenland, Gilmanton, N. H., and
Parsonsfield, Me., and his wife Mercy (Randlett), had
born in Greenland
Children :

(65) i Noah,[5] b. 25 Oct., 1767; m. Anna Pendexter; d. 30 Oct., 1808.
Nine children.
ii Anna P.,[5] b. 6 June, 1769.
(66) iii Eliphalet,[5] b. in Newmarket, 6 June, 1770, farmer in Parsonsfield, Me.; m., 1st, Susan (dau. of Joseph) Perry, b.
in Scarboro, Me., 1773; d. 23 Aug., 1813; m., 2nd, Martha
Kennerson, and d. in Parsonsfield, 6 May, 1838, æ. 68.
Had seven children.
iv James G.,[5] b. 22 Feb., 1772; m. and lived but a few weeks.
v John,[5] b. in Gilmanton, 21 Feb., 1774; m. Sarah Huff
[Hough]? Children:
1 *Polly*.[6]
2 *Hannah*.[6]
3 *Samuel*,[6] m. Sargent, and had Nettie, w. of Jury White.

4 *Susan.*[6]
5 *Sally.*[6]
vi Mary,[5] b. 6 Feb., 1776; d. Nov., 1786.
vii Susanna,[5] b. 23 Mar., 1778; [d. 19 Apr., 1780]?
viii Samuel,[5] b. 19 Feb., 1780; m. Mehitable Knight, had seven sons, " moved down East " and is not traced.
ix Ichabod,[5] b. 25 Nov., 1782; d. 23 Oct., 1784.
(67)x Matthias,[5] b. 4 Mar., 1785; m., 1st, —— Day; m., 2nd, Olive Guptail (or Mrs. Hammond). Had eight children.
xi Levi,[6] b. 11 Feb., 1788.
(68)xii Benjamin,[5] b. 24 Jan., 1791; m., 1814, Nancy (dau. of Abram) Barnes of Cornish, Me., who d. 13 Apr., 1883. He was a farmer in E. Parsonsfield, Me., where he d. 4 Sept., 1836. They had nine children.

Elder Samuel Weeks married, second, in Parsonsfield, Mrs. Sarah Barnes (widow of S.) Guptail, and had :

xiii Mercy,[5] b. 16 April, 1803, who m., 1st, Daniel Pendexter; 2nd, Wm. Chamberlain of Jefferson, N. H.
Child by first marriage :
    1 *Hannah* (Pendexter) who m. Joshua Knight and had two children.
Child by second marriage :
    2 *William* (Chamberlain), jr., who m. Has four children.

29

Benjamin Weeks[4] (*Matt.,*[3] *Sam.,*[2] *Leon.*[1]) born 1751, died 1829, and his wife Sarah (Weed), had born in Gilmanton

Children :

i Hon. Daniel,[5] b. 28 Dec., 1775, opened a store at the home place in 1801,— traded in Boston and Portsmouth, then a farmer in Gilford, and d. there in 1851. He m. Hannah Gale of Salisbury, and had
    1 *Isabella,*[6] b. in Portsmouth, 1804; m. in Gilford, 26 Mar., 1828, Morrill Thing, and d. in Gilford, 18 July, 1886, æ. 81 yrs. and 9 mos. She was called "an executive woman."
    2 *Julia M.,*[6] m. 16 June, 1829, Benj. Frank (son of Capt. Benj.) Weeks, and had five sons (see No. 68a-iii).
    3 *George William,*[6] m. 3 June, 1838, Mehitable (dau. of Capt. B.) Weeks. Children : (1) Winfield Scott,[7] m. 1 Jan., 1866, Clara M. Philbrick, b. 10 June, 1847. He d. April, 1866, *s. p.* (2) Geo. Wm. of Lakeside house, Weirs; m. Mary Sinclair, *s. p.* (3) Levi R. ; m. Narcissa Fellows, and had (a) Grace Louisa,[8] (b) Alice C., (c) Ann Laurie.
    4 *Thos. Benton,*[6] m. 1 Nov., 1873, Jennie S. Morrill, res. in Laconia. Children : (1) Albert Morrill.[7] (2) Geo. Isaac, res. in Laconia.

5 *John G.*,[6] a hatter; m. Sally H. (dau. of Capt. Benj.)
Weeks, in Gilford, 16 Jan., 1829, and had nine children,
who lived to mature age: (1) Carrie E.;[7] m. in 1847,
Chas. Swain, who d. of disease contracted in the army.
They had four sons: (*a*) C. Frank,[8] m. Della Goodwin,
and had Mamie M. and Chas. F. (Swain);   (*b*) Fred M.,
m. Lena Ellis, *s. p.*;   (*c*) John H., m. Mary Folsom, and
has Gracie May; (*d*) William T. These are all manu-
facturers of knit goods.   (2) John H., b. 1838; m. 11
Dec., 1855, Lizzie A. Kelley, and res. on the homestead
of his great grandfather, Benj. Weeks. (3) Sarah J.,
m. Sylvester Swain, res. in Illinois, with two children,
Lillie A., w. of A. J. Ploughman, lawyer in Deadwood,
Dakota, and Geo. (Swain). (4) Lydia A., m. Wm. T.
Batchelder, who d. *s. p.*, March 1888. (5) Mary E., b.
1841, graduated in St. Louis, Mo.; m. 12 Dec., 1864,
Barton Munsey, M.D. Both are homeopathic physicians,
(6) Hannah G., b. 1843; m. 16 Jan , 1863, J. W. Follett.
b. 1838, *s. p.* (7) Elvora Josephine, b. 1846; m. 7 Oct.,
1865, Jewell Gove, b. 1838. and has Clara E. (Gove).
(8) Rebecca W., b. 1848, M.D.; m. 15 July, 1868, Rev.
Fred. L. Wiley, b. in Maryland, 1836, grad. No. Hampton.
Theol. Sem., 1868. She graduated at Boston Univ,
School of Med., 1882; res. in Laconia.   Child: Maurice
G. Wiley.

6 *Susan.*[6]
7 *Emily C.*,[6] m. Cummings.
8 *Daniel.*[6]
9 *Albert Gallatin*,[6] b. 8 Feb. 1819; Dart. Coll. 1844, studied
law, then medicine, M.D. 1849; m. Mary D. (dau. of
Meshek) Sanborn, rem. to Barnstead, and practised there
" till death took away the beloved physician," 25 Feb.
1853.

ii   Matthias,[5] b. 2 Feb. 1778; studied law; and had a tan yard;
rem. to Clinton, Me. and died there. He m. 4 Nov. 1802,
Mary Bodge of Gilmanton, who d. in Augusta, Me. (Aug.
22. 1815, a Mary, widow. administered on the estate of Matthias Weeks, dec'd.)   Children :

1 *William.*[6]
2 *Mary Ann*,[6] d. Strafford, N. H., unm.
3 *Elizabeth*,[6] m.——Hinds, and d.
4 *Harriet*,[6] m.——Rideout.

iii Sally,[5] b. 3 Dec. 1779, "a woman of literary taste;" m. 14
Oct., 1800, Henry Wadley, a blacksmith, who came to Gilmanton in 1787.   Their children were:

1 *Benjamin* (Wadley), blacksmith and stone cutter, of Gilford,
a skilful workman and a useful citizen, living in 1888.
2 *William*, a blacksmith; m. and d. in Gilford.
3 *Catharine Betsey*, m. Mark Thing.
4 *Isabella.*

iv   Elisha,[5] b. 13 Sept., 1781, began trade Gilmanton, 1802; m. 19
Jan., 1806, Polly (Mary) Potter of Gilmanton, b. July,1783;
rem. to a farm in Strafford, where he d. 4 June, 1866. She
d. Sept. 1852. Children :

1 *Joseph Potter*,[6] b. May, 1809 ; m. Mar., 1831, Betsey (Eliz. L.)

Reynolds, who d. May, 1885; res. on the homestead, in
Strafford, s. p.

2 *William*,[6] m. May, 1842, Maria Clark; res. Barrington.
Children: (1) Ellen M.,[7] b. Apr., 1843; m. Chas. Hayes of
Madbury. (2) Chas. W. b. April, 1850; m. Anna Glidden,
and lives with his parents; has son Geo. In 1886, Chas.
W. was member of the Legislature.

3 *Elisha Warren*,[6] b. May, 1811; an invalid; d. 1855, unm.

4 *Mary Susan*,[6] b. Oct., 1825; m. Jan. 1848, David B. Winkley
of Barnstead, and has had: (1) Mary L.[7] (Winkley), b.
July, 1852; m. E. F. Abbot, and has a dau. (2) Lauren
W., b. July, 1854; d. an infant. (3) Laura R., b. Mar., 1863,
d. Oct., 1873.

v William,[6] b. Gilmanton, 17 June, 1784; A. B. Dart. Coll. 1806;
a teacher, feeble in health, read law, settled in Philadelphia; d. Pottsgrove, Pa., 21 Aug., 1810, æ. 26, "in the
dawn of a promising life."

(68a) vi Capt. Benjamin,[5] b. 4 Apr., 1788, farmer and merchant in
Gilford, m. in Gilmanton, 30 June, 1806, Betsey Hoyt of G.
and had eight children.

vii Levi R.,[5] b. 9 Apr., 1793, a trader in Gilford; m. 9 June,
1814, Lydia Sleeper of Gilford, and had six children. In
1829, he was adm. on the estate of his father, Benj. Weeks
of Gilford. His children were:

1 *Lydia*.[6]
2 *Benjamin*.[6]
3 *Sarah*[6] (twin sister of Benj.).
4 *Harriet Fayette*.[6]
5 *Mary Ann*.[6]
6 *George*,[6] graduated at West Point, and was an officer in the
U. S. Army.

30

Noah Weeks[4] (*Matt.*,[3] *Sam.*,[2] *Leon.*[1]) born 1754,
died 1825, farmer, and his wife Betsey (Meed), had born
in Gilmanton (now Gilford)

Children:

(69) i William,[5] b. 12 Dec., 1781; in 1805 published a paper in Kennebunk, then in Saco and in Portland; m., 23 July, 1809,
Abigail Hubbard of Kennebunk, Me., who d. 7 Nov., 1871.
In 1809, he came from Portland, Me., to Portsmouth, and
bought the N. H. Gazette, which he published till 1813,
when he was succeeded by Beck & Foster. He was printer,
editor, etc. "He held an able pen and wrote more than his
predecessors." He had seven children and died 8 Aug., 1839.

ii Mary,[5] b. 24 Sept., 1784; d. 26 July, 1806.

iii Sally,[5] b. 18 Nov., 1786; d. 3 Mar., 1875; m. 24 Feb., 1811.
Daniel Kelley, farmer, both of Gilmanton.* Their children
were:

*They lived seven miles from the church at Gilmanton Centre, and yet were
constant in attendance at public worship.

1 *Betsey Mead*, b. abt. 1815; a teacher; unm.
2 *Sarah*, d. unm., 1878.
3 *Mary Ann* (Kelley), b. 11 Apr., 1817; m., 1st, John S. Darrell, who.d. in Sanbornton, 1859; m., 2nd, C. Sargent, who was in Feb. 1887, killed on the railroad.
4 *Ellen W.*, b. 1821; m., 1851, Wm. Bell; d. 16 Mar., 1862; had four children.
5 *James S.*, b. Sept., 1823; m., 1847, Susan J. Drew; res. Franklin Falls; farmer, etc. Has been representative, etc. Children: (1) Emily Bird, b. 1850, (2) Joseph Olin, (3) Chas. H., (4) Dan'l E., (5) Nellie B., (6) Jn. Irving, b. 1870.
(69a) iv Dea. Matthias,[5] b. 13 Dec., 1788; m., in Gilford, 4 Oct., 1812, Betsey (dau. of Jere.) Thing; lived in Gilford, and d. there 4 May, 1847, æ. 58 years and 5 months. She d. 3 Mar., 1854, æ. 65. They had five children.
(69b) v Dea. Asa,[5] b. Aug., 1790, a farmer in Gilford; m. there 7 Dec., 1815, Jemima (dau. of Caleb) Marston of Gilmanton, b. 11 Nov., 1788, and d. Nov., 1862, æ. 72. She d. 6 June, 1872. They had two children:
1 *Stephen M.*[6]
2 *William B.*[6]
vi Betsey,[5] b. 14 Aug., 1792; m. in Gilford, 7 Mar., 1815, Ephraim Mason; d. 9 Jan., 1818, at the birth of her son, Lemuel B. (Mason). He studied theology, preached in N. H. Then edited a paper in Ills. Chaplain of Ills. Reg't; d. of disease contracted in the army. He m. in New Jersey, and left three sons.
vii Hannah,[5] b. 18 June, 1794; d. 24 Mar., 1813.
(69c)viii Dea. Noah,[5] jr., b. 29 March, 1797; farmer, in Gilford; m., 23 Apr., 1820, Mary Dudley, and had nine children, b. in Gilford.
ix Eleanor,[5] b. 12 Jan., 1801; m., 1st, in Gilford, 23 Jan., 1826, John G. Sanborn of Gilmanton, who d. 19 July, 1832. She m., 2nd, Hazen Prescott, b. 1798, of Belmont, farmer, who d. 15 June, 1840. Child:
1 *John G.*, jr., b. 1827; d., 20 Sept., 1852, unm.

30a

Dudley J. Weeks[5] (supposed son of *Josiah*,[4] *Matt.*,[3] *Sam.*,[2] *Leon.*[1]) born, 1788, in Gilmanton, died Oct., 1868, cooper, married Lucy Sampson, born in 1791, who died in Boscawen, 1 Aug., 1825.

Children :

i Mary Jane,[6] b. 16 Dec., 1814; m. Benj. J. (s. of Richard C.) Gile, b. 1817, harness maker, and res. in Hooksett, N. H.; has held town offices and been representative to the Legislature. They had four daughters and one son. She d. 25 Mar., 1887. Children:
1 *Lucy G.* (Gile), m. S. Ames.

    2 *Frances A.*, m. Albert Wells, and d. *s. p.*
    3 *Wm. H. H.*, m. Lottie Wells; res. in Denver, Col.
    4 *Sarah S.*, m. Henry Hamilton, of Concord, *s. p.*
    5 *Mary*, m. Chas. Jones, engineer on Concord R. R.
ii   Arvilla L.,⁶ b. 12 Dec., 1818; m. June, 1844, B. A. Stanley, of
    Lynn, Mass., and d. in Lynn, Mass., 29 Oct., 1844.
iii   Charles,⁶ b. 1820; d. 1 Sept., 1825.
iv   Elizabeth F.,⁶ b. 6 May, 1822; m. 7 Apr., 1842, J. W. Dodge,
    b. 18 Mar., 1815. In 1871, removed and resided in Henni-
    ker. Children:
    1 *John B.*, b. 30 Mar., 1848; m. 18 Oct., 1869, Mary S. Mor-
    rill, of Penacook and has one son (1) Fred. (Dodge).
    2 *Geo. H.*, b. 6 May, 1850; m. 14 Nov., 1874, Abbie F. Straw,
    of Hopkinton, and res. in Henniker. These children
    were b. in Hopkinton, where J. W. Dodge lived till 1871,
    when he rem. to the farm in Henniker.
v   George W.,⁶ b. in Boscawen, 12 Aug., 1824; of Manchester. On
    the death of his mother, being less than twelve months old,
    he was taken into the family of Rev. Parker O. Fogg, whose
    wife cared for her motherless nephew till he was about 15
    years of age. He was called Geo. W. Fogg. About 1839
    he found work in the mills, in Manchester. Afterward he
    spent two years in the East Indies. Returning he studied
    and became a teacher. Then spent some years in the shoe
    business; but is now agent for real estate, insurance, etc.
    He m. 27 Sept., 1846, Sarah E. Mead, b. in Hopkinton, 13
    Nov., 1827, and had:
    1 *Laura A.*,⁷ b., 1847; d. 4 Nov., 1853.
    2 *Medora*,⁷ b. in Manchester, 2 Jan., 1855; m. Alonzo Elliot
    of Manchester.
    3 *Geo. Perley*,⁷ b. 22 Feb., 1863; student in Exeter; graduated
    from Dart. College in 1885.

30b

John Weeks⁵ (supposed son of *Josiah*,⁴ *Matt.*,³ *Sam.*,²
*Leon.*¹) (see No. 11–iii), born about 1765; married, first,
in Meredith (or vicinity) about 1786 Sarah Abbot; removed to Walden, Vt., and died in Woodbury, Vt., about
1846.

Children:

I   William,⁶ b. abt. 1788; d. 1875, æ. 87.
ii   Sarah,⁶ b. 1790; d. 1810, æ. 20.
iii   Robert.⁶ b. 1 July, 1793; d. 16 Apr. 1864, at Walden, Vt., æ.
    71. He m. in Walden, 8 Apr., 1819, Polly (Mary), dau. of
    Dan'l Johnson of Walden and had:
    1 *A son*,⁷ b. 7 Feb. 1820, d. young.
    2 *William Abbot*,⁷ b. 7 July, 1821; m. 27 Apr., 1865, Jane (dau.
    of Edw. W.) Farrington of Walden; b. 27 Apr., 1829.
iv   Betsey,⁶ b. abt. 1795; d. 1854, æ. 59.
v   Daniel,⁶ b. abt. 1797.

By a third wife, John Weeks[5] had born in Walden :

vi Clara,[6] b. 26 Mar. 1818; m. 1st, Wm. Williams in Cabot, Vt. ;
 m. 2nd, in 1855 Eli Aiken, in Patten, Canada; m., 3rd, Orin
 Pratt, and was living in 1885.
 Children by second marriage :
 1 *Mary* (Aiken).
 2 *Frank.*
 3 *Merrill.*
vii Merrill A.,[6] b. 1825; res. Danville, Vt.; m. and had :
 1 *Clara May.*[7]

31

John Weeks[5] [*Joshua*,[4] *Jed.*,[3] *Jos.*,[2] *Leon.*,[1]]? born
[1763], d. 1825, of Bartlett, and his wife Comfort
(Clarke), had born in Greenland and Bartlett
Children :

i Robert,[6] m. Bethia Smith (wid. Lombard); seven children;
 res. in Gorham, Me.
 1 *Sally.*[7]
 2 *Bethia.*[7]
 3 *Maria.*[7]
 4 *Almeda.*[7]
 5 *Hannah.*[7]
 6 *Robert.*[7]
 7 *Randall.*[7]
ii Josiah,[6] m. Mary Libbey of Porter, Me. ; res. at Kezar Falls,
 Oxford Co., Me. Children :
 1 *Mary*,[7] d.
 2 *Josiah.*[7]
 3 *John.*[7]
 4 *Jemima.*[7]
 5 *Livonia.*[7]
 6 *Rollins.*[7]
 7 *William.*[7]
iii Joseph Clark,[6] b. 25 Dec., [1782]? and died 13 Dec., 1874.
 He m., in 1810, Hannah (dau. of Nich. and Eunice Doe)
 Lunt of Newbury, Oldtown, who d. 20 Mar., 1848. Children :
 1 *John Little*,[7] b. 19 Nov., 1811; d. 15 Aug., 1818.
 2 *Joseph C.*,[7] b. 29 May, 1815; d. 24 Aug., 1818.
 3 *Jane Little*,[7] b. 3 July, 1817; m. 13 Dec., 1839, Thos J.
 Willey, of Brookfield. Children : (1) Lydia Jane[8]
 (Willey), b. in Conway; (2) Maranda Sophonia; (3)
 Abby Hill, d. 13 July, 1852; (4) Joseph Clark, d. 22 Oct.,
 1884; m. Emma C. Whipple of Salisbury, Mass. ; (5) John
 Nicholas, m. Hattie M. Marston of Conway; (6) Chas.
 Henry, not m.
iv Joshua,[6] m. Jemima Libbey, of Porter, Me.; resided there
 and had :
 1 *Effie.*[7]

2 *Thankful.*[7]
3 *Clark,*[7] d.
4 *Henry,*[7] d.
5 *William.*[7]
6 *Judith,*[7] d.
7 *Mary Ann.*[7]
8 *Jane Chick.*[7]
9 *Maranda Delano.*[7]

v Polly Perkins,[6] m. William Pickering of Bartlett. Children :
  1 *Sally* (Pickering).
  2 *John S.*

vi John,[6] b. in Greenland, 1793, a soldier in 1812; m. Hannah M. Stone of Ipswich, Mass., and d. in Newburyport, 1865, æ. 72. Children :
  1 *Hannah,*[7] b. Newburyport, 1823; m. Jn. Burnham of Conway Centre. Two children.
  2 *Abigail M.,*[7] b. 1825; m. Nicholas Vella of Lynn, Mass.
  3 *Mary,*[7] b. 1827; m. John Reed, res. 6 Violet St., Lynn, *s. p.*
  4 *John,*[7] b. 4 Mar., 1829 (Dr. in Cleveland, O.) ; m. Eunice E. Bailey of Wakefield, Mass. Children: (1) John Franklin;[8] m. Nellie Draper of De Payton, N. Y. (2) Hannah, m. Wm. T. Leighton of Cleveland, O. (3) Geo. W., d. (4) Mary E. (5) Arthur B. (6) Hervey. (7 and 8) Alvina and Clara, both d.
  5 *Dr. Joseph,*[7] b. 5 Aug., 1831; m. 23 Apr., 1853, Elizabeth Ann Lewis of Newburyport, res. in Lynn, Mass. Children: (1) Caroline Stone,[8] b. 8 Mar., 1854; m. 8 Oct., 1871, F. B. Dennis of Lynn, Mass. (2) Elizabeth, b. 11 July, 1856; d. 10 July, 1857. (3) Joseph Wm., b. 22 July, 1858.
  6 *Caroline,*[7] b. 1833; d. 1852.

vii George,[6] m. Mary Ann Putnam of Lancaster, and had :
  1 *Caroline.*[7]
  2 *Emeline.*[7]
  3 *Mary Elizabeth.*[7]
  4 *George.*[7]

viii Henry,[6] b. 1797; m. Mary Willey, of Bartlett, and had :
  1 *Alice P.,*[7] d.
  2 *Martha.*[7]

ix Nathaniel,[6] m. Lydia Thompson of Lee ; res. Concord. Children :
  1 *Abby.*[7]
  2 *John.*[7]
  3 *Caroline.*[7]
  4 *Thomas.*[7]
  5 *Joseph.*[7]
  6 *Isaac,*[7] d. æ. 2 yrs.
  7 *George.*[7]
  8 *Henry.*[7]

x Eleanor[6] (Nellie), m. Job Holland Burley; res. Elk River, Minn. Eleven children.
  1 *Clarissa* (Burley), d.
  2 *John.*
  3 *Belinda,* d.
  4 *Barker,* d.

6

5 *Joseph.*
6 *Richard.*
7 *Mary,* d.
8 *Martha.*
9 *Nathaniel,* d.
10 *Job,* d.
11 *Ransom.*

32

Josiah Weeks⁴ (*Jed.*,³ *Jos.*,² *Leon.*¹) born [1743]? or 1749, of Bartlett, and his wife Polly (Emery), had born in Bartlett

Children :

  i Hannah,⁵ b. 2 Feb., 1793; m. Thomas Willey, and had:
    1 *Levi* (Willey).
    2 *Sophia.*
    3 *Andrew.*
    4 *John.*
    5 *Sarah.*
    6 *Samuel.*
    7 *Catharine,* d.
    8 *Caroline.*
    9 *James,* d. unm.
  ii Joshua,⁵ b. 27 Jan., 1795; m. Mrs. Maria Farnham (*née* Hawkins) and d. *s. p.*; res. at Bartlett, a farmer.
  iii John,⁵ b. 7 Aug., 1799; d. an infant.
  iv Polly,⁵ b. 27 Jan., 1802; m. Lyman Vincent and d. *s. p.*
  v Ellie⁵ (Ally), b. 3 May, 1804; m. Benj. Richardson, and had:
    1 *Joseph* (Richardson), m., and was killed in army.
    2 *Angeline,* m. Granville Brown; res. Conway, *s. p.*
    3 *Eben,* m. Miss Abbot, and has six children.
  vi Nancy,⁵ b. 14 Aug., 1808; m. Mr. Bugbee; res. Conway; d. *s. p.*
(69d)vii Josiah,⁵ b. in Bartlett, 18 May, 1812; res. there 1837; m. Mar., 1839, Mary K. (dau. of Job) Eastman, and had five children.

33

Jedediah Weeks⁴ (*Jed.*,³ *Jos.*,² *Leon.*¹) born 1761, died ——, of Northwood, and his wife Lydia (Knowlton), had born in Northwood

Children :

  i Dr. Nathaniel,⁵ b. 1 Feb., 1791; m. Alma Harolton, had eight children; settled first in Loudon, rem. to Illinois and d.
  ii Polly,⁵ b. 21 Sept., 1795; m. Joseph Johnson, had one child; d. Joliet, Ill.

lii Jedediah, jr.,[5] b. 1 Apr., 1807; m. 23 Mar., 1842, Belinda
(dau. of Jn.) Yeaton, b. in Epsom. Children:
1 *Emily Jones*,[6] b. 19 Mar., 1844.
2 *Mary Ella*,[6] b. 4 Sept., 1846.
3 *John Gardner*,[6] b. 16 Sept., 1847; m. 1872, Hannah Jane
Shaw, and has: (1) Geo. W.,[7] b. 7 Apr., 1879; (2) G. Fay,
b. 12 Nov., 1882; (3) Eugene, b. 23 Aug., 1885.
4 *Andrew J.*,[6] b. 2 June, 1849.
5 *Augusta*,[6] b. 2 June, 1851.
6 *Flora L.*,[6] b. 11 Oct., 1856.
7 *Frank Douglass*,[6] b. 26 Mar., 1860.

34

Phineas Weeks[4] (*Leon.*,[3] *Jos.*,[2] *Leon.*[1]) born 1745,
a cooper in Greenland, removed to Loudon.

Children :

i Abram,[5] m.; settled in Meredith, and had:
1 *John Henry*,[6] b. in New Haven, 5 Oct., 1832; d. 5 June,
1878, æ. 46; m. 27 June, 1854, Araminta D. Robinson of
Meredith, and had: (1) Fred. R.,[7] b. 14 Aug., 1855; d. 16
Feb., 1856, æ. 6 mos.
John Henry W. was an engineer, then steamboat captain,
dealer in lobsters, etc.
2 *David.*[6]
3 *Frederick.*[6]
4 *Sarah.*[6]
5 *Mary Eliz.*[6]
6 *Mary Emeline.*[6]
All dead in 1886.
ii Sarah,[5] m. ———. " Paul Twombly & Sally Weeks both of
Loudon m. 12 Jan., 1809."
iii John S.,[5] b. ———; (res. at 13 Princeton St., E. Boston, 1867).
iv Eben.[5]
v Thomas.[5]
vi Phineas.[5] "Phineas Weeks m. in Loudon 5 June, 1808, Lydia
Rogers."
In 1820 Phineas Weeks, cooper of Chichester, sold land
in Loudon.
vii George.[5]

35

John Weeks[4](*Leon.*,[3] *Jos.*,[2] *Leon.*[1]) born 1747, died
1832, and his wife Deborah (Allen), had born in Greenland

Children :

(69e) i Levi,[5] b. abt. 1773; m., 1st, Betsey Stanton Willey; res.
Brookfield. She d. and he m., 2nd, her sister Dolly and d.
25 Dec., 1811. Four children.

il   Deborah,[5] b. 12 May, 1776; m. —— Brown. She res. in
      Tuftonboro; was killed by lightning with her babe in her
      arms. Children:
      1 *Deborah.*
      2 *Rachel.*
      3 *John.*
      4 *Levi.*

(70) iii   John,[5] b. in Wakefield, 19 Feb., 1778; m. Abigail Colomy;
      and d. 11 Oct., 1842; had five children b. in Wakefield.

      iv   Margaret,[5] b. 8 July, 1781; m. —— Frost. Children:
      1 *Thomas* (Frost).
      2 *Amasa.*
      3 *John.*
      4 *Nancy.*
      5 *Margaret.*

      v   Elizabeth,[5] (Betsey), b. 12 Aug., 1783; d. 2 Apr., 1841; m.
      Joseph Jenness of Wolfboro, b. 25 July, 1777; d. 12 May,
      1860; had eleven children:
      1 *Mark* (Jenness), b. 9 Jan., 1804.
      2 *Daniel,* b. 4 Jan., 1806; d.
      3 *Nathan,* b. 5 Dec., 1807; d. 13 Jan., 1877.
      4 *Deborah,* b. 20 Feb., 1810; m. —— Hobbs; d. 13 Sept.,
      1886.
      5 *Cornelius,* b. 2 Nov., 1811; d.
      6 *Joseph,* b. 18 Sept., 1813; d. 19 Feb., 1885.
      7 *Betsey,* b. 16 Sept., 1815; d. 2 Apr., 1841.
      8 *Johnson,* b. 16 May, 1818.
      9 *Belinda,* b. 16 Sept., 1820; m. —— Nute; and d. 15
      Aug., 1874.
      10 *Chesley,* b. 14 Mar., 1823.
      11 *Samuel,* b. 18 Sept., 1825.

(71) vi   Phineas,[5] b. 12 Dec., [1786]?; m. Dec., 1814, Martha Cot-
      ton of Wolfboro, who d. 16 Feb., 1869. He d. 2 May, 1859.
      Seven children. ·

(72) vii   Nathan,[5] b. 6 Nov., 1788; m. Sally (dau. of Jacob) Clarke of
      Wakefield, who d. 12 Sept., 1847.
      They res. in Wolfboro and in Wakefield, where he d. 10
      May, 1872, æ. 83 yrs. and 6 mos. In Aug., 1818, he was
      guardian to Jn., Josiah, Amos and Levi, minor sons un-
      der 14, of Levi Weeks, late of Brookfield, dec'd.

(73) viii   Caleb,[5] b. 20 June, 1793; m. Aug., 1817, Patience Dudley of
      Waterboro, Me.; res. in Wakefield; had seven children;
      and d. — May, 1844. She d. in Wakefield, Sept., 1886, æ.
      91.

36

Rev. Joshua W. Weeks[4] *(Jn.,[3] Joshua,[2] Leon.[1])*

born 1738, died 1804, of Marblehead, Mass., and of Halifax, N. S., and his wife Sarah (Treadwell), had born in
Marblehead

Children :

      i   John,[5] was in the British army, then settled in the W. Indies.

ii Martha W.,[5] m.—Stone, settled in Sidney, Cape Breton. Her
    dau. m. Rev. Hibbard Burney, and their son, in 1857, was
    Bishop of Prot. Epis. Church of Nova Scotia; res. in Hali-
    fax.
iii Sarah W.,[5] m. Rev. Wm. Twining, and their son was a chap-
    lain of the Garrison at Halifax.
iv Helen,[5] m., 1st, an officer in the British army; and 2nd,——
    Simpson, a merchant of Loudon.
v   Capt. I. W.[5] (Weeks), left a large family: one son who was
    editor of a paper in Halifax, and two others who were far-
    mers in Cape Breton.
vi C. W.[5] (Weeks), was an Episcopal minister, at Weymouth,
    then at Manchester, and d. in Halifax, N. S.
vii Foster,[5] a major in the army, and settled in Canada.
viii James,[5] was commissary in the British army, and died young.

37

Dr. Coffin Moore[4] (*Wm.*,[3] *Wm.*,[2] *Col. Jona.*[1]) born
1739, died 1784, and his wife Comfort (Weeks), had
Children :

i   Martha[5] (Patty) (Moore), b. Newmarket, 12 July, 1761: m.
    Dea. Caleb (s. of Rev. J.) Prince, of Candia; d. 1821. Chil-
    dren:
    1 *Martha* (Prince), m.—— Webster.
    2 *Joseph*, m.—— Eaton of Candia.
    3 *Caleb.*
    4 *A dau.*, Mrs. Eaton.
ii William[5] b. in Brentwood, 5 Oct., 1763; m. Ann Carr of
    Candia, settled in Lancaster; res. there in 1823. Children :
    1 *Mary.*
    2 *Joshua Carr.*
    3 *Martha.*
    4 *Wm. Weeks.*
    5 *Ann.*
    The sons died and the daughters married and left Lancaster.
iii John W.,[5] b. 1765, Georgetown; 25 July — was killed in a
    storm at sea, being struck by lightning, in the shrouds of
    the vessel.
iv Coffin,[5] b. Georgetown, Me., 30 Apr., 1768; in 1787, moved
    with Gen'l E. Bucknam to Lancaster; whose daughter,
    Polly Bucknam, he m. there in 1789; was a farmer in Lan-
    caster, where he had twelve children, and d. 22 Aug., 1842.
    1 *Jacob Bailey*, d. in the army, in the war of 1812.
    2 *John Weeks*, rem. to Genesee Co., N. Y. [Batavia]?
    3 *Sukey*, m. Enoch Kinney of Whitefield, and had children.
    4 *Polly*, m., 1st, Nathan Morrill of Whitefield; 2nd, S. B.
      Johnson of Littleton, and d. *s. p.*
    5 *Geo. W.*, m. Miss Hicks of Burke, Vt., and had: (1) Har-
      riet and (2) George. He d. in Stewartstown.
    6 *Dr. Edward Bucknam*, (M.D., Bowdoin Coll. 1828), b. in

Lancaster, 1801; left home at the age of 19, studied medicine with his relative Dr. Thos. Brown of Deerfield; in
1830, m. Elizabeth (dau. of Samuel) Lawrence of Epping,
where he practised till, late in life, he rem. to Chelsea,
Mass., and d. there 16 Sept., 1874. "Dr. Moore was a
true man, too true to seem what he did not feel, to say
what he did not think, or to do what was only good pol-
icy."—(Hist. Gen. Register XXII, p. 344.) His ch. were:
(1) Mary E., (2) Sam'l. L., (3) Edward N. B., all b. in.
Epping.

7 *Simon French*, settled in Batavia, N. Y.

8 *Joseph Brackett*, m. Eunice McIntire, and had: (1) Or-
ville, (2) Selden, res. in Lancaster.

9 *Wm. Harvey*, settled in Billerica, Mass.

10 *Adino Nye*, ⎰ b. abt. 1809; a merchant in Boston; d. *s. p.*
11 *Martha*, ⎱ twin; m. Enoch Rogers of Concord, d. *s. p.*

12 *Comfort*, m., 1st, Asa Kimball of Concord; 2nd, Willard
Carleton; res. Derby Line, Vt.

v   Comfort,[5] b. 24 Jan., 1770; m. 20 Dec., 1793, John (s. of
Simon) French, b. 25 Mar., 1770, of Candia; lived and
died on the homestead, where Simon French settled in 1765.
She d. 1 Dec., 1834, and her husband d. 24 Dec., 1845.
Their children, b. in Candia, were:

1 *Martha* (French), b. Oct., 1794; d. 27 June, 1811, æ. 17.

2 *Simon*, b. 2 Feb., 1796; d. 25 May, 1871. He m. Ann B.
Evans, and had: (1) Mary Ann, who m., 1st, —— Seavey; 2nd, —— Dawkins.

3 *Dea. Coffin Moore*, b. 6 Apr., 1799; m. 8 Dec., 1825, Dolly
Pillsbury, who d. 20 Nov., 1879. He was a farmer in
Candia where he d. 15 Dec., 1881. Children: (1) Jn.
Pillsbury, b. 14 Sept., 1826, farmer in Candia; m., 1st,
Edee Knight, 20 June, 1861; 2nd, 20 Feb., 1872, Mary E.
Craig of Auburn, Mass., *s. p.* (2) Mary Celina, b. 6 May,
1832; m. 1 Jan., 1862, Rev. J. H. Fitts, of So. New-
market, in 1887, *s. p.* (3) Rev. Samuel Franklin, b. 22
Dec., 1835 (D. Coll., 1860; Andover Sem., 1864); m. 22
Dec., 1864, Martha Jane (dau. of Geo.) Upton, Andover,
Mass., *s.p.* (4) George Henry, b. 27 July, 1838 (Dart.
Coll., 1863; And. Sem., 1868); m. 28 Sept., 1871, Fan-
nie E. Kilburn, of Holden, Mass. Their children were:
(*a*) Warren K., (*b*) Irving J., and (*c*) Geo. F., res. in
Charlestown, N. H., 1888.

4 *Lucinda*, b. 18 June, 1803; m. 21 Oct., 1824, Fred Fitts, who
d. 3 Nov., 1837. Children: (1) Martha Ann (Fitts), (2)
Alfred Dana, (3) Sarah Jane, (4) Chas. Frederick.

5 *Evelina*, b. 5 Sept., 1805; m. Sam'l Murray of Auburn. She
d. there 28 Jan., 1848. Their children: (1) Martha French
(Murray), (2) Wm. Henry, (3) Lucinda Fitts, (4) Mary
Comfort, (5) Samuel Francis.

vi   Dr. Jacob Bailey,[5] b. in Georgetown, Me., 5 Sept., 1772; m.
Polly (dau. of Ephraim) Eaton of Candia, settled in 1796.
in Andover; was surgeon in U. S. Army in 1812; d. 10
Jan., 1813. He was a man of talent, and of literary taste,
wrote poetry, composed music, etc. His children were:

1 *Jacob B. Moore*, jr., b. 31 Oct., 1797, was an apprentice of

Isaac Hill of the N. H. Patriot, Concord, then his part-
ner, whose sister he m. In 1823, with John Farmer he
edited the N. H. Gazetteer. In 1826-9, edited the N. H.
Journal. He was an able political writer, and wrote
"The Laws of Trade in the United States." He was
Librarian of the N. Y. Historical Society and d. in New
York in 1853. His son (1) Frank Moore, of New York,
was Ed. of "Songs and Ballads of the Am. Revolution,"
"Rebellion Records," etc.

  2 *Henry E.*, a musician.
  3 *Mary*, w. of Dr. Thos. Brown; d. in Manchester, abt. 1870.
  4 *John W.*, once ed. of Bellows Falls Gazette.
vii Polly,[5] b. in Pownalboro, 23 July, 1774; m. John Quimby and
    rem. to Canada; had children.

38

Capt. John Weeks[4] (*Jn.,*[3] *Joshua,*[2] *Leon.*[1]) born in
1749, died 1818, and his wife Deborah (Brackett), had
born in Greenland

Children :

  i   Martha,[5] b. 20 Dec., 1771; m. Edward Spaulding of Lancas-
     ter, and d. there 10 Jan., 1871. They had b. in Lancaster:
    1 *Edward Cummings* (Spaulding), m. Sally Moore.
    2 *John Weeks*, m. Electa Stebbins.
    3 *Wm. Dustin*, m., 1st, Deborah Stephenson, who d., 1824;
     m., 2nd, Sarah Ann Goss.
    4 *Eliza W.*, m. Wm. Moore.
    5 *Jas. Brackett*, d. unm., 1824.
    6 *Martha B.*, b. abt. 1806; m. Chas. B. Stebbins, and was
     living in 1886.
  ii Deba,[5] b. 21 Nov., 1773; d. 27 July, 1774.
 iii Deborah,[5] b. 29 Feb., 1776; m. 1st, Wm. Ayres, and had
     Deborah, wife of Myron Chandler. She m., 2nd, Jacob
     Emerson, and d. in Lunenburg, Vt., 21 Nov., 1860, æ. 84.
  iv Elizabeth,[5] b. 10 March, 1778; m., in Lancaster, Jan., 1801,
     Judge Azariah Webb, jr., of Lunenburg, Vt., b. 3 Nov.,
     1775, who d. 19 May, 1849. She d. in Maidstone, Vt., 1
     April, 1844, æ. 66. Their children, b. in Lunenburg, were :
    1 *Marcus A.* (Webb), b. 7 Oct., 1802; m. 3 Apr., 1832, Ange-
     line Perkins, and d. 30 Dec., 1865.
    2 *Eliza A.*, b. 9 June, 1804, lives unm. with her brother Jn.
     W. Webb.
    3 *Martha W.*, b. 21 Feb., 1808; d. 7 Feb., 1832.
    4 *Mary Ann*, b. 17 Mar., 1810; m. 3 Dec., 1837, Wm. Cushing
     Gates, and d. 11 Jan., 1848.
    5 *Lucy Andrus*, b. 15 June, 1812; m. 11 Feb., 1838, Foster
     Thomas, and d. 9 Oct., 1866. Had six children: (1)
     Adelaide, (2) Deborah, (3) Lucian, (4) Folsom, (5)
     Elizabeth W., (6) Foster.
    6 *John Wingate*, b. 8 Nov., 1814; m. 17 Jan., 1850, Lucretia

Gates Webb, b. 20 Aug., 1819. Children: (1) Chas. F., (2) Isabel L., (3) Geo. Wingate, (4) Sarah Eliza, (5) Mary Brackett.

v Hon. John Wingate,[5] b. in Greenland, 31 March, 1781; m., 1st, his cousin, Martha W. Brackett; 2nd, Persis F. Everett, and res. in Lancaster. From 1829 to 1833, he was member of Congress from New Hampshire. Owing to pecuniary circumstances, he did not acquire a liberal education, but he was a man of superior talents. He d. 3 April, 1853, æ. 72, *s. p.* (See Note VII, Appendix).

(74) vi James Brackett,[5] b. 14 June, 1784, farmer in Lancaster; m. 1 Jan., 1810, Elizabeth (Betsey) (dau. of Dennis) Stanley, b. in Lancaster, 4 Aug., 1785, who d. there 24 Dec., 1854. He d. 19 March, 1858, æ. near 74. They had three sons and four daughters.

vii Mary Wiggin,[5] b. in Lancaster 4 Mar., 1787; d. 1863; m. 1 Nov., 1808, her cousin Adino Nye Brackett (son of Joseph B.), b. in Lee, Nov., 1777, d. 1847; farmer; clerk of Coos Co. Court, etc., and had b. in Lancaster:

1 *John* (Brackett), who d. early.

2 *Adino Nye, jr.*, b. 11 July, 1822 (D. Coll., 1844; M.D., in Woodstock, Vt., 1851); a doctor at Negrofoot, Hanover Co., Va., where he m. 6 Mar., 1855, Lucy A. Bumpass, and has three daughters: (1) Mary Fanny, (2) Persis Amelia, (3) Lucy Thompson.

3 *James S.*, b. about 1825; m. Mary E. Emerson; lives on the homestead and had: (1) Mary Nye, (2) Lucy Jane, (3) Sarah Helen, (4) Martin W., (5) James Adino.

viii Sally Brackett,[5] b. 13 Aug., 1789; is living in 1888, æ. 99; m. 25 Jan., 1816, Edwards (son of Gen'l Edwards) Bucknam, of Lancaster, b. 15 Feb., 1780; d. 16 Sept., 1861. His father was a surveyor, justice of the peace, and his sister Eunice was the first white child b. in Lancaster. Their children were:

1 *Edward F.* (Bucknam), b. 19 Feb., 1818; m., 1st, Emeline Burbank; 2nd, S. P. Bissel and had: (1) Emeline B., b. Sept., 1852; d. Apr., 1884; m. Jesse Wilson. (2) Helen M., b. July, 1854; m. Frank Harris. (3) Eddie A., b. May, 1856; d. 27 Nov., 1879. (4) John F. and (5) Martha B., twins, b. 17 Apr., 1859; d. early. By second wife he had: (6) Jn. F., b. 1867. (7) Chas. E., b. Aug., 1868; d. Aug., 1878. (8) Nellie B., b. Aug., 1869; d. Apr., 1870. (9) Wm. E., b. Jan., 1871; d. July, 1878. (10) Geo. B., b. Aug., 1872; d. Aug., 1878. (11) Albert J., b. Feb., 1874; d. Aug., 1878. (12) Lilla W., b. July, 1876; d. July, 1878. (13) Minnie W., b. 30 Dec., 1877. (14) Edw. H., b. 16 Dec., 1879.

2 *Deborah Weeks*, b. 7 Dec., 1821; m. 15 March, 1843, Jas. McIntire. Children: (1) Jas. (McIntire), b. 12 March, 1845; d. 5 March, 1862. (2) Sarah E., b. Oct., 1850; d. Feb., 1862. (3) Mary Ella, b. Sept., 1853; m. 22 Sept., 1880, Wm. G. Baker; d. 6 Aug., 1881. (4) John E., b. March, 1857; d. Feb., 1862. (5) James E., b. 23 Feb., 1863.

3 *Mary Nye*, b. 10 Mar., 1826; m. 3 Dec., 1846, Sam'l H. Legro; res. in Lancaster, *s. p.*

4 *Martha B.*, b. 8 Nov., 1830; m. 24 Jan., 1867, Proctor Jacobs, farmer in Lancaster, and has, b. there: (1) Clara Weeks Jacobs, b. 21 Jan., 1869.
5 *Dr. John Wingate*, b. 4 Dec., 1833 (M.D., Dart. Coll., 1860); m. 12 June, 1861, Anna Celia Buckland, and had: (1) Annie Weeks, b. 4 Oct., 1865. Her father, Dr. J. W. Bucknam, d. in Great Falls, 18 Dec., 1870, and her mother d. soon afterward.
Dr. B. was, in 1862, surgeon of the 5th N. H. regiment.

39

William Weeks[4] (*Jn.*,[3] *Joshua*,[2] *Leon.*[1]) born 1751, died 1821, joiner and farmer, and his wife Susanna (Haines), had born in Portsmouth

Children:

i John,[5] b. 14 Sept., 1773; m.; rem. to Bangor; had one son, *Jn.*,[5] and three daughters.
ii William, jr.,[5] b. 15 Aug., 1775; d. early; m.
iii Benin,[5] b. in Chester, 17 Feb., 1779; m. Hannah Hill of Chester, N. H.; removed to Bangor, Me.; he enlisted a soldier in 1812 and was lost; had five children:
1 *A dau.*,[6] m. Abner Clark.
2 *John*,[6] went to New Brunswick, British Prov.
3 *Harriet*,[6] m. Phineas Fogg of Searsmont, Me.
4 *Caroline*,[6] m. ——— Rivers of Boston.
5 *Malinda Myra*,[6] b. in Old Town, Me., 8 June, 1806; m. in Montville, Me., 2 Aug., 1827, Alex. Vose,* who was b. 8 Mar., 1806. He went to California, and it is said that at the mouth of Petaluma Creek 9 July, 1856, he was swept from the deck of his vessel and drowned. Children: (1) Harriet Hannah[7] (Vose), b. in Montville, Me., 26 April, 1828; m. in Franklin, Mass., 30 May, 1850. Alvah Metcalf,† b. in Appleton, Me., 12 Apr., 1824. He is a boxmaker in Ashland, Mass., where she d. 15 Sept., 1858. Their children were: (a) Adelbert Alvah,[8] b. 10 Apr., 1851; m. June, 1874, Estella M. Wyman of Livermore Falls, Me. He is a mechanic in Ashland, Mass., and has three children: Alvah E.,[9] Alice and Maud. (b) Geo. Ernest, b. 30 June, 1853; m. 30 Dec., 1880, Clara E. Smith of Middletown, Conn. He was a grad. Com. Class, Wesleyan Univ., 1880, and is travelling salesman; res. in Worcester, Mass. They have Mabel, b. 25 May, 1882;

* Alex. Vose was of the seventh generation from Robert and Abigail Vose who came from Lancashire, Eng., and were among the first settlers of Milton, Mass. His grandfather, Seth Vose, rem. in 1763 from Milton to Maine, and d. in Cushing, Me. His father, Ebenezer, was b. 1774; m., 1st, in 1802, Nancy Lermond of Warren.
† Alvah Metcalf was the eighth in descent from Michael Metcalf one of the original settlers of Dedham, Mass. His father, Junia, was b. in Franklin, Mass.; m., 1821, Melinda Phillips, descended from Rev. Geo. Phillips, first Cong. minister of Watertown, Mass.

7

Emeline O., b. Feb., 1884; Frederick K., b. 1885; a son, b. in Worcester, Sept., 1887. (c) Nora Ardelia, b. 1 Apr., 1856; m. 22 June, 1874, Alfred Seelye Roe of Ashland, Mass., b. in Rose, N. Y., 8 June, 1844, a descendant of John Roe, an early settler in Brookhaven, L. I., N. Y. He is a son of Rev. Austin M. and Polly (Seelye) Roe of Fulton, N. Y. His mother is dau. of Geo. Seelye of Rose, N. Y., descended from the famous Seelye family in Conn. He served near two years in the 9th N. Y. Heavy Artillery.; was captured on the 9 July, 1864, at Monocacy Junction, Md., and held a prisoner till 22 Feb., 1865; grad. 1870, Wesleyan Univ.; taught in High School, Worcester, Mass., from 1875 to 1880, then became principal of the same; had : Adelaide Estelle, b. in Ashland, Mass., 6 Apr., 1875; d. there 24 Apr., 1878; Annabell Catherine, b. in Worcester, 3 Sept., 1879; Delos Metcalf, b. 8 Jan., 1883; Harriet Eudora, b. 5 June, 1885. (2) Ebenezer S., b. 15 Dec., 1829; res. in New Orleans, m. there three times and had children. (3) George Henry, b. 30 Dec., 1831; m. 26 Dec., 1852, Susan E. Hendrick of Smithfield, R. I., b. 24 Aug., 1833; served three years in the 32nd Mass.Vols. in the Rebellion; res. in Worcester, Mass., with one child : (a) Fred. E., b. 8 Mar., 1861, who m. 24 Aug., 1881, Clara Gray of Boston, b. Dec., 1863. (4) Americus John, b. in Union, Me., 9 Aug., 1834; d., unm., in Woonsocket, R. I., 1862. (5) Arethusa M., b. 21 May, 1836; m. 8 July. 1854. Dexter Bates of Woonsocket, R. I., b. in Bellingham, Mass., 15 May, 1835, and has three children. (6) Caroline, b. 28 Feb., 1839; m. Wm. Carr, a soldier during the war of the rebellion; had three children. (7) Charles F., b. 18 Oct., 1842; a soldier in Co. I, 2nd R. I. Vols., and d. at Brandy Station, Va., 12 Nov., 1863.

iv Mary,[5] b. 14 Dec., 1782. She m. Edward Moore Preston and went west.

v Susan Haines,[5] b. 26 Aug., 1788; d. 27 Oct., 1842; m. 10 July, 1827, James Calef, b. in Chester, 14 Apr., 1792, teacher and farmer, who d. 25 July, 1858, res. in the part of Chester, now Auburn. Child :

1 *Charles Weeks*[6] (Calef), b. in Chester, 5 Apr., 1829; m. 21 Apr., 1864, Venelia M. Richards of Quincy, Mass., a teacher descended from Peregrine White of the Mayflower.

(75) vi Noah,[5] b. 14 June, 1790, farmer in Chester; m. Charlotte (dau. of Bradbury) Quimby, b. 25 May, 1800, who d. 13 June, 1870, "an excellent Christian." He d. 20 Mar., 1875. They had eight children.

39a

Capt. John Wingate Weeks[5] (*Ward C.,*[4] *Jn.,*[3] *Joshua,*[2] *Leon.*[1]) born 1784, died 1872, and his wife —— (Durgin), had

REV. JACOB CHAPMAN.

Children :

i   Cotton,[6] res. in Wellington, Piscataquis Co., Me.
ii Gilman,[6].
iii John,[6] b. in Cornville, Me., Feb., 1806; m. in Athens, Me., 1828, Amanda (dau. of Jas.) Lord, and died in Springfield, Mass., 22 Feb., 1882, æ. 76. Children :
1 *John Milton*,[7] b. in Brighton, Me., 31 Aug., 1840, is a commercial traveller; m. in Ware, Mass., 1 June, 1862, Sarah P. Shumway.
2 *Hannah*,[7] m. F. D. Richards, lawyer in Ware, Mass.
3 *Jane Eliza*.[7]
iv Alvah.[6]
v   Noah.[6]
vi Bradford.[6]
vii Caroline.[6]
viii Joanna.[6]

40

Levi Folsom[5] (*Jere.*,[4] *Jere.*,[3] *Jn.*,[2] *Jn.*[1]) born 1753, died 1844, farmer in Tamworth, and his wife Joanna (Weeks), had nine children, all, except Ward and Levi, born in Tamworth.

Children :

i   Ward Weeks[6] (Folsom), b. in Newmarket, 4 Sept., 1778, who m. 15 Nov., 1802, Lydia Allen Hayford, b. 17 Mar., 1782; d. 20 Apr., 1876, æ. 94; a farmer, much respected and often in town office in Tamworth, where he d. of consumption, 25 June, 1829. They had eleven children, some of them widely known as business men at the West.
ii Jeremiah,[6] b. in Tamworth, 16 Sept., 1780; m. in Machias, Me., 4 Apr., 1805, Octavia Howe, who had ten children, and d. in Brownfield, Me., 6 Sept., 1872. He was a man of much enterprise, engaged in various occupations and closed his eventful life in Brownfield, Me., 12 Dec., 1859, æ. 79. Children :
1 *Levi H.*, b. 1806; d. 1883.
2 *Joanna W.*, b. Sept., 1808; d. 1884.
3 *Jeremiah*, b. 1810; d. 1869.
4 *Jn. H.*, of Prairie du Chien.
5 *Geo. B.*, b. 1815.
6 *Hon. W. H. C.*, b. June, 1817, of Taylor's Falls, Minn.
7 *Simeon P.*, of St. Paul, Minn.
8 *Chas. B.*, b. 1822.
9 *Ward W.*, b. 1824, of St. Paul, Minn.
10 *Susan O.*, d. 1831, æ. 3 yrs.
iii Elizabeth (Betsey) Smith,[6] b. 29 Mar., 1785; m. 10 Feb., 1808, Samuel (S. Job) Chapman of Tamworth, b. Greenland, 11 May, 1781, who d. 30 Oct., 1857, æ. 76. She had five children, and d. Tamworth, 5 Aug., 1821, æ. 38.

1 *Rev. Jacob* (Chapman), b. 11 March, 1810 (A.B., Dart. Coll., 1835, and Theo. Sem., 1839); m., 1st, 27 May, 1840, Mary C. Howe, of Bridgton, Me., who d. *s. p.*, 6 April, 1869. He m., 2nd, 14 Sept., 1871, Mary E. Lane of Stratham. He taught in Bridgton, Me., Franklin College, Lancaster, Pa., in Harrisburg, Pa., and Terre Haute, Female College, Ind.; preached in Marshall, Ill., Deerfield and Kingston, N. H. At the age of 70, he resigned his pastoral office, retired to Exeter and compiled "The Folsom Genealogy," "The Philbrick Family" and the Genealogy of "Leonard Weeks and family."

2 *Eliza F.*, b. 14 Mar., 1812; m. Dea. Jas. J. Chesley of New Durham, and settled in Tamworth, where for forty years he was a prominent and useful citizen. They had seven children.

3 *John*, b. 17 June, 1814; m. Sept., 1839, Mary P. Swasey of Meredith, practised law in Benton, Scott Co., Mo., and d. there, *s. p.*, 26 Aug., 1845, of consumption.

4 *Samuel, jr.*, a doctor, b. June, 1816, was murdered in Bloomfield, Stoddard Co., Mo., 10 June, 1843; unm.

5 *Mary Ann*, b. 19 Nov., 1819; d. unm. 8 Dec., 1848, æ. 29.

iv John Weeks,[6] b. 7 Nov., 1785, lived in Maine, near New Brunswick and was lost in 1812; unm.

v Col. Levi, jr.,[6] b. Sandwich, 11 April, 1788; m. Lydia Dodge of Wenham, Mass., who d. 7 May, 1824. He d. 9 Dec., 1841, æ. 53. Children:
1 *Elizabeth.*
2 *Joanna.*
3 *John T. D.*
4 *Levi W.*
5 *Lydia.*

vi Joanna,[6] b. Tamworth, 29 Sept., 1790; m. 11 Feb., 1816, Thos. Chesley of Lee. She d. 7 Aug., 1879, æ. 89. Children:
1 *Levi F.* (Chesley).
2 *Martha Ann.*
3 *Eliza A.*
4 *Benjamin*, d.
5 *Jas. Ezra.*
6 *Thomas B.*
7 *Geo. Edward.*

vii Mary,[6] b. 29 May, 1793; m. 20 July, 1815, Jere. D. Ballard, b. 1792, a farmer in Tamworth, and had seven children. She d. 29 Mar., 1849.
1 *Mary N.* (Ballard).
2 *Jeremiah D.*, b. 1820.
3 *Wm. Ward*, b. 1822.
4 *Susan S.*, b. 1830.
5 *Levi W.*, b. 1833.

viii Martha Wingate,[6] b. 24 June, 1795; m. 21 Sept., 1825, Benj. Durgin of Limington, Me., who d. in Brownfield, Me., 29 Aug., 1870; æ. 73. She d. in Brownfield, 22 Dec., 1885, æ. 90 yrs., 6 mos. They had:
1 *Benj. F.* (Durgin).
2 *Martha A.*
Others that d. young.

William Weeks

ix Geo. Frost,⁶ b. 7 July, 1797; m. 24 Mar., 1825, Miriam Dow
and d. 16 May, 1831, leaving:
1 *George*, drowned in childhood.
2 *Clara A.*, who m. and d. early.

41

Capt. William Weeks⁴(*Wm.*,³ *Joshua*,² *Leon.*¹)born
in 1755, died in 1843, of Hopkinton, and his wife Nabby
(Rogers), had born in Berwick, Me.

Children:

i Dea. William,⁵ b. 21 Aug., 1781, a farmer on the homestead,
at the Bay Side, Greenland, where he d. 20 Feb., 1864, æ.
82 years and 6 mos. He m. 26 May, 1835, Louisa (dau.
of Rev. H.) Porter of Rye, b. 18 May, 1803. He was an
amiable man, a useful citizen, and for many years a faithful officer in the Cong. Church. His children were:
1 *Ann Louisa*,⁶ b. 22 Mar., 1836.
2 *Ellen Maria*,⁶ b. 23 Jan., 1838.
3 *Sarah Porter*,⁶ b. 27 Oct., 1839.
4 *Geo. William*,⁶ b. 8 Sept., 1841; m. in Exeter, 22 May, 1878,
Sarah L. Robinson and has:(1)William R.,⁷b. 1 May, 1880.
5 *John Porter*,⁶ b. 24 Jan., 1844; m. 26 April, 1870, Ellen (dau.
of Hon. Chas.) Hatch, who d. 3 June, 1874. He m., 2nd,
26 Sept., 1876, Laura A. (dau. of Nathan R.) Foss and
had: (1) Mabel Porter,⁷ b. 26 July, 1878. (2) Carrie Foss,
b. 26 Mar., 1881. (3) Alice Huntington, b. 27 Oct., 1882.
ii George,⁵ lost at sea, æ. 20.

By second wife, Sarah Cotton Weeks, Wm.⁴ had:

(76)iii Charles,⁵ b. 26 Oct., 1790; m. Phebe Henry; had eight children; d. 14 Dec., 1863, æ. 73. He was a farmer in Hopkinton.
iv Abigail,⁵ b. 15 July, 1792; d. 18 Feb., 1875, unm., æ. 82.
v Mary,⁵ b. 1 Nov., 1794; m. Frank Parker; d. *s. p.*, 22 Aug.,
1832, æ. 38.
vi Jacob,⁵ b. 9 Nov., 1796; m., 1st, Mary Colby, who d. in Hopkinton; m., 2d, Mary Lancaster, who d., *s. p.*; m., 3d, Mary
Rand. Child by first marriage:
1 *Nathaniel.*⁶
Child by third marriage:
2 *George W.*⁶
vii Washington,⁵ b. 14 Feb., 1798 (or 1799), went in 1829 to Me-
redosia, Ill.; m. 1849, in Ill., and had seven children:
1 *Wm. Henry Harrison.*⁶
2 *Jn. Langdon.*⁶
3 *Geo. Washington.*⁶
4 *Thos. Jefferson.*⁶
5 *Benj. Franklin.*⁶
viii Thos. Jefferson,⁵ b. 11 May, 1801; m. Apr., 1825, Hannah
Cogswell Smith of Ipswich, Mass., who d. Sept., 1885, and
had five children b. in Hopkinton:
1 *Isaac*,⁶ d. unm.

2 *Harriet*,[6] m. Eli Boutwell of Hopkinton, and had: (1) Harvey[7] (Boutwell), m. 28 Dec., 1886, Nellie Booth. (2)
Henry, m. 31 Dec., 1885, Alice Montgomery. (3) Arthur,
not m. (4) Ella, d. in 1884, æ. 12.

3 *Louisa*,[6] m. Dea. J. H. Ballard, and had four sons b. in Concord: (1) Everett Cogswell[7] (Ballard), (2) Fred Goss,
(3) Milton Henry, (4) Gilbert Newton.

4 *Lavinia P.*,[6] unm., classed with the N. H. poets.

5 *Cogswell*,[6] m. Jennie Hubbard of Webster and has two children: (1) Lida M.,[7] (2) Carrie Eveline.

ix Sarah Ann,[5] b. 1803; m. 17 Mar., 1846, Dea. Daniel Fitts, of
Boscawen.

x Susan,[5] b. 23 July, 1807; d. unm., Dec., 1844.

xi Hannah,[5] b. 10 July, 1810; m. Eben French, and d. 1871. She
had:
1 *John L.* (French), res. and d. in Hopkinton; had 1 ch.

xii Emily,[5] b. 2 Sept., 1815; d. 28 May, 1839, unm.

xiii John Langdon,[5] b. 26 Mar., 1819; d. 9 Sept., 1843; m. Lavinia Allison, and had:
1 *Sarah L.*,[6] m. W. Frank Stark, and lives in Cambridge, Mass.

41a

David Weeks[5] (*David*,[4] *Jona.*,[3] *Jn.*,[2] *Leon.*[1]) born
1774, died 1842, farmer, and his wife Matilda (Child),
had born in Bath:

i Laura.[6]

ii John C.[6]

iii Mary.[6]

iv Dudley C.,[6] b. 23 Dec., 1804; d. 22 Mar., 1884; m. Lucy Top-
liff, b. 20 May, 1809; d. 15 Sept., 1873. Children:
1 *Horace T.*,[7] b. 17 Nov., 1832; m. 13 Feb., 1873, Mary H.
(dau. of Benj. H.) Poor, b. 16 May, 1854, and had b. in
Bath: (1) Nora T.,[8] b. 15 Dec., 1875. (2) Horace, b. 3
June, 1877. (3) Maud, b. 29 Jan., 1879. (4) Deborah A.,
b. 15 June, 1880.
2 *Adaline B.*,[7] b. 15 Oct., 1834.
3 *Annette*,[7] b. 29 Sept., 1836.

v Alfred.[6]

vi Jonathan,[6] m. Betsey Chamberlain and had:
1 *Emily M.*,[7] b. Bath, 10 Feb., 1853, who m., 1875, Edw. C.
Poore (*v.* Poore Family).

vii Moses M.,[6] res. Haverhill, N. H.

viii Willard.[6]

ix Emily.[6]

x Eliza.[6]

xi Ezra.[6]

41b

Joseph Weeks[5] (*Jona.*,[4] *Jona.*,[3] *Jn.*,[2] *Leon.*[1]) born
1780, died 1834, of Dover and his wife Charity D. (Hurd),
had born in Dover

Children :

i   William,⁶ b. 1802; d. 1884; m. Mary Hopkinson of Hollis, Me., where they lived and d. *s. p.*

(77) ii   Jonathan,⁶ b. 1804; d. 1865; m. 1823, Mary Dame of Farmington, N. H., b. 2 June, 1805 (dau. of Tim. and Betsey L. Dame), res. and d. in Lowell, Mass., 28 June, 1861. Had nine children of whom two are now living, viz. :

     1 *Joseph Dame*,⁷ of Pittsburg, Pa., editor of Am. Manufactures and Iron Age.

     2 *Mary Ella*,⁶ of Cambridgeport, Mass.

iii   Stephen H.,⁶ b. 1805; d. unm.

iv   Margaret,⁶ b. 1806; d. 1807.

v   Joseph,⁶ b. 1807; m., 1st, abt. 1831, Mary Loud of Portsmouth, N. H.; in 1844 he m., 2nd, Mary A. Bryant of Bristol, Me., d. 1886 in Bristol, Me. Children by first marriage :

     1 *Mary A.*,⁷ m. —— Norton of Cambridgeport, Mass.

     2 *Albert*,⁷ d. in Boston, 1871.

     3 *Mehitable*,⁷ m. —— Stockwell, and is a widow in Boston.

     4 *Susan H.*,⁷ unm., in Cambridgeport.

     5 *William*,⁷ d. early.

     Children by second marriage :

     6 *Sarah*,⁷ d. 1865.

     7 *Wm.*,⁷ res. in Boston.

vi   Mary Ann,⁶ b. 1809; m. 4 Sept., 1831, Benj. Welch, of Cambridgeport, Mass., and d. 1851. He m., 2nd, in Cambridgeport, her sister, Hannah Rust Weeks of Dover, Dec. 25, 1851. He d. 13 Sept., 1874. Had by first marriage nine children, seven b. in Boston :

     1 *Joseph W.* (Welch), b. in Dover, N. H., 10 July, 1832; d. in Cambridgeport, Mass., 3 Feb., 1868.

     2 *George S.*, b. in Boston, 8 July, 1834; d. in Boston, 16 Dec., 1835.

     3 *Benj. Scott*, b. in Boston, 9 Jan., 1837; m.; res. in Cambridgeport, Mass., with three children.

     4 *Charles Pike*, b. in Boston, 1 May, 1839; m.; res. in Cambridgeport. Two children.

     5 *Hannah Rust*, b. in Boston, 3 Apr., 1841; d. in Boston, Feb., 1844.

     6 *Martha White*, b. in Boston, 25 Aug., 1843; d. in Cambridgeport, 30 June, 1863.

     7 *Wm. Henry Hatch*, b. in Boston, 15 Aug., 1845; d. in Cambridgeport, 26 July, 1864.

     8 *George Pickering*, b. in Boston, 2 Aug., 1847; d. at Point of Rocks, Va., 9 Apr., 1865.

     9 *Ezra Mudge*, b. in Cambridgeport, 7 Jan., 1850; d. there 26 Apr., 1851.

     By second marriage had :

     10 *Frank Mudge*, b. 18 Feb., 1853, who m. and resided in Marlboro, Mass., with one child.

     11 *Mary Elizabeth*, b. 3 Apr., 1856, res. in Marlboro, Mass.

vii   Benjamin,⁶ b. 1811; m., abt. 1832, Sarah Ham of Dover, N. H.; d. 1876, æ. 64; left one son, James Kingsbury (Weeks), of Campello, Mass.

viii   Thomas,⁶ b. 1813; d. 1814.

56   LEONARD WEEKS AND FAMILY.

ix   Hannah Rust,[6] b. 1815; m. 25 Dec., 1851 (as 2nd wife), Benj.
     Welch and had two children:
     1 *Frank Mudge*[7] (Welch).
     2 *Mary E.*

42

Joseph Weeks[5] (*Jn.*,[4] *Jn.*,[3] *Sam.*,[2] *Leon.*[1]) born
1755, died 1847, farmer, and his wife Margery (Hussey),
had born in Jefferson, Me.
    Children :

    i   John,[6] m. Sarah Peaslee of Jefferson and had:
         1 *Sarah Jane.*[7]
         2 *Rebecca*,[7] d. unm.
         3 *Eleanor*,[7] d. unm.
         4 *Ira*,[7] m. Ann Gray of Newcastle, and had: (1) John E.,[8]
           who d. in the army.
         5 *Albert*,[7] m. Harriet Kennedy of Jefferson.
         6 *Margery*,[7] d. unm.
         7 *Alden*,[7] b. 1821; m. Lois Noyes, res. in Jefferson.
    ii   Abigail,[6] m. Joseph Partridge of Jefferson, and had thirteen
         children:
         1 *Margery* (Partridge), m. Jas. Weeks of Jefferson.
         2 *Jenny*, d. young.
         3 *Hiram W.*, a farmer; m. Reliance Taylor.
         4 *Jane*, m. Nathaniel Mahew, a wheelwright.
         5 *Mary*, m. Eben Farnham, a farmer.
         6 *Joseph*, m. Eliza Bean of Washington, Me.
         7 *Lydia.*
         8 *Abram W.*, m. Elizabeth Weeks.
         9 *Lucinda*, m. J. D. Newhall.
         10 *Arletta*, went to Missouri.
         11 *Everett*, m. Miss Hussey.
         12 *Abigail*, m. in Boston and went to France.
         13 *Albert W.*, res. in Jefferson, Me.
    iii June,[6] m. Wm. Kennedy, and had:
         1 *Joseph* (Kennedy), m. Miss Richardson.
         2 *Samuel*, d. at sea.
         3 *Alden.*
         4 *John H.*, m. Didania Kennedy.
         5 *Martha J.*, m. Luther Kennedy of Whitefield, Me., res. on
           the homestead.
    iv   Eleanor,[6] m. Enoch Weeks[5] (*Jn.*,[4] *Jn.*[3]), res. in Jefferson.
         Children:
         1 *Orinton* (Weeks), b. in 1817; d. in 1868.
         2 *Martha*, b., 1819; m. Mr. Shepard.
         3 *Nettie*, m. Frank (s. of Elbridge) Weeks, and has: (1)
           Ellwood.
    v   Margery (Kennedy),[6] m. Jas. Kennedy and had:
         1 *Horace*, d. unm.
         2 *Emily*, m. Elijah Hussey, farmer, of Newcastle.

3 *Harriet*, m. Anthony McCobb of Boothbay, Me.

4 *Maria*, m., 1st, Nathan Ware of Whitefield, Me. ; 2nd, Horace Chapman, farmer in Jefferson.

vi Lydia[6] (twin sister of Margery), m. John Moody of Belfast; d. in Jefferson, 1880, *s. p.*

(78) vii Joseph H.,[6] m. 1818, Asenath (dau. of Geo.) Barstow of Newcastle, b. 1797, who d. in 1848; res. in Jefferson, and had five children.

viii Martha,[6] m. in 1818, Col. Jn. Hussey, b. 10 Sept., 1793, lawyer in Newcastle. Their children were :

1 *Emily G.* (Hussey), b. 6 Oct., 1820; d. 16 Sept., 1826.

2 *John Augustus*, b. 5 Dec., 1827; m. Mary E. Burnham, and was killed on board of steamer Ocean, by collision, in Boston harbor.

3 *Joseph W.*, b. 13 Mar., 1829; res. in N. Y.

4 *Marcus L. M.*, b. 30 Apr., 1833; m., 1856, Mariah H. Winslow of Bath, Me. ; a soldier in the 16th Reg. Me. Vols., and Capt. of Co. I, 32d Me. Vols.

5 *Fred E.*, b. 28 Mar., 1835, Lieut. Co. C, 4th Reg. Me. Vols.

ix Sally,[6] m. Thomas Kennedy of Waldoboro, Me. ; had :

1 *Sophronia* (Kennedy), m. Mr. Williams of St. George.

2 *Margery*, m. John Orff, farmer in Waldoboro.

3 *Mary Jane*.

4 *Almira*, m. Alfred Davenport, farmer in Chelsea, Me.

5 *George*, m., 1st, Mary Hussey; 2nd, Susan Haskell; 3rd, —— Jones of Montville, Me.

6 *Lydia*, m. Alfred Trask, wheelwright, of Jefferson, Me.

7 *Didania*, m. John H. Kennedy (see No. 42–iii).

8 *Lucinda*, m. Alanson Pond, farmer of Jefferson.

9 *Clarinda*, m. Jas. W. Jackson, farmer in Jefferson.

43

Thomas Weeks[5] (*Jn.*,[4] *Jn.*,[3] *Sam.*,[2] *Leon.*[1]) born 1762, died 1846, and his wife Ruth (Taylor), had born in Jefferson, Me.

Children :

(79) i Ephraim,[6] b. 30 Nov., 1786; m. Abigail Peaslee of Jefferson, and d. Jan., 1867; had nine children.

ii David,[6] b. 31 Dec., 1788; d. unm. 31 Aug., 1838.

(80) iii Thomas, jr.,[6] b. 5 Apr., 1791; m. Mary (dau. of Amos) Otis, b. 1792, both of Jefferson, where he d. Mar., 1881, near 90. They had five children.

(81) iv Hon. Joseph,[6] b. 7 Mar., 1793; m., 8 Dec., 1819, Jane Jackson of Jefferson, who had five children; and d. 22 Nov., 1866, æ. 78. He d. Oct., 1870, æ. 77.

(82) v Benjamin,[6] b. 27 June, 1795; m. his cousin Jane (dau. of Winthrop) Weeks of Jefferson, and had nine children (see No. 47–iv).

vi Thankful,[6] b. 8 Sept., 1797; m. Joseph (son of John) Weeks, b. 1795; called "Joseph Weeks 4th of Jefferson;" had seven children, and d. 20 Oct., 1834. He d. 1875 (see No. 46–iv).

8

vii John T.,⁶ b. 29 May, 1799; m. 10 Feb., 1836, Aurelia Allen of
    Jefferson, and had:
    1 *Sarah E.,*⁷ m. Benj. Ladd of Jefferson.
    2 *Emma H.*⁷
    3 *Isa A.*⁷
viii Abigail,⁶ b. 26 Apr., 1801; m., Nov., 1823, Leonard Cooper of
    Whiting, who d. at Montville; had eight children:
    1 *Thomas* (Cooper), m. Ursula Stevens of Montville, Me.
    2 *Hannah*, m. Dan'l Stevens of Montville, Me.
    3 *Leonard*, m. Miss Keating of Searsmont.
    4 *Edward*, m. Julia Weeks of Whiting.
    5 *Marcellus*, m. Olive Haford of Belfast, Me.
    6 *Freeman*, m. Sarah Gunn.
    7 *Laura*, m. Wm. Cooper of Montville.
    8 *Alexander.*
(83) ix Hon. George,⁶ b. 15 Oct., 1803; d. 2 Mar., 1879; res. Jeffer-
    son, Me.; trader, etc.; was often in town office; m., 9 Feb.,
    1837, Caroline (dau. of Capt. Elias and Susan) Haskell, and
    had seven children. She was b. 12 Apr., 1817, and d. 29
    Sept., 1886, æ. 69.
  x Washington,⁶ b. 10 May, 1805; m., 1 Oct., 1833, Louisa Allen
    of Jefferson, and had:
    1 *Anna L.*⁷
    2 *Clara A.*⁷
    3 *Eliz. C.,*⁷ m. Jan., 1862, Jn. F. Hilton of Damariscotta.
    4 *Sarah A.*⁷
    5 *Dana Boardman.*⁷
    6 *Delia.*⁷

44

Major Daniel Waters, born 1768, died 1850, of Newcastle, Me., and his wife Mary (Weeks), had Children :

i Jane (Waters), b. 19 Nov., 1790; m. Milton Goodenow,
    lawyer of Nobleboro, Me.; d. 12 Mar., 1812.
ii George G., b. 4 Apr., 1792; not m.; first mate of a ship and
    was washed overboard, 21 Feb., 1812.
iii James S., b. 4 Oct., 1793; m. Margaret Kavanaugh; res. in
    Jefferson; d. 11 Mar., 1841, and had:
    1 *Edward.*
    2 *Sarah.*
    3 *Minnie.*
    4 *Mary.*
iv Mary, b. 22 Dec., 1795; m. Jas. Sawyer of Saco, and res. in
    Dorchester, Mass.
v Samuel, b. 12 Apr., 1798; m. 28 Feb., 1820, Hannah Shibles
    of Knox; d. 21 Apr., 1845; was a merchant, and had:
    1 *Mary.*
    2 *Clara.*
vi Daniel, jr., b. 10 June, 1800; d. 26 Feb., 1801.
vii Abigail, b. 9 Sept., 1802; d. 15 Aug., 1804.

viii Clarissa, b. 8 Sept., 1805; m. Henry Carleton of Wisconsin, and d. 21 Mar., 1828.
ix William, b. 27 Mar., 1807; d. 22 Sept., 1808.
x Daniel, jr., b. 26 Mar., 1808; d. in Cincinnati, 3 Sept., 1830.

45

Mark Weeks[5] (*Jn.*,[4] *Jn.*,[3] *Sam.*,[2] *Leon.*[1]) born 1766, died 1850, farmer in Jefferson, Me., and his wife Sally (Moody), had born in Jefferson

Children :

(84) i John,[6] b. 22 Nov., 1789; m. Sarah (dau. of Joseph) Jackson, b. 8 Dec., 1792, who d. 20 Jan., 1883, æ. 90. He d. 1844. Had six children.
ii Mary,[6] b. 26 June, 1792; m. Sam'l (son of Sam'l) Jackson; d. 30 May, 1876. Children :
    1 *Geo. W.*, m. Rosilla Kennedy of Jefferson.
    2 *Sally Emily*, m. Matthew Jones of Nobleboro.
iii David,[6] b. 20 May, 1794; m. Eunice Jackson and d. 1 June, 1834. Children :
    1 *Erastus F.*,[7] b. [1820]?; m. Janette Richardson and d. Oct., 1883.
    2 *Eliza*,[7] m. Samuel Heyer of Jefferson.
    3 *Hannah*,[7] d. unm.
    4 *Lot M.*,[7] m. Matilda Haskell of Jefferson.
iv Lot,[6] m. Betsey Kennedy, and had :
    1 *Nathaniel*,[7] d. æ. 20.
    2 *Ambrose*,[7] m. and res. in Mass.
    3 *Leonora*.[7]
    4 *Elvira*,[7] d. young.
v Joseph G.,[6] b. 3 May, 1800; m. Sarah Cleaves of Whitefield and d. 28 May, 1882, and had :
    1 *Harriet N.*,[7] m. John A. Weeks (see No. 84–iv).
    2 *Susan J.*,[7] m. Isaac Moody of Nobleboro, Me.
    3 *Jane*.[7]
    4 *Lot*,[7] d. unm.
    5 *Sarah*,[7] m. Leander Peaslee.
    6 *Mary*,[7] m. Otis T. (son of Thomas) Weeks (see 80–v).
    7 *Luella*,[7] m. Joseph Flagg of Nobleboro.
vi Sally,[6] b. 27 Sept., 1802; m. David S. Hilton, b. 1798, and d. 17 Jan., 1882. Children :
    1 *Mary* (Hilton), b. 1819; m. Elijah Sykes of Newcastle, Me.
    2 *Sally*, b. 1820; m. Thos. Jennings of Lynn, Mass.
    3 *Julia*, b. 1823; m. D. Dickinson and is in 1886 a widow.
    4 *Anastatia*, b. 1825; m. Capt. S. C. Whitehouse of Newcastle.
    5 *Statira*, b. 1829; m. Stephen Whitehouse.
    6 *Leonora*.
    7 *Ellen*, b. 1834; m. Gould Bailey.
    8 *Clara*, b. 1837; m. Geo. Galusha of Mass.
vii Mark,[6] jr., b. 14 July, 1810; m. Statira Murphy of Jefferson, and res. in La Grange, Me. Children :

1 *Sarah A.,*[7] m. Enoch Day of Jefferson.
2 *Elvira B.,*[7] m. 18 Aug., 1854, Simeon Dunbar of Thomaston, Me., b. abt. 1834, a mariner.

46

John Weeks[5] (*Jn.,*[4] *Jn.,*[3] *Sam.,*[2] *Leon.*[1]) born 1768, died 1799, farmer and his wife Rachel (Avery), had born in Jefferson, Me.

Children :

 i Enoch,[6] b. 9 May, 1788, and d. 9 May, 1872; m. Eleanor (dau. of Joseph) Weeks, b. 14 Jan., 1796, who d. 3 Mar., 1875. Children born in Jefferson :
  1 *Orrington J ,*[7] b. 11 Nov., 1815; d., unm., 7 Jan., 1871.
  2 *Martha,*[7] b. 12 June, 1817; m. Llewellyn Shepard of Jefferson.
 ii Mary,[6] b. 13 Nov., 1791; m. Thos. Mowry of Jefferson, and had children :
  1 *Rachel* (Mowry).
  2 *Nancy.*
  3 *Thomas.*
  4 *Mary.*
 iii John,[6] b. 16 Dec., 1793; d. 1799.
 iv Joseph,[6] b. 5 Mar., 1795 (called Joseph Weeks the 4th); d. 1875; m. his cousin Thankful (dau. Thos. and Ruth) Weeks (see 43-vi). Children :
  1 *Ruth,*[7] m., 1st, Jn. Boynton of Alna; 2nd, Joseph Hilton of Alna.
  2 *John Farley,*[7] m. Miss Williams of Australia.
  3 *Rachel,*[7] m. Robt. L. Kincaid of Whitefield.
  4 *Enoch,*[7] m. Ruth A. Flagg of Waldoboro or Nobleboro.
  5 *Adalaide*[7] (Adaline)?
  6 *Geo. W.,*[7] m. —— Cuyler of Alna.
  7 *Thankful.*[7]
 v James,[6] b. 10 Jan., 1797; d., Derry, N. H., 1 June, 1880, æ. 83; m. Margaret Partridge of Jefferson, and had :
  1 *Margaret,*[7] b. 1825, res. in Jefferson, Me.
  2 *Harriet,*[7] b. 1827; unm.
  3 *Hiram Partridge,*[7] b. 1832; res. Derry, N. H.; m., 1855, Sarah H. Stuart. Children : (1) Anna B.,[8] b. Jefferson, Me., 1857. (2) Charles F., b. Jefferson, 1859; m. at Cold Spring, N. Y., 1881, Ida Van Tastle of Cold Spring, N. Y.
  4 *Emily K.,*[7] b. 1838; m., 1859, J. E. Howe of Hallowell, Me.; res. in Boston, Mass.
  5 *Lucinda,*[7] b. 1841; m. J. W. Dudley.
 vi Thomas,[6] b. 26 Feb., 1799 (called Thomas 3rd, the blacksmith); m. Hannah Young and had :
  1 *Serena Young,*[7] who m. Jas. P. (s. of Dan'l H.) Weeks, b. 1819; d. 1875 (see No. 85-1).
  2 *Benjamin.*[7]
  3 *John,*[7] m. Miss Dunton of Whitefield.
  4 *Henry D.,*[7] m. Miss Peaslee of Jefferson.
  5 *Rev. Geo. Weeks,*[7] b. Cooper's Mills, Me.

47
Winthrop Weeks[5] (*Jn.*,[4] *Jn.*,[3] *Sam.*,[2] *Leon.*[1]) born 1770, died 1856, farmer, etc., and his wife Hannah (Hopkins), had born in Jefferson, Me.

Children:

  i   David,[6] b. 2 Nov., 1793; m. Susan Noyes of Jefferson, and d. 2 Mar., 1816. His widow d. 2 Mar., 1866, *s. p.*

(85) ii   Daniel H.,[6] b. 19 Apr., 1796; d. 18 Feb., 1882; farmer and cement mason; m., in Brunswick, 2 June, 1818, Margaret Spear (dau. of Josiah) Simpson of Brunswick, Me., gr. dau. of Wm. and Agnes L. Simpson. He was living in 1885, æ. 88, a large, robust man weighing 250 lbs.; was teacher, then innkeeper in Fairfield; a farmer in Vassalboro, where he died.

 iii   Nancy,[6] b. 26 Sept., 1798; m., 1st, Abiel Noyes, and had:
   1 *Hannah* (Noyes).
   2 *Susan.*
   3 *Louise.*
   4 *Jane.*
   5 *Abiel*, etc.

 iv   Jane,[6] b. 9 Aug., 1801; d. 3 May, 1879; m. Benj. (s. of Thomas) Weeks, b. 1795, and had eight children. (See No. 43–v, and No. 82.)

  v   Winthrop,[6] b. 25 Nov., 1803; m. Lois (or Louise) Noyes of Jefferson, and had:
   1 *Everett.*[7]
   2 *Joseph.*[7]
   3 *David.*[7]
   4 *Louise.*[7]

 vi   Abigail P.,[6] b. 1 Mar., 1806; m. Nov., 1830, Dan'l Hopkins of Newcastle, b. 23 Mar., 1801, who d. 19 Apr., 1875. Children:
   1 *Martha* (Hopkins), b. Aug., 1831; res. in Boston.
   2 *James S.*, b. 1834; m. Jane Hutchings.
   3 *Ophelia*, b. 16 Apr., 1835; m., 1859,D. S. McLean of Plympton, Mass.
   4 *Franklin W.*, b. 1836; m. A. Noyes.
   5 *George*, b. Nov., 1838.
   6 *Hannah*, b. July, 1840; d. 1841.
   7 *Mary R.*, b. June, 1843.
   8 *Dan'l W.*, b. Dec., 1844.

 vii   Hannah E.,[6] b. 10 June, 1808; m. Alexander Glidden of Jefferson. Children:
   1 *Rosanna* (Glidden), m. Mr. Avery.
   2 *Abigail.*
   3 *Albert.*

viii   William,[6] b. 18 Sept., 1810, member of Legislature, 1857; m. Hannah Grindle of Sedgwick, Me., and had:
   1 *Hannah*,[7] m. and res. in California.
   2 *Margaret*,[7] m. Mr. Martin.
   3 *John G.*,[7] not m.
   4 *Vesta.*[7]
   5 *Louis*,[7] m. Ida Ramsel, res. in California.
   6 *Almeda.*[7]

7 *Georgia.*[7]
8 *William.*[7]

ix   Stinson,[6] b. 1 Dec., 1813; m. Susan T. (dau. of Eph. and
Abigail) Weeks of Jefferson; res. in Bristol, Me. Children:
1 *Julia,*[7] m. Moses Pickering of Bristol.
2 *Marshall,*[7] m. Nancy Erskine.
3 *Emma A.*[7]
4 *Chas.,*[7] m. Mary Bryant of Bristol.
5 *Stinson, jr.,*[7] clerk in Boston.

48

Dea. Daniel Weeks[5] (*Jn.,*[4] *Jn.,*[3] *Sam.,*[2] *Leon.*[1]),

born 1774, died 1854, farmer, and his wife Martha (Taylor), had born in Jefferson, Me.

Children:

i   Hon. Thaddeus,[6] b. 10 Feb., 1799; m., 1st, 2 Feb. 1830, Mary
Turner of Whitefield; m., 2nd, 21 Mar., 1833, Esther Hustin of Bristol, Me., and had seven children; d. 1878.
1 *Esther H.*[7]
2 *Mary Turner,*[7] d. an infant.
3 *Frank.*[7]
4 *Amanda.*[7]
5 *Laura.*[7]
6 *Charles.*[7]
7 *Frederic.*[7]
ii   Daniel T.,[6] b. 20 Dec., 1800; m. 6 Jan., 1826, Betsey Barstow
of Newcastle, and d. 1873.   Children:
1 *Alexander B.,*[7] m. 1866, Myra W. Acorn.
2 *Daniel A. P.,*[7] d. 1855.
3 *Helen E.,*[7] m. Capt. Jn. G. Barstow.
4 *Geo. H.,*[7] m. Ella A. Barstow.
iii   Freeman,[6] b. 4 Jan., 1803; m. 4 Dec., 1845, Mary J. Wallace
of Montville, and d. May, 1847, *s. p.*
iv   Asenath,[6] b. 3 Feb., 1805; m., Sept., 1827, Capt. Jn. Hopkins, b. 9 Mar., 1798, who d. *s. p.* in California. She d. 13
Aug., 1831.
v   Horace,[6] b. 20 June, 1807; m., 1st, Nov., 1835, Louisa Turner. He m., 2nd, 1840, Caroline Woodbury of N. Y. Children:
1 *Julia,*[7] m. Edwin Cooper of Montville, Me.
2 *Rhoda A.*[7]
vi   Ruth,[6] b. 1 Jan., 1811; m., May, 1831, Dr. E. A. Brainard, and
d. 10 Apr., 1842, *s. p.*
(86) vii   Myrick L.,[6] b. 7 Feb., 1813; m. in Montville, 5 Feb., 1846,
Harriet (dau. of James) Wallace of Montville, a farmer
in Jefferson; had seven children. He rendered much aid in
securing these records.
viii   Barzena E.,[6] b. 28 Oct., 1814; m. Oct., 1836, Alden Johnson
of Jefferson and d. 3 Aug., 1837, *s. p.*
ix   Martha Jane,[6] b. 25 Dec., 1821; m., Oct., 1845, Hon. Wm.
Rust of Belfast, Me., who d. 1888.   Children:

1 *Maria* (Rust).
2 *Frederic.*
3 *Eugene.*

49

Chase Weeks[5] (*Cole,*[4] *Jn.,*[3] *Sam.,*[2] *Leon.*[1]) born 1762, died 1847, farmer, and his first wife Patty (Cawley), had born in Sanbornton
Children :

   i Sally,[6] b. 26 Nov., 1785; m. 17 Nov., 1808, Joseph Colby, farmer in Sanbornton, where she d. 20 Oct., 1820, æ. 34 yrs. and 11 mos. He d. 12 Aug., 1822, æ. 42. Children :
     1 *Melinda* (Colby), b. 20 Oct., 1809; d. 26 May, 1845.
     2 *Chase Weeks,* b. 9 Jan., 1812.
     3 *Aaron,* } b. 21 Oct., 1816; { d. 1821.
     4 *Moses,* } dealer in furniture in So. Boston, unm.
  ii Hannah,[6] b. 23 Sept., 1787; m., 6 Mar., 1806, David Brown, and d. 1809. Children :
     1 *Chase Weeks* (Brown), b. 2 Nov., 1807.
     2 *Lucinda,* b. and d. 28 July, 1809.
  iii Betsey,[6] b. 22 July, 1789; m. 4 May, 1810, David Brown, as his 2nd wife. Children :
     1 *Samuel* (Brown), b. 1811; d. 1813.
     2 *Samuel,* b. 16 Mar., 1814; m. Nancy C. Swain and res. in Sanbornton.
  iv Patty[6] (Martha), b. 18 Oct., 1791; m., 9 June, 1814, Joseph G. March, b. 1789. Children :
     1 *Mary* (March), b. 16 July, 1817; d. 1818.
     2 *Mary,* 2nd, b. June, 1820; d. 1821.
  v Nancy,[6] b. 14 Oct., 1793; d. 28 June, 1820, in her 27th year.
  vi Polly,[6] b. 9 Nov., 1795; m., 1st, 3 Jan., 1819, Stephen S. Hersey, who d. 9 Feb., 1830, æ. 38, leaving :
     1 *Peter* (Hersey), b. 13 Dec., 1819.
     She m., 2nd, Moses Farnham who d. 8 May, 1852. She d. 29 Nov., 1869.
  vii Chase, jr.,[6] b. 27 Feb., 1798; d. 4 Dec., 1816, æ. near 19.
(87)viii Mark,[6] b. 14 Sept., 1800; m., 30 Mar., 1821, Clarissa Osgood of Gilford, b. in Loudon. He was a farmer and d. in Sanbornton, 2 Nov., 1851, æ. 51.
  ix Charlotte,[6] b. 13 Nov., 1802; d. 13 Apr., 1831, æ. 28.
  x Lucinda,[6] b. 16 and d. 19 Feb., 1805.
  xi Curtis,[6] b. 6 Dec., 1806; m., 15 Nov., 1832, Julia (dau. of Sam'l) Dustin,— an efficient farmer, a selectman, and a worthy citizen who d. 22 Oct., 1870, æ. 64. Children :
     1 *Samuel Dustin,*[7] b. 21 Oct., 1834; m., 10 Mar., 1860, Ellen F. Marshall of Hill, and succeeds his father on the homestead. Children : (1) Myrtie Augusta,[8] b. 20 Aug., 1861. (2) Belinda Julia, b. 22 June, 1863; d. same day. (3) Bertha Elizabeth, b. and d. in 1867.
  xii David,[6] b. 11 Feb., 1810; d. 13 Sept., 1816, æ. 6.

50

William Weeks[5] (*Cole,*[4] *Jn.,*[3] *Sam.,*[2] *Leon.*[1]) born
1764, died 1839, farmer, and his first wife, Sally (Calley), had born in Sanbornton
Children :

  i   Hannah,[6] b. Sept., 1784; m., 10 Mar., 1813, Jas. M. Clark of
Dorchester; and had two children.

  ii   Comfort,[6] b. 20 May, 1786; d. 29 Nov., 1861; m., 2 Nov., 1813,
Levi (son of Jotham) Rollins, farmer in Sanbornton, who
d. 31 Dec., 1872, æ. 83, "one of the old standard men of
Sanbornton." Their children were :

    1 *Lucretia T.* (Rollins), b. 11 May, 1815; d. 7 Jan., 1817.

    2 *Levi W.*, b. 12 Aug., 1818; d. 7 Oct., 1839, æ. 21.

    3 *Robinson Colby*, b. 28 Dec., 1822; m. 22 Dec., 1842, Sarah
Jane Thompson, b 1823, and had : (1) Levi B. b. 1843;
of Boston. (2) Martha J., b. 1853; d. 1872.

    4 *Marianne Weeks*, b. 28 Aug., 1827; m. 15 Nov., 1849,
Daniel A. Sanborn, and res. in Franklin.

  iii   Levi,[6] b. 29 Sept., 1788; farmer on the homestead, who m.,
12 May, 1811, Abigail (dau. of Eben.) Swain, and d. 8 July,
1814, æ. 26. Child :

    1 *Sally,*[7] b. 10 Oct., 1812; m., Sept., 1831, Harvey N. Ingalls
of Bristol. She d. in Franklin, leaving five children.

  iv   Dolly,[6] b. 19 Sept., 1791; m., 29 Apr., 1813, Wm. Durgin, carpenter, etc. She d. 10 Dec., 1822, æ. 31, leaving three
children:

    1 *Abigail* (Durgin), wife of Capt. —— Andrews of Salem,
Mass.

    2 *William, jr.*

    3 *Cyrus*, who was lame through life.

  v   Ezra,[6] b. 11 Dec., 1794; drowned 9 Oct., 1798.

  vi   Susanna,[6] b. 15 Aug., 1798; m., 30 June, 1831, John Kimball
of Northfield; had two children.

  vii   Jeremiah[6] (Jerry), b. 16 Mar., 1802; m., 13 Apr., 1826, Electa
(dau. of Chase) Osgood, and occupied the homestead; a
farmer and "a man of intelligence and conscientiousness."
He furnished valuable records of the Weeks family for the
History of Sanbornton. His children were :

    1 *Jerusha,*[7] b. 1 Feb., 1828; d. 13 Mar., 1828.

    2 *Norris Manly,*[7] b. 5 May, 1829; m., 5 May, 1861, Diana Foss
of Northfield. He is a farmer on the homestead and a pillar in the First Baptist Church. He has :(1) Fidelia Foss,[8]
b. 31 Dec., 1864. (2) Mary Bell, b. 24 Feb., 1868. (3)
Herman Norris, b. 29 Sept., 1875.

    3 *Rosilla,*[7] b. 10 Nov., 1831; m., 24 Feb., 1863, David B. Mason of Loudon, a soldier in the 7th N. H. Reg., who d.
in service, 28 May, 1865. Child : (1) Eldora, b. 15 July,
1864.

    4 *Matilda,*[7] b. 19 July, 1835; m., 31 Aug., 1853, Mark Hersey
Piper, and has b. in Sanbornton : (1) Laura Eliz., b. 5
Sept., 1856; m. Chas. A. Wallis. (2) Willie M., b. 12 Jan.,

Jan., 1861; d. 1 Nov., 1867.   (3) Leland Huntley, b. 5
July, 1863.   (4) Elmer Mark, b. 15 Mar., 1868.
viii Joseph,⁶ b. 18 Jan., 1804; d. 8 May, 1817.

51

John Weeks⁵ (*Cole*,⁴ *Jn.*,³ *Sam.*,² *Leon.*¹) born,
1769, died ——, and his wife —— (Calley), had born in
Jefferson, Me.,
Children :

   i David,⁶ settled in St. John's, N. B.
  ii Josiah.⁶ One Josiah Weeks m., in Gilmanton, 11 May, 1828,
      Dorothy French.
 iii Cole,⁶ a soldier in the war of 1812–14, in 1826–28 he was a
      voter in Chicago with only thirty-four others.   He m. a
      widow Caldwell and d. s. p.—Hon. J. Wentworth.
 iv Archelaus Mooney.⁶
  v Joseph.⁶
(88)vi Wm. Brackett,⁶ m., 1st, Miss Weeks, settled in Warren, Graf-
      ton Co., N. H.   He m., 2d, Sally (dau. of Joseph) Farn-
      ham, b. 5 Nov., 1824.
 vii Betsey.⁶
viii Polly⁶ (Molly).
 ix Hannah.⁶
  x Jesse.⁶
 xi Andrew C.⁶
xii Silvenus.⁶

52

Joseph Weeks⁵ (*Cole*,⁴ *Jn.*,³ *Sam.*,² *Leon.*¹) born
1773, died 1840, farmer, and his wife Huldah (Chapman),
had born in Sanbornton
Children :

(89)i Moses Welch,⁶ b. 17 May, 1792; m. 20 Sept., 1811, Rebecca
      (dau. of Lowell) Sanborn of Gilford, b. 27 Dec., 1791. "He
      was a farmer on the homestead, and a pioneer in the Tem-
      perance movement."   He d. 12 July, 1868, æ. 76.   They had
      nine children.
 ii Mehitable,⁶ b. 10 Feb., 1796; m., 1819, Samuel Gile, b. in
      Northwood, 1795; d. 25 Oct., 1851, æ. 55.   Her children
      were :
    1 *Betsey Bowdoin* (Gile), b. 12 Nov., 1820; m. A. Farnham,
      of Hill, and had two children.
    2 *Joseph Weeks*, b. 3 July, 1823; m., 1st, Ruth Ann Hilliard;
      2d, S. C. Clark; 3rd, Mrs. C. P. ——.
    3 *Mary Jane*, b. 7 Sept., 1828; d. 26 May, 1849.
    4 *Curtis K.*, b. 16 June, 1831; m. 8 Oct., 1854, Mary C. Rol-
      lins of Fisherville, and rem. from Hill to Urbana, Ill.;
      was a carpenter and d., 1879, æ. 48; had four children.

9

5 *Susan G.*, b. Sept., 1833; d. Sept., 1835.
6 *Mehitable A.*, b. 3 Aug., 1836; m. 29 Jan., 1863, J. Francis
   Bamford, a farmer.
iii Huldah,[6] b. 6 Aug., 1800; d. 26 Aug., 1800.
iv Joseph,[6] jr., b. Dec., 1801; d. 26 Oct., 1810.
v   Ezra,[6] b. 5 Oct., 1802; d. 11 July, 1803.
vi Asa,[6] b. 16 Apr., 1804; d. 7 Sept., 1816.

53

Jonathan Weeks[5] (*Cole*,[4] *Jn.*,[3] *Sam.*,[2] *Leon.*[1]) born
1776, died 1850, farmer, and his wife Polly (Call), had
born in Sanbornton

Children :

(90) i   Jonathan, jr.,[6] b. 16 Dec., 1796, a farmer in Sanbornton, then
    in Hill; m. 28 Nov., 1822, Mahala (dau. of Moses) Colby,
    and d. on a visit to Tamworth, 23 May, 1872, æ. 75. She
    d. in Waltham, Mass., 19 Sept., 1880, in her 77th year.
    They had five children.
ii   Daniel,[6] b. 4 June, 1798; m. Sally Wiggin; was forty years
    a farmer in Tamworth where he d. 11 Nov., 1879, æ. 81, *s. p.*
iii Eliza,[6] b. 15 Aug., 1804; m. Nathan Smith of New Hampton;
    d. in California in 1879, æ. 75. She had :
    1 *Dana* (Smith), of Laconia.
    2 *Eliza Jane*, who m. Dan'l Drew and rem. to California.
    3 *Martha*, m. D. Cummings, and d. in Ashland, July, 1878.
iv Polly C.,[6] b. 6 Dec., 1806; m., 1st, Reuben Beckman and had :
    1 *Martha E.* (Beckman).
    Married 2nd, John Smith of Tamworth and had :
    2 *Monroe* (Smith).
    3 *Abigail.*
    4 *Lucy*, m. —— Whiting and d.
    5 *John Byron.*
v   Hannah,[6] b. 20 Aug., 1808; m. Amos Webster of Tamworth,
    cabinet maker. Children :
    1 *Mary Ann* (Webster), b. 1830; m. Simeon Johnson of Tam-
    worth.
    2 *Martha*, m. Wm. W. Weeks (son of Jere. D.) Ballard of
    Tamworth, and had : (1) Mary, (2) Hollis, of Tamworth.
    3 *Hiram*, m. Lydia Bennett of Tamworth.
vi Joseph,[6] b. 26 July, 1813; once a Free Baptist preacher, res.
    in Tamworth and in 1880 in Hubbardston, Mass. Children :
    1 *Rosetta*,[7] m. —— Plumer and res. in Providence, R. I.
    2 *Sarah*,[7] m. David Blake, stationary engineer in Boston.
    3 *Ai.*[7]
    4 *Hiram*[7] [Harry]?. In 1881, Harry was manager of Tivoli
    Garden, Pittsburg, Penn.
    5 *Nathan Smith.*[7]
vii Josiah,[6] b. 10 Aug., 1816; } went together from Boston, on a
viii Rufus,[6] b. 17 Nov., 1819; } sea voyage, about 1840 and have
    never returned.
    Three other children died in infancy.

54

Capt. Cole Weeks[5] (*Cole*,[4] *Jn.*,[3] *Sam.*,[2] *Leon.*[1]) born 1778, died 1854, farmer, and his wife Eliza (Elkins), had born on the homestead in Sanbornton

Children :

i   Huldah,[6] b. 13 Oct., 1802; d. 18 Aug., 1803.

ii Curtis Elkins,[6] b. 24 Dec., 1804; d. 23 Oct., 1805.

iii Cyrus,[6] b. 16 Nov., 1806; a physician in New York City forty years; m., 1st, Maria L. Child of Portland, Me., 25 Sept., 1834, b. 21 Mar., 1810; d. 12 Sept., 1849. He m., 2nd, 2 Sept., 1852, Caroline E. Coles of New York. He was M.D. (Harv. Coll.), and member of N. Y. Academy of Medicine till his death at Hoboken, N. J., 20 Sept., 1875, by falling under the cars.   Children :

1   *Mary Elizabeth*,[7] b. 28 June, 1836; d. 25 Sept., 1836.

2   *Grenville M.*,[7] b. 22 Nov., 1837; a physician in the army, then in his father's office in New York. He was some years surgeon among the Indians and afterward secretary of the N. Y. Indian Commission. He wrote "The Last Cruise of the Monitor" in the Atlantic Monthly, March, 1863.

3   *John C.*,[7] b. 28 July, 1848, and d. 3 Aug., 1848.

4   *Caroline M.*,[7] b. 18 Nov., 1857 (by second wife) ; res. 1879, E. 45th street, New York.

iv Alpheus E.,[6] b. 29 Mar., 1809; inherited the homestead in Sanbornton, and d. there 2 Aug., 1862, æ. 53; "a faithful member of the Congregational church, living 4 miles from the place of worship." He m., 1st, Sept. 29, 1837, Susan (dau. of Eliph.) Ordway, who d. 4 July, 1853, æ. 37. He m., 2nd, May 29, 1855, Anna Coe of Newport, R. I. His children were :

1   *Sarah Ward*,[7] b. 13 Feb., 1839; m. 5 May, 1857, George H. Lane, a merchant in Boston, and had : (1) Fred. A.[8] (Lane), d. 1858. (2) Chas. S., b. 1860; entered Amherst College. (3) Charlotte G., b. Mar., 1863. (4) Lillie F. W., b. Sept., 1865. (5) Mary M., b. 1867. (6) Sarah Weeks, b. 21 Feb., 1869. (7) Geo. H., b. 1 Sept., 1871.

2   *Eliza Elkins*,[7] b. 30 Aug., 1840.

3   *Susan O.*,[7] b. 10 Aug., 1843; m. in Brookline, Mass., 14 Nov., 1867, F. A. Arnold, boot and shoe maker in Boston. She d. in Braintree, Mass., 19 May, 1876. Children : Eliza S., b. Aug. 29, 1868. (2) Frank Russell, b. 1 Oct., 1871.

4   *Maria C.*,[7] b. 17 Mar., 1846; m. 23 Dec., 1869, Russell Lane of a clothing store in Boston, then of Braintree.

5   *Lillian A.*,[7] b. 1 Nov., 1851.

6   *Mary M.*,[7] d. in infancy, 5 May, 1856.

55

John Weeks[5](*Benj.*,[4] *Jn.*,[3] *Sam.*,[2] *Leon.*[1]) born 1762, died 1841, farmer, and his wife Esther (Spencer), had born in Piermont

Children :

(91) i Enoch R.,[6] b. 5 Mar., 1787; d. 26 Jan., 1867; he m. 2 Mar., 1814, Sally Merrill, b. 9 May, 1793; was a farmer and hotel-keeper in Warren, and had ten children.

(92) ii John,[6] b. 19 Apr., 1789; m., 1st, 11 Mar., 1811, Abigail Currier, b. 9 Oct., 1792, who had five children and d. 20 Feb., 1821. He m., 2nd, 6 May, 1821, Rosina Brown, b. 4 Apr., 1801, who had eight children, and d. 19 Oct., 1877. He d. 19 Oct., 1845.

iii Nehemiah,[6] b. 11 Apr., 1792; m. 1 Nov., 1817, Lucinda Brown, and d. June, 1869. Children :

1 *Sophia*,[7] b. 10 June, 1819; m., res. and d. in St. Johnsbury, Vt.; three children.

2 *Hiram*,[7] b. 9 Nov., 1820; m. Sarah Butler; res. St. Johnsbury Centre, Vt.

3 *Catharine E. G.*,[7] b. 18 Mar., 1834; m. Roswell C. Vaughn.

(92a) iv Jonathan,[6] b. 29 June, 1794; d. 11 Nov., 1836; m. 25 Jan., 1818, Betsey Brown Huse, b. 4 June, 1794, who d. 30 Jan., 1847. He was tanner and shoemaker in Lyndon, Vt., and had six children.

v Betsey,[6] b. 30 Dec., 1796; d. 15 Nov., 1815.

vi Eunice,[6] b. 29 June, 1799; d. 24 Apr., 1870.

(93) vii Capt. Brainard Spencer,[6] b. 13 Dec., 1801; d. Edenville, Iowa, 16 June, 1875; m., in Wentworth, N. H., 17 Sept., 1840, Sarah Minerva Chamberlain, b. in Norwich, Vt., 18 Aug., 1820; res. on the homestead and had seven children; was a Universalist; was respected and trusted with office by his townsmen.

viii Benj. F.,[6] b. 24 May, 1804; d. 16 July, 1845; a doctor; d. in Sigourney, Iowa, unm.

ix Mary Hunt,[6] b. 29 May, 1814; m. 18 June, 1838, Jn. W. Brown of Lyndon, Vt.; d. 26 Jan., 1848. Children :

1 *Geo. F.* (Brown), b. 23 Feb., 1839.

2 *Charles S.*, b. 1 Nov., 1840.

3 *Betsey L.*, b. 8 Apr., 1842.

4 *Sophia A.*, b. 9 Apr., 1844.

5 *Ella S.*, b. 2 May, 1846.

55a

Joseph Weeks[5] (*Benj.*,[4] *Jn.*,[3] *Sam.*,[2] *Leon.*[1]), died 1841, of Piermont, and his wife Lucy (Lund), had born Children :

i Sally,[6] m. Peter Whitman; rem. to Canada; d. abt. 1840.

ii Sybil,[6] m. Oram Randall, rem. to Indiana, then to Marshall Co., Iowa, and d. there.

iii Ann,[6] m. B. C. Whitcomb, res. in Lawrence, Mass., then in De Kalb Co., Ill., where he d. She res. in Chicago.

iv Timothy,[6] m. Phebe ———; rem. and d. in Kendall Co., Ill., 1864.

v Daniel,[6] b. 28 Nov., 1811, farmer; m., 1st, Mary (dau. of Joseph) Rollins, b. 1812; d. 1854; m., 2nd, ———. Children of Daniel and Mary (Rollins) Weeks were :

1 *Wm. G.*,[7] b. 1841; d. 1843.
2 *Henry*,[7] d. 1843.
3 *Henry M.*,[7] b. in Grafton Co., N. H., 19 Aug., 1844; rem.,
   1863, to Ill., in 1865 to Marshall Co., Iowa; was twelve
   years a teacher; m. there 28 Nov., 1868, Clara J. Nichols,
   b. in Green Co., Penn., 17 Apr., 1850, and has nine children, b. in Rhodes, Iowa. Children: (1) Mary E.,[8] b.
   8 Oct., 1869, teacher. (2) Lela B., b. 1 Oct., 1871,
   teacher of music. (3) Dan. P., b. 16 Oct., 1873. (4)
   Paul Revere, b. 19 Mar., 1876. (5) Ida E., b. 10 Mar.,
   1878. (6) Nellie A., b. 10 June, 1880. (7) Katie E., b.
   14 Oct., 1882. (8) Agnes C., b. 18 Oct., 1884. (9) James
   A., b. 5 Oct., 1886.
4 *Emily B.*,[7] b. 17 June, 1848; m., in Iowa, Chas. Bartlett,
   and d. 1878. Four children.
5 *Mary E.*,[7] b. 2 Aug., 1851, a teacher six years at Omaha,
   Neb.; m. in Vineland, N. J., 1880, A. W. Thorndyke of
   that city who in 1887 rem. to San Diego, Cal., where
   she d. 5 Feb., 1888.
   Children of Daniel Weeks by second wife:
6 *Kate.*[7] b. 1858; m. C. H. Libbey of Iowa and d. 1879.
7 *Carrie,*[7] b. 1860; m. J. W. Garis, and res. in Rhodes,
   Iowa.
vi Miriam,[6] m. Hosea Lund who d. in Piermont in 1856. She
   rem. to Vineland, N. J., and d. there in 1884.
vii Irene,[6] m. James Stevens and rem. to De Kalb Co., Ill.; d.
   there in 1863.
viii Joseph,[6] m. Mary J. Chamberlain who d. and he res. in Boston.
ix Emily,[6] m. Zenas Bartlett, who d. from a wound at the battle
   of Shiloh. She res. at Oberlin, Kansas.

56

Stephen March Weeks[5] (*Ich.* [4] *Walter,*[3] *Sam.,*[2]
Leon.[1]) and his wife Mary S. (Gookin), had born in
Greenland

Children :

i Dr. Charles March,[6] b. 16 Mar., 1809 (Dart. Coll., 1830; M.D.,
   Bowdoin, 1833); m. in Roxbury, Mass., 6 Dec., 1839, Elvina
   (dau. of Rev. H.) Porter of Rye. He practised in St. Clair,
   Mich., in Eliot, Me., Lynn, Mass., and d. in Crawford, Ga.,
   27 June, 1882, æ. 73. Children :
   1 *Albert H.*,[7] m. Naomi ——— ; res. Crawford, Ga.
   2 *Edgar,*[7] d.
   3 *Caroline Porter,*[7] d. about 1879.
ii Caroline,[6] an invalid in Greenland; d. 1887.
iii Stephen March,[6] b. Dec., 1812; d. 31 Dec., 1868. He m. 1
   Feb., 1852, Ellen Henderson of Greenland, and had b. in
   Greenland :
   1 *Stephen Henderson,*[7] b. 20 Mar., 1853.
   2 *Edward Robie,*[7] b. 6 Jan., 1855.
   3 *Ellen Adalaide,*[7] b. 12 Feb., 1858.

iv Capt. Nath'l G.,[6] m. Elizabeth Lord of So. Berwick, Me., and
    had :
    1 *Walter M.*,[7] m. Mary Brett.
    2 *Stephen D.*,[7] lost at sea; unm.
    3 *Laura*,[7] res. Rollinsford.
v   Ichabod.[6] d. *s. p.*, Kalamazoo, Mich., about 1850.
vi Rufus W.,[6] b. 1819; m. 27 Jan., ;861, Ellen Janette (dau. of
    Wm. B.) Belknap of Lisbon, N. H.; is a farmer and had b.
    in Greenland :
    1 *Belknap*,[7] b. 28 Jan., 1863.
    2 *Goldwin Ichabod*,[7] b. 29 Jan., 1866.
    3 *Arthur Hale*,[7] b. 4 Feb., 1868.
    4 *Rufus Wm., jr.*,[7] b. 18 Apr., 1871.

57

Walter Weeks[5] (*Wm.*,[4] *Walter*,[3] *Sam.*,[2] *Leon.*[1]) born
——, died 1848, shoemaker, and his first wife Sarah
(Tarleton), had born in Greenland

Children :

i   Walter,[6] b. 25 Mar., 1795; m. 2 Aug., 1819, Elizabeth White
    (dau. of Jn. and Eliz.) Haines of Greenland who was b. 6
    June, 1800. He rem. to Levant, Me., where he d. 16 Sept.,
    1884, and his wife in 1878. Their children :
    1 *Mary Elizabeth*,[7] b. 6 June, 1820.
    2 *Martin R.*,[7] m. Mary Greeley of Kenduskeag, Me.
    3 *Sarah Georgiana*,[7] b. 11 Nov., 1831; teacher; m. 8 Oct., 1859,
    in Stetson, Me., Cleveland Caverly, a carpenter, of No.
    Newport, Me., who d. 2 Feb., 1879. Children : (1) May
    E. (Caverly), b. 8 Aug., 1863. (2) Walter W., b. 29 May,
    1865.
ii Joseph,[6] a carpenter, m. 14 Feb., 1825, Nancy Hilton, b.
    1804, d. 1870, of Newmarket and settled in Portsmouth,
    where he d. 24 Mar., 1864. Children :
    1 *Ann Sarah*,[7] b. 5 Aug., 1828; m. 29 Jan., 1861, Capt.——
    Warsaw, who d. San Francisco, Cal., 1 June, 1880, leav-
    ing (1) Hattie L. (Warsaw).
    2 *Martha*,[7] b. 3 Jan., 1835; m. 15 June, 1857, Capt. Wm. Lester,
    Stratham, and has no children.
iii William,[6] a cooper, m. Mary Blake and d. in Hampton, *s. p.*
iv Elizabeth,[6] m. Thos. Norton, b. 1800, of Greenland, and d.
    there, 1872. Children :
    1 *Ellen* (Norton).
    2 *Walter*. res. Greenland.
v   Ann P.,[6] m. John H. Hilton, cabinet maker; res. in Ports-
    mouth, and d. there 1 Dec., 1870. Children :
    1 *John Calhoun* (Hilton).
    2 *Geo. Washington*.
    3 *Gustavus Adolphus*.
    4 *Georgiana*, m. Joseph F. Smart of Stratham.
    5 *Walter Harrison*.

Walter Weeks[5] married, second, Nancy Presby of Newmarket, and had

Children :

   vi Caroline,[6] m. —— Ham, carpenter, of Portsmouth, and res.
     there. Children :
     1 *Hubbard* (Ham).
     2 *Nellie G.*

58

Joshua Weeks[5] (*Wm.,*[4] *Walter,*[3] *Sam.,*[2] *Leon.*[1])
born 1792, died 1872, blacksmith, and his wife Nancy
(Rollins), had born in Greenland

Children :

   i Comfort,[6] b. 1804 ; m., 1st, 1828, P. Coleman of Newington ;
     m., 2nd, Gen. Theodore A. Burleigh. Children by first
     husband :
     1 *Mary* (Coleman) ; m. —— Cate.
     2 *Jacob James.*
     3 *Phineas N.*
   ii Abigail,[6] b. [1806] ?, m. John Pickering of Newmarket and
     had :
     1 *Caroline* (Pickering).
     2 *John Albert.*
   iii John Calvin,[6] m. Mary Greenough of Portsmouth, and had :
     1 *Helen,*[7] m. Charles Drake of Rye.
     2 *Anna,*[7] m. Mr. Bryant of Manchester.
     3 *Mary Abbie,*[7] not m.
   iv Joshua,[6] m. and had :
     1 *A daughter,*[7] in Oregon.
   v Lydia Ann,[6] m. Wm. Bennett of Greenland, and had :
     1 *Ada Jane* (Bennett), m. Mr. Lane, farmer in Greenland.
     2 *Willie S.*
     3 *Joshua E.*

59

Nathaniel Weeks[5] (*Jn.,*[4] *Matt.,*[3] *Sam.,*[2] *Leon.*[1]) ?
born 1760 ?, died 1815, tanner and shoemaker of Gilmanton, Stratham, etc., and his wife Huldah (Pottle), had

Children :

(**94**) i Samuel P.,[6] b. 1784 ; [m. 1807] ? Huldah, b. 1787 (dau. of
     Josiah) Knight of Falmouth, Me. ; rem. to Buckfield, 1813,
     and to Paris, Me., in 1815, where she d. 16 Jan., 1828, having
     had eight children. He d. 16 Mar., 1829.

Nathaniel Weeks[5] married, second, in Exeter, 6 May,
1787, Polly Pottle, both of Exeter, and had :

ii   Jane,[6] } twins; d.
iii   Nicholas,[6]

iv   Mary (Polly),[6] m. —— Clark of Allenstown and d. there.

v   Nicholas,[6] 2nd, d.

vi, Joseph[6] (changed to George), moved to N. Y. state.

(95) vii Maj. Nathaniel,[6]* b. in Gilmanton, 1796. His father d. when he was about 18 years of age, leaving a widow and several children younger than himself, without much means for their education or support. He came to Exeter, and on the 6 August, 1820, m. Harriet Byram Gilman, b. 1802, of Exeter, and had six children. He was a well known merchant, and a Christian. His wife d. in Exeter, 11 Aug., 1870, and he followed her, 29 Mar., 1874, æ. 78.

(96) viii Timothy,[6] b. in Bridgewater, N. H., 13 Nov., 1801; m. 6 Oct., 1825, Eliz. Barnard (dau. of Joel) Whitney, b. in Westminster, Mass., 27 May, 1804, who d. 17 Apr., 1887, in Everett, Mass., at the home of her son-in-law, N. W. Frye, æ. 83. Had seven children. He d. in Lowell, Mass., 1 July, 1854, æ. 52.

ix Joshua,[6] b. 1806; m. Dorcas Neally of Exeter, b., in 1815, who d. 13 June, 1857, æ. 42; he d. in Exeter, 30 June, 1866, æ. 60. Six children.

1 *Nath'l*,[7] not m.

2 *Joshua, jr.*,[7] m.

3 *Henry*.[7]

4 *Mary*,[7] m. Geo. Chase and had a son, in Amesbury, Mass.

5 *Julia*,[7] m., 1st, Mr. Pollard; 2nd, Mr. Burns of Providence, R. I.

6 *Dorcas Maria*,[7] b. 1848; d. May, 1885, æ. 37.

60

John Lang Weeks[5] (supposed *Jn.*,[4] *Matt.*,[3] *Sam.*,[2] *Leon.*[1]) born 1763, died 1853, and his wife Judith (Plummer), had born in Tamworth

Children :

i   John,[6] b. 11 Dec., 1800; m. Miss —— Nickerson; had five children; d. in Minneapolis, Minn.

ii   Hannah,[6] b. 27 Apr., 1802; d. in Gilford, æ. 9 yrs.

iii Mehitable,[6] b. 6 May. 1803; d. 1826; unm.

iv Sally,[6] b. 15 May, 1804; m. in Maine and d. there.

v   Judith,[6] b. 2 Aug., 1805; m. Amasa Howard, blacksmith of Tamworth; rem. to Maine; d. in Bangor, 25 Jan., 1877; left two children.

---

*Maj. Nath'l Weeks. one of a large family, had few advantages for an education, in early life, being obliged to provide mostly for himself. Before they were old enough to bear arms, he and his brother entered the army as musicians, in the war of 1812. Amidst many discouragements and difficulties he rose to become a prominent and useful citizen of Exeter. In 1829, he and his wife united with the First Congregational church. Afterward he became a Christian Baptist, serving the Master with such a commendable zeal as placed him among the leading members of that church.

vi Noah,[6] b. 7 Oct., 1806; d., unm., in Tamworth, 1 Feb., 1842.
vii Martin,[6] b. 29 Nov., 1808; m. 14 Dec., 1848, Nancy Berry; d. on the homestead, 23 May, 1884.
viii Elisha,[6] b. in Gilford, 26 Aug., 1810; d. in Lawrence, Mass., 20 May, 1866. He m. Mary A. Johnson of Bucksport, Me., and had :
    1 *Geo. F.,*[7] b. 23 Aug., 1853; educated at Tilton, N. H., Boston and Michigan Univ. Law Schools; a miner in Colorado, an engineer; unm.
    2 *Henry A.,*[7] b. 10 June, 1855; a farmer in Dakota.
    3 *Lizzie A.,*[7] at home with her mother in Waltham, Mass.
ix Lydia,[6] b. in Gilford, 20 Jan., 1812; d. in Tamworth, 19 Aug., 1824, æ. 12.
(97) x Gilman,[6] b. in Gilford, 27 July, 1813; m., 1st, in Tamworth, 6 Oct., 1837, Sarah Fairfield, b. in New Hampton, 4 June, 1812, who had seven children, and d. 31 July, 1854. He m., 2nd, Mrs. Hannah Head of Madison, who d. 1872; m., 3d, Mrs. Elvira Davis of Tamworth; d. 15 Sept., 1879. She d. May, 1881.
xi Plummer,[6] b. in Tamworth 23 Mar., 1815; m.. 1848, Nancy Hart and d. in E. Boston, Mass., 10 Sept., 1884, *s. p.*
xii Levi,[6] b. 30 June, 1817; m. in Lawrence, Mass., Mrs. Abigail ———; d. in Salem, Mass., 1840, leaving one child.
xiii Dorothy,[6] b. 25 Feb., 1819; m. Jas. Dunton; res. in Hampden, Me.
xiv Benjamin,[6] b. 30 Dec., 1820; m. Fidelia Jennings of Methuen, Mass.; d. in Lawrence, Sept., 1881. Their children were :
    1 *Benj. L.*[7]
    2 *Lyman A.*[7]
    3 *Orin.*[7]
    4 *Joseph E.*[7]
    5 *Jonathan E.*[7]
    6 *Rhoda,*[7] d. early.
xv Hannah,[6] b. in Tamworth 16 Feb., 1824; d. 24 Dec., 1826.
xvi Lavinia,[6] b. 26 May, 1826; m. 24 Dec., 1847, Atkinson Moody of Ossipee; res., 1885, in Tamworth, and had nine children :
    1 *Chas. A.* (Moody), b. 23 Jan., 1849; m. Lizzie Durgin of Madison.
    2 *Levi W.,* b. 3 Oct., 1850; m. Jennie Davis of Ossipee; d. 24 Dec., 1884.
    3 *Emma F..* b. 30 Jan., 1855; m. David Clay of Newmarket.
    4 *John F.,* b. 22 July, 1856; d. in Tamworth, 1 Feb., 1887.
    5 *Hattie A.,* b. 26 Apr., 1858; m. 31 Dec., 1880, Onslow L. Ross of Tamworth.
    6 *Abbie E.,* b. 21 Aug., 1859; m. Albert Adams.
    7 *Fred. L.,* b. 15 Oct., 1861; m. Miss Nellie ———; is a lawyer in Boston.
    8 *Melissa A.,* b. 9 Dec., 1863.
    9 *Nettie A.,* b. 6 May, 1865; d. in Tamworth 16 June, 1866.

60a

Noah Weeks[5] [*Jn.,*[4] *Matt.,*[3] *Sam.,*[2] *Leon.*[1]]? born Feb., 1771 [in Greenland]?, died in Alton, Dec., 1804,

æ. 33 yrs. 10 mos. (married in Gilmanton, 12 Mar., 1793),
and his wife Sarah (Morrill), had born in Alton
Children :

   i   Susanna,[6] b. 26 Feb., 1794.
   ii   Henry,[6] b. 27 Apr., 1796; d. 1861; m. Hannah Chapman.
       Children :
       1 *Sarah*,[7] b. 7 Mar., 1819; m. Moses S. Gale, b. May, 1815.
         Children : (1) Joseph E.[8] (Gale), b. 13 Mar., 1841; d. 31
         Oct., 1863. (2) Laurenia A., b. 22 July, 1842; d. 16 Dec.,
         1846. (3) Henry M. b. 2 Aug., 1845; d. 16 May, 1849.
         (4) Laurenia A., b. 28 Apr., 1849; m. Geo. Eastman, and
         has : (*a*) Moses G.[9] Eastman.
       2 *Noah*,[7] b. 26 Mar., 1821; m. Sarah A. McNeal. Children :
         (1) Mary K.,[8] b. 21 Apr., 1846; d. 13 Feb., 1869. (2)
         Marcus S., b. 2 Mar., 1848; m. Sylvia F. Kimball. Chil-
         dren : (*a*) Ira F.,[9] b. 1 Dec., 1876; (*b*) Blanche, b. 2 Jan.,
         1883. (3) Chas. T. Weeks, b. 26 Apr., 1854; m. Alice A.
         Berry. Children : (*a*) Eva A , b. 14 Dec., 1878; (*b*)
         Ira A., b. 27 Dec., 1881; (*c*) Henry P., b. 11 May, 1884.
         (4) John L., b. 26 May, 1857; m. Nellie Page. Child:
         (*a*) Winfred A., b. 29 Feb., 1884. (5) Herbert N., b.
         27 Jan., 1860; unm.
       3 *Nathaniel*,[7] b. 10 Nov., 1824; m. Cordelia Merrill. Children :
         (1) Martha,[8] (2) Henry, (3) George, (4) Ellen, (5) Mary.
   iii John L.,[6] b. 27 Jan., 1799; res. in Alton; m. in Gilmanton
       2 Mar., 1823, Judith E. Gilman of Gilford.
   iv Nathaniel,[6] b. 10 Jan., 1801.
   v   Noah,[6] b. 17 Oct., 1804.

61

John Weeks[5] (*Matt.*,[4] *Matt.*,[3] *Sam.*,[2] *Leon.*[1]) born
1762, died 1852, farmer in Gilmanton and Canaan, Vt.,
and his wife Hannah (Moody), had born in Gilmanton
Children :

   i   Moody,[6] b. 20 Mar., 1787 ⎫
   ii   Peter,[6] b. 28 Feb., 1793   ⎬ went to Ohio and we have no
   iii Leavitt,[6] b. 5 Feb., 1796 ⎭ records of them.
   iv Abigail,[6] b. 2 Aug., 1797; d. early.
   v   Dorothea,[6] b. [Canaan, Vt.]? 2 Mar., 1803; m. Jotham Saw-
       yer of Stewartstown, N. H., and had :
       1 *James Weeks* (Sawyer), d.
       2 *Darius*, d.
       3 *Mary H.*, b. July, 1838; m. 25 Aug., 1856, Jas. Woodbury
        Weeks (see No. 63-i).
       4 *Peter*, d.
       5 *Celestia*, res. in Wisconsin.

vi Matthias,⁶ b. 27 June, 1806; m., 1st, Olive Dennet, who d.
s. p.; m., 2nd, Emily Morison, and had:
1 *Stephen E.*,⁷ m. —— Piper; lives in Canaan, Vt., with several children.
vii Mary,⁶ b. 15 May, 1809; m. in Canaan, Vt., 2 Dec., 1830, Sam'l
G. Bishop, jr. Children:
1 *Mary Jane* (Bishop), b. 2 Aug., 1838; d. 1 Mar., 1840.
2 *Wm. Bramwell*, b. 3 Nov., 1840.
3 *Mary Eliza*, b. 18 July, 1843.
4 *John Weeks*, b. 16 Nov., 1845.
5 *Samuel Tuck*, b. 12 Mar., 1848.
6 *Martha Abigail*, b. 10 Aug., 1851.
7 *Geo. Almazo*, b. 1 May, 1854.
viii Olive,⁶ b. 28 Feb., 1812; m. —— Dennis.

62

Matthias Weeks⁵(*Matt.*,⁴ *Matt.*,³ *Sam.*,²*Leon.*¹) born
1767, died 1815, of Gilmanton, and his wife Mary (Bennett), had born in Gilmanton
Children:

i Polly.⁶ b. abt. 1795; m., 1st, 23 Nov., 1815, Josiah Robinson
of Gilmanton. After the death of her sister Malinda, she
m., 2nd, Dan'l Goss, and d. 24 Sept., 1879.
ii Matthias,⁶ b. 17 Dec., 1797; m. 26 Mar., 1821, Fanny Morgan,
both of Gilmanton. He was a stone mason in Moultonboro and in Tamworth. In 1885, res. in Franklin, Mass.
Children:
1 *Frank Silvester*,⁷ b. 1821; m. Harriet Carter of Wakefield,
and d. Oct., 1879. His wife d. a few years afterward.
They had: (1) Anna Frances;⁸ (2) Mary Carter, m. Frank
Howe of Milton; (3) Lizzie Franklin, m. Chas. Smith
of Tamworth.
2 *Frances Annville*,⁷ b. 1822; m. Chas. P. Carter, merchant
of Wakefield, and res. Franklin, Mass.
3 *Nancy Malinda*,⁷ b. 1832; m. Rev. D. F. Savage, and d.
soon after s. p.
4 *Ellen Arminda*,⁷ b. 1842; m. 13 May, 1874, Randolph P. De
Lancey; res. No. Beach, Hampton, s. p.
iii Malinda B.,⁶ b. 20 Feb., 1800; m. Dan'l Goss and d. 23 Jan.,
1831. Children:
1 *Alonzo* (Goss), of Salem.
2 *William.*
3 *John.*
4 *Melissa*, m. Sargent.
iv Judith,⁶ b. 1 Apr., 1802; d. of spotted fever, 23 Feb., 1815.
v John B.,⁶ b. Apr., 1804; d. July, 1805.
vi Charles G.,⁶ b. 29 May, 1807; m. in Meredith Village, 3 June,
1838, Mary (dau. of Asa) Kelcey, b. Croydon, 21 June, 1815;
a teacher, No. Branch, Somerset Co., N. J., and d. Somerville, N. J., 30 Nov. (1884). Children:
1 *Edward Alphonso*,⁷ b. Gilford, 2 Mar., 1839; m. 21 July,

1863, Gertrude (dau. of Peter) Melick, of Pepack, N. J.,
and had: (1) Chas. F.,[8] b. Sept., 1864; d. July, 1867. (2)
Wilbur Kelcey, b. 23 Oct., 1871. (3) Lewis Berg, b. 28
Nov., 1873. The mother, Gertrude, d. 13 May, 1882, and
Edward A. m., 2nd, 10 Nov., 1885, Elizabeth Trotter of
Bound Brook, and res. Somerville, N. Jersey.
2 *John Tappan*,[7] b. Hempstead, N. Y., 29 Dec., 1845; d. 26
May, 1867, æ. 21.
3 *Mary Ella*,[7] b. No. Branch, Branchburg township, N. J., 19
Aug., 1854.
vii Samuel Greeley,[6] b. Gilmanton, 14 Apr., 1809: studied divinity at Princeton, N. J., was a home missionary, preached
in Michigan, then at So. Bend, Ind., where he d. 21 May,
1846, æ. 37, *s. p.*

62a

Samuel Weeks[5] (*Matt.*,[4] *Matt.*,[3] *Sam.*,[2] *Leon.*[1]) born
1770, died 1854, farmer, in Gilmanton, and in Canaan,
Vt., and his wife Abigail (Moody), had born in Gilmanton
Children :

i   Judith,[6] m. Barnes Hilliard of Colebrook, N. H.; res. and d.
there; had twelve children :
1 *Abigail* (Hilliard), m. Asahel Brainard, and had no children.
2 *Melinda*, m. Jn. Ingals of Canterbury (Gilmanton), and had
children : (1) Arianna B., d. æ. 24. (2) Orilla, m. Chas.
Dalton of Belmont. (3) Frank, b. 1854; d. æ. 12. (4)
Helen Mar, b. 4 Sept., 1859. (5) Elmer, b. 1861; killed
by a tree, 1870.
3 *Ira*, a brickmaker, m. and settled in Iowa. Children: (1)
Lewis, (2) Archie.
4 *Jn. Moody*, a farmer in Canaan, Vt.; m. Mary Ann Hibbard
of Canada; d. in Canaan, Vt. She lives in W. Stewartstown with several children.
5 *James*, m. Lucy Neal of Canaan, and was killed in the war
of the Rebellion. His son Ino, b. 1853, was killed on the
R. R.
6 *Persis*, m. Drew Little of Colebrook, N. H., and has : (1)
Irving D., b. 1872. (2) Etta May, b. 1875.
7 *Laurinda*, b. Dec., 1831; m. Matthias Weeks of Gilmanton,
and have nine children (see 64–v).
8 *Lovina* W., m. Jas. Little of Colebrook, N. H.; no children.
9 *Sarah*, b. Jan., 1834; m. Orrin Tuttle of Stewartstown, N.
H., and has no children.
10 *Martha*, m. Othniel Stillings of Stewartstown. Child : (1)
Flora, b. 1856; m.——Forest; three children.
11 *Fidelia*, unm., res. in Colebrook.
12 *Susan*, m. Osmond Forest of Colebrook, *s. p.*
This large family is said to be "all industrious and respec-
table."
ii   John Lyford,[6] b. 1797; m. Mary Hughs of Colebrook, N. H.,
and had b. in Canaan, Vt., five children :

1 *Abigail*,[7] m. Wm. Morrill; d. Mar., 1888. They had b. in
Canaan six children: (1) Geo., d. young. (2) Mary,
not m. (3) Wm. E., m. Hattie Davis of Haverhill, Mass.,
and has: (*a*) Fred, (*b*) Hattie. He, with his uncle, C.
H. Weeks, is dealer in marble, etc., in Haverhill, Mass.
(4) Charles, m. Mary Watkins of Canaan. (5) Ray. (6)
Fred. d. young.

2 *Geo. H.*, d., æ. 22.

3 *Wm. E.*, m. Miss Butler and had: (1) Lilla Belle,[8] (2) a
dau.; both d. young.

4 *Calvin H.*,? m.; res. in Haverhill, Mass.; has been mayor
and alderman of the city; works on marble.

5 *John*,[7] enlisted at the first call for volunteers, served three
years in the army and was killed in the Battle of the
Wilderness.

iii Hannah.[6] d. young.

iv Samuel,[6] b. 10 Nov., 1803, is living, 1887, in Canaan, Vt.;
m. 9 Mar., 1829, Genett (dau. of Joseph and Naomi) Hilliard, b. 8 Jan., 1810, and had b. in Canaan, Vt.:
1 *C. H.* (Weeks).[7]
2 *J. A.* (Weeks).[7]
3 *Mrs. D.* Heath.[7]

v Eliza.[6] m. Winthrop Young of Canaan, Vt., and had:
1 *Alvah* (Young), of Prairie du Sac, Sauk Co., Wis.

vi William,[6] d. in Canaan, Vt., unm.

vii Sarah,[6] m. —— Brooks.

viii Susan,[6] m. —— Dennet, res. in Wisconsin. Children:
1 *Albert* (Dennet).
2 *Sarah.*
3 *William.*

ix Abigail,[6] m. Jonathan Clough; res. in Canaan, Vt.

x Dorothy,[6] d. young.
The last four daughters went west and their history is un-
known.

63

Dea. William Weeks[5] (*Matt.*,[4] *Matt.*,[3] *Sam.*,[2] *Leon.*[1])

born 1772, died, 1852, tanner, in Gilmanton, and his first
wife Mary (Beede), had born in Poplin

Children:

1 James,[6] b. 25 Dec., 1795, a farmer in Gilmanton, where he d.
1 Dec., 1874; m. Miss Sally Towle, b. 2 May, 1795, who d.
3 Dec., 1861. They had:
1 *Betsey*,[7] b. 21 May, 1824; m. Jn. Foster who d. in Belmont,
25 Mar., 1874, æ. 46.
2 *Jas. Woodbury*,[7] b. 31 Oct., 1827; m. 25 Aug., 1856, Mary
H. Sawyer, b. July, 1838, res. in Columbia, and has:
(1) Chas. W.,[8] b. 13 Jan., 1861. (2) James Irving, b. 18
Sept., 1866. (3) Mary L., b. 15 June, 1874.
3 *Olive Jane*,[7] b. 13 Aug., 1830; m. A. H. Greene, of Lynn,
Mass., res. in Gilmanton. Children: (1) A. H., b. 1858;

d., 1865. (2) Mary A. P., b. June. 1865, grad. Gilmanton
Acad.; a teacher.

4 *Wm. II.*,[7] b. 2 Dec., 1840; m. 17 Dec., 1864, Olive A. Buswell, b. in Franklin, 1844; res. in Andover, 1888. Children: (1) Anna S.,[8] d. æ. 12. (2) James Albert, d. 23
May, 1885, æ. 18.

ii Mary,[6] b. 19 July, 1799; m. 20 Jan., 1819, Peter Moody, res.
in Bethlehem, and d. in Gilmanton, 24 Oct., 1835. Children:

1 *Wm. Weeks* (Moody), b. 21 Nov., 1821; engineer, went to
Wisconsin.

iii William, jr.,[6] b. 23 Oct., 1800, tanner; m. 1 Nov., 1828, Mary
Folsom Beau, and d. in Lyndon, Vt., 20 Aug., 1877. She
d. 18 Aug., 1881. Children:

1 *Frances H.*,[7] b. in Gilmanton, 13 Feb., 1830; d. 1841.

2 *Charlotte E.*,[7] b. in Craftsbury, Vt., 12 Oct., 1839; d. 3 Apr.,
1868.

3 *Mary Almira*,[7] b. 21 Mar., 1841; m. James S. Shaw, and d.
in Lyndon, Vt., 30 Apr., 1875. He m., 2nd, Mrs. Sarah
Hutchinson, and is a doctor in Boston.

iv Betsey,[6] b. 1 Sept., 1802; d., unm., 5 Nov., 1823.

v Thomas Beede,[6] b. 6 July, 1806, and d. in Sandwich, 25 Apr.,
1874. He m., 1st, in Sandwich, Feb., 1828, Philinda Way,
b. in Lempster, 6 Apr., 1805, who d. 11 July, 1844; m., 2nd,
26 Apr., 1846, Irene A. Webster, b. July, 1808, who d. 19
Aug., 1883. Children:

1 *Mary Eliz.*,[7] b. 27 Dec., 1831, in Sandwich, and d. 15 Nov.,
1887; m. Isaac Harris, who d. 15 Nov., 1876. Children:
(1) Mark A.[8] (Harris), b. 20 Aug., 1850; m. 14 Aug., 1878,
Mary L. Taylor. Children: (*a*) John[9] and (*b*) Willie.
(2) Philinda Way, b. 24 Aug., 1853, a teacher, m. in
Belmont, 17 Sept., 1875, A. L. Barton, grocer, etc., now
a broker in Kansas, with one dau.: (*a*) Cora A., b. 17
Sept., 1887. (3) Ann Maria, b. 15 July, 1855; m. 4 Feb.,
1877, Dana D. Maxfield of Belmont, *s. p.*

2 *Benj. Way*,[7] b. 31 July, 1836; m. Julia A. Whitcher of
Northfield. He enlisted, Sept., 1862, in Co. D., 12th N.
H. Reg't and d. in Falmouth, Va., 26 Nov., 1862. His
children: (1) Sallie L.,[8] d. an infant. (2) Geo. M., b. 6
Oct., 1861; res. Lake Village, carpenter, d. there unm.,
22 Mar., 1888. (3) Fred C., house painter, res. unm. in
Lake Village, with his mother.

3 *Daniel Way*,[7] b. 18 June, 1843; m. in Manchester, 24 Apr.,
1869, Eliz. (dau. of Benj.) Lane, b. in Alna, Me., 29 June.
1838; res. in Sandwich with one child: (1) Ella Francis,[9]
b. 3 Jan., 1871.

vi Samuel,[6] b. 13 Sept., 1810; d. 27 July, 1847; tanner, res. in
Gilmanton on the homestead; m. 21 Nov., 1838, Abigail
Towle (dau. of Tim.) French of Loudon, who d. 7 Aug.,
1849. Children:

1 *Mary Lovina*,[7] b. 3 Oct., 1839; m. Dan'l L. Moore, farmer
of Loudon Ridge, and d. 3 May, 1880. Children: (1) Alfred
D. (Moore), b. 7 July, 1867; and six others d. young.

vii John,[6] b. 3 Feb., 1813; a millwright, d. unm., 20 Mar., 1842.

viii Filinda,[6] b. 5 Mar., 1815, a milliner, etc.; m. 18 Jan., 1844,

Josiah R. (son of Benj.) Morrill, b. in Gilmanton, 18 Jan.,
1820, farmer, and res. in Belmont; had three children:
1 *Mary Louisa* (Morrill), b. 15 Oct., 1844; grad. N. Hampton,
1868, a teacher; m. 16 June, 1878, Frederick E. Copp of
Loudon, b. 1 Sept., 1843; in 1888 was postmaster at Grafton Centre, N. H.
2 *Wm. Weeks*, b. 31 Aug., 1851; grad. at Dartmouth College,
1874, taught at Lancaster, at Norwich, Vt., and at
Cooperstown, N. Y.; m. in Windsor, Vt., 14 Sept., 1876,
Nina Marie Louise (dau. of Col. Wm. E.) Lewis, of Norwich, Vt. He is a lawyer in Troy, New York. In 1886
he published a work on "The Competency and the
Privileges of Witnesses," which has been highly com-
mended.
3 *Elizabeth Abigail*, b. 14 July, 1858; taught in Belmont,
Sandwich and Sanbornton; m. 10 Apr., 1879, Dr. Harry
G. Lincoln of Boston, b. 3 Oct., 1850, d. in Belmont, 11
May, 1885. Mrs. Lincoln now res. with her parents in
Belmont and has contributed to the Granite Monthly and
other publications, under the *nom de plume* of " Lizzie
Linwood." For the records of this family and several
others we are indebted to her faithful and persevering
researches.
ix Lovina,[6] b. 22 Oct., 1817; d. unm., æ. 20.

(Clarissa Colby, b. 7 Jan., 1791, came from Poplin with this
family and remained with them till her death at the home
of Mrs. J. R. Morrill, Belmont, 4 June, 1873.)

64

Stephen Weeks[5] (*Matt.*,[4] *Matt.*,[3] *Sam.*,[2] *Leon.*[1]) born
1785, died 1862, and his wife Betsey (Weed), had born
in Gilmanton

Children :

i David Weed,[6] b. 22 Feb., 1809; m. 1838 (Betsey) Elizabeth
W. (dau. of Josiah) Fifield, who d. in Oran, Iowa, 11
May, 1888. He was a farmer and rem., abt. 1857, to
Oran, Fayette Co., Iowa, where he d. 16 July, 1886. Children :
1 *Mary E.*,[7] b. 1 Oct., 1839; m. 15 Jan., 1861, Morrill Sanborn,
farmer in Fairbank, Fayette Co., Iowa, *s. p.*
2 *Frances J.*,[7] b. 20 Dec., 1840; m. 1865, Wm. Codling, farmer,
from England; res. in Fairbank, Iowa. Three daughters.
3 *Lyman G.*,[7] b. 5 June, 1842; d. 1862 in the army.
4 *Jesse S.*,[7] b. 10 June, 1851; not m.; res. in Oran, Iowa
(P. O. Olewein, Iowa).
5 *Ella M.*, b. 24 Apr., 1856; not m. in 1888.
ii Dea. Stephen, jr.,[7]* b. 15 Jan., 1811; d. 28 Jan., 1885; m., 1st,

---

* Dea. Stephen Weeks, of Loudon Ridge, a teacher in early life, was a prosper-
ous and useful citizen, a friend of education and of missions, a worthy member
of the church, always at his post, faithful in words and in deeds. His loss was
deeply felt. Many of the pupils who have been under his instruction remember
him with grateful affection.

24 May, 1844, Mary Adeline (dau. of Moses) Stevens of
Gilmanton. His P. O. address was Loudon Ridge, Merrimac Co., N. H. He m., 2nd, Elizabeth (dau. of Stephen)
Haines, of Canterbury, b. 27 Apr., 1817, who was sister of
Hon. Wm. P. Haines of Biddeford, Me. Children :
1 *Adaline E.*,[7] b. 27 Feb., 1845; d. in Loudon, 22 Apr., 1857.
2 *Wm. H.*,[7] b. 28 Aug., 1847; res. unm. on the homestead.
3 *Martha H.*,[7] b. 24 Feb., 1850; m. 1873, Oscar Hill of Loudon,
   and has child : (1) Archie, b. 1877.
4 *Mary J.*,[7] b. 24 Sept., 1852; d. in Loudon, 4 Nov., 1867.
5 *Sarah A.*,[7] b. 19 July, 1853; m. in Loudon 3 June, 1877,
   Lauren S. Clough, of Loudon and had : (1) Gracie.
6 *Dora V.*,[7] b. 10 May, 1858, a teacher at sixteen years of
   age, and by over-exertion became the victim of nervous
   prostration.
iii Jesse W.,[6] b. 6 Mar., 1813; d. young.
iv   Dr. Lorraine True,[6] b. 4 Nov., 1819; (M.D. Dart. Coll.,
     1843) m. Hannah Clifford of Gilmanton; d. in Laconia, 19
     July, 1876. He had :
     1 *A son*,[7] who d. æ. 18.
v   Matthias,[6] b. 15 Nov., 1824; farmer on the homestead in Gil-
     manton; m. in Canterbury 7 Jan., 1855, Laurinda (dau. of
     Barnes) Hilliard of Stewartstown, and had b. in Gilman-
     ton nine children :
     1 *Ermina*,[7] b. 8 July, 1856; d. 23 Aug., 1868.
     2 *Jesse Fremont*,[7] b. 1 Nov., 1857; is in Randolph, Mass.
     3 *Lorraine Edwin*,[7] b. 17 Sept., 1859, grad. Dart. Coll., 1885.
     4 *Albert Matthias*,[7] b. 9 June, 1861; grad. Dart. Coll., 1888.
     5 *James Henry*,[7] b. 9 Mar., 1865; in a lumber mill.
     6 *Annie Eliza*,[7] b. 27 Mar., 1867; a teacher.
     7 *Stephen Leavitt*,[7] b. 30 Oct., 1870.
     8 *John Moody*,[7] b. 13 Dec., 1871; d. 10 June, 1881.
     9 *Mary Ellen*,[7] b. 21 May, 1874.
vi   Mary Jane,[6] b. 26 July, 1827; m. 29 Mar., 1853, Timothy B.
     French, b. 1825; res. and d. in Sanbornton, where she had
     eight children :
     1 *Lorraine True* (French), b. Sept., 1854; d. æ. 2 mos.
     2 *Laura Abigail*, d. Aug., 1867, æ. 11 yrs. and 7 mos.
     3 *Benj. Herbert*, b. 22 Jan., 1858; res., 1879, on the ances-
        tral farm in Loudon.
     4 *Adaline Eliz.*, b. Feb., 1860; d. Sept., 1865.
     5 *Timothy S.*, b. Dec., 1861; d. Sept., 1867.
     6 *Isabella*, b. 6 Feb., 1864.
     7 *Joseph Dana*, b. 27 Apr., 1866.
     8 *Cyrus Edgerly*, b. 10 Aug., 1868.

65

Noah Weeks[5] (*Sam.*,[4] *Matt.*,[3] *Sam.*,[2] *Leon.*[1]) born
1767, died 1808, and his wife Anna (Pendexter), had born
in East Parsonsfield

Children :

i   Ichabod,[6] b. Dec., 1793; m. Anna Pendexter, and d. 4 Mar.,
    1859; had children :

1 *James M.*,[7] m. Mary F. Kenneson, and had: (1) Marshall,[8] m.; (2) Stephen m., Alice Howe and had one child.

2 *Austin*,[7] m. Sally Pendexter, and had: (1) Anna,[8] (2) Nathaniel.

3 *Nancy.*[7]

4 *Henry.*[7]

5 *Anna.*[7]

ii Henry,[6] b. 2 Feb., 1797; m. Anna Pendexter, and d. 3 July, 1825. His children were:

1 *Mercy*,[7] m. Moses Brackett, and had: (1) Eunice,[8] (2) Alice, (3) Sarah.

2 *Edmund*,[7] m. Harriet Pendexter, and had: (1) Henry,[8] (2) Lewis, m. with five children, (3) Sarah, m. Frank Day, (4) Mercy, (5) Harriet, (6) Charles.

iii Mercy R.,[6] b. 1 Mar., 1800; m. David Johnson, and d. 9 Feb., 1856. Children:

1 *Noah* (Johnson), m., and had one child.

2 *Lydia A.*, m., with one child.

3 *Nath'l J.*

4 *Henry.*

5 *David.*

iv James Wesley,[6] b. 2 Aug., 1802; m. Sarah Frye, and d. at Kalamazoo, Mich., 3 Mar., 1875. Their children b. in East Parsonsfield, Me., were:

1 *Almira W.*,[7] b. 5 May [1830?]; m. Isaac Brackett; d. Portland, 19 Sept., 1861; had two children: (1) Margaretta,[8] (2) Alice.

2 *Lucinda*,[7] b. 4 June, 1832; m. Mr. —— Humphrey of Columbus, O., and had one child.

3 *Sarah M.*,[7] b. 22 Feb., 1835; m. Isaac Brackett; res. Brunswick, Me; two children.

4 *James Edwin*,[7] b. 9 Apr., 1837; res. No. 59 Blackstone St., Jackson, Mich.

5 *Mercy Jane*,[7] b. 17 Jan., 1839; m. and res. in Jackson, Mich.

v Sarah,[6] m. Henry Pendexter, and had children:

1 *John M.* (Pendexter), who m. Sarah Berry, and had three children.

2 *Joseph*, m. Hannah Cole, and had three children.

3 *David.*

4 *Henry.*

vi Noah,[6] m. Polly Haley, and had children:

1 *Mary E.*,[7] m. Mr. Knight.

2 *Benjamin*,[7] m.

3 *Sarah.*[7]

4 *Henry.*[7]

5 *Noah.*[7]

6 *David.*[7]

7 *Eddie*,[7] m. Etta (Lang)? one child.

66

Eliphalet Weeks[5] (*Sam.*,[4] *Matt.*,[3] *Sam.*,[2] *Leon.*[1])

born 1770, died 1838, farmer, and his first wife Susan (Perry), had born in Parsonsfield

11

Children :

(98) i Joseph,[6] b. 17 Mar., 1796; m. in Cornish, Me., 1819. Sally
        (dau. of Nath'l) Barker, b. 1791, who d. 9 Dec., 1870. He
        d. there 31 July, 1832; had three children.
     ii Anna,[6] b. 15 Sept., 1798; d. about 1814.
(99) iii James H.,[6] b. 18 Feb., 1801; m. Lois Ballard of Fryeburg,
        Me.; had seven children; res. and d. in Chatham, Dec.,
        1880.
(100)iv Rev. Eliphalet,[6] b. 4 June, 1803; m. Lydia Ballard of Fryeburg,
        Me.; lived and d. in Chatham 24 July, 1881; had five chil-
        dren; a local Methodist preacher and farmer in Chatham.
(101) v Samuel,[6] b. 23 Sept., 1805; lived and d. in Parsonsfield,
        Me.; m. twice and had a large family.
     vi Eben E.,[6] b. 4 Jan., 1808; m. Serena Willey of Fryeburg;
        had five children; lived in Fryeburg, Me., 1885; retired
        merchant. Children :
        1 *Weston W.,*[7] b. 1848; d. 1864.
        2 *Marshall,*[7] b. 1850; d. 1851.
        3 *Seth,*[7] b. 1854; m.; farmer; and res. in Fryeburg, *s. p.*
        4 *Ella,*[7] b. 1856.
        5 *Anna J.*[7]
(102)vii John,[6] b. 26 Oct., 1810; farmer; d. in Chatham, 22 Apr.,
        1880. He m. Mehitable Holmes, b. in Cornish, Me., 27
        Mar., 1808.

Eliphalet Weeks[5] married, second, in 1814, Martha
Kenneson, and had

Child :

     viii Susanna,[6] b. 1 May, 1815; m. Nathaniel Barker; res. in
        Limerick, Me., *s. p.*

67

Matthias Weeks[5] (*Sam.,*[4] *Matt.,*[3] *Sam.,*[2]*Leon.*[1]) born
1785, died ——, and his first wife —— Day, had :
Children :

     i Catharine,[6] m. Timothy Guptail and had :
        1 *Harrison* (Guptail), m., 1st, Mrs. Paul ; 2nd, Lucania Pen-
        dexter, and had seven daughters.
        2 *Martha*, m. Enoch Abbey, and had five children.
        3 *Alna*, m. Mr. Abbey, and had two daughters.
     ii Noah.[6]
     iii Susan.[6]
     iv Olive,[6] m. Hiram Guptail, and had :
        1 *James* (Guptail).
        2 *Louisa.*
        3 *Mary.*
        4 *Susan.*
        5 *Hattie.*

Matthias Weeks[5] had by second wife, Mrs. Hammond:

v   Albion,[6] m. Martha Pray and had four children.
vi James,[6] m. ———— Guptail and had one child.
vii Alvira.[6]
viii Moses,[6] m. Mrs. Jane Morison and had four children.

68

Benjamin Weeks[5] (*Sam.,[4] Matt.,[3] Sam.,[2] Leon.[1]*)
born 1791, died 1836, farmer, and his wife Nancy (Barnes),
had born in E. Parsonsfield, Me.,
Children:

i   Warren W.,[6] b. 21 June, 1815; d. 19 Feb., 1844; m., 1840,
     Sally B. Benson, who d. 19 Feb., 1847, *s. p.*
ii Sally W.,[6] b. 27 Jan., d. 15 Aug., 1817.
iii Benjamin R.,[6] b. 9 Feb., 1818; m. Lydia Bodge, and had:
     1 *Edith,[7]* who d.
iv Nancy B.,[6] b. 9 May, 1820; m., 1840, Hiram Staples, who d.
     Their sons:
     1 *Albert S.* (Staples) } both d. in infancy.
     2 *Lewis H.,*   }
     We are under obligations to Mrs. N. B. Staples of E.
     Parsonsfield, Me., for valuable records of this family.
v   Abraham W.,[6] b. 9 Jan., 1822; d. 27 Feb., 1848.
vi Mary J.,[6] b. 22 Apr., 1824; m. Henry Merrill; d. 4 May,
     1848, in a few weeks from the day of marriage.
vii Moses S.,[6] b. 3 Mar., 1827; d. 5 Nov., 1846.
viii Albert S.,[6] b. 7 Jan., 1830, and d. 22 Sept., 1865. He m.
     Mary Fay, and had:
     1 *Lewis A.[7]*
     2 *M. Ella.[7]*
ix Harriet A.,[6] b. 2 Mar., 1832; m. David W. Severance; d. 11
     Aug., 1859, *s. p.*

68a

Capt. Benj. Weeks, jr.[5] (*Benj.,[4] Matt.,[3] Sam.,[2] Leon.[1]*) merchant, and his wife Betsey Hoyt, had
Children:

i   Hazen,[6] m. 1835, Prudence G. Sleeper and had:
     1 *Benj.,[7]* of Gilford.
     2 *John Murray,[7]* d., left a son Eddie with one child.
     3 *Betsey,[7]* d.
     4 *Harriet,[7]* m. Benj. Gale of Salisbury. Children: (1) Elmer,
     (2) Ernest, (3) Grace.
ii Sally,[6] m. 16 Jan., 1829, Jn. G. Weeks, both of Guilford. Nine
     children (see No. 29–i).

iii Benj. Frank,[6] m. in Gilford, 16 June, 1829, Julia M. (dau. of
      Daniel) Weeks. Children :
      1 *Charles H.,*[7] of Thornton ; m. ; one daughter.
      2 *Francis,*[7] m. Sarah Saltmarsh of Plymouth, *s. p.*
      3 *Geo F.,*[7] m. Abbie Shaw, res. in Northfield, *s. p.*
      4 *Henry,*[7] m. Jennie Holmes ; two children.
      5 *Parker,*[7] m. Martha, *s. p.*
iv   William,[6] b. 1812, farmer ; m. 18 Feb., 1835, Eliza Hutchinson ;
      d. 9 June, 1878, æ. 66. Children :
      1 *Eliz. A.,*[7] m. Jas. R. Morrill, and had : (1) Flora,[8] w. of
        Chas. Collins.
      2 *Harrison W.,*[7] m. Mary Potter. Children : (1) Julia,[8] (2)
        Nath'l, (3) Milly, (4) Stark.
      3 *Orrin,*[7] m ; four children.
      4 *Annette,*[7] b. 1844 ; m. 2 Sept., 1865, Edwin Munsey, b. 1844,
        s. p.
      5 *Fred,*[7] m. Laura (dau. of Daniel) Gilman of Gilford.
      6 *Rufus.*[7]
      7 *Arthur,*[7] m.
v   Mehitable,[6] m. 3 June, 1838, Geo. Wm. (son of Daniel) Weeks.
      Seven children, two living in 1888 (see No. 29-i).
vi   Thos. H.,[6] b. 1816 ; m. Nancy Hill, and d. in Gilford, 12 June,
      1884, æ. 67 yrs. and 10 mos. Children :
      1 *Frances,*[7] m. Geo. Wm. Morrill and had : (1) Leon.
      2 *S. Amanda,*[7] m. Thos. Haskins, *s. p.*
      3 *Austin B.,*[7] b. 1858 ; m. 24 Nov., 1880, Nellie W. (dau. of
        Theodore) Dodge ; two sons.
vii Harriet,[6] m. Daniel Gilman and had :
      1 *Laura,* m. Fred Weeks.
      2 *Georgiana,* m. Marston Sanborn and has : (1) Lizzie.
viii Nathan H.,[6] b. 9 Mar., 1826 ; m. 30 June, 1859, Martha G. Phil-
      brick. Children :
      1 *Annie May,*[7] b. 30 Nov., 1860.
      2 *Fred P.,*[7] b. 18 Nov., 1862.
      3 *Lela G.,*[7] b. 17 Mar., 1865.
      4 *Scott,*[7] b. 22 July, 1867.
      5 *Mary B.,*[7] d. Oct., 1872, æ. 3 mos.
      6 *Mattie J.,*[7] b. 12 Oct., 1873.

69

William Weeks[5](*Noah,*[4] *Matt.,*[3]*Sam.,*[2] *Leon.*[1]) born
1781, died 1839, printer, editor, etc., and his wife
Abigail (Hubbard), had born in Portsmouth
Children :

i   James Hubbard,[6] b. 5 May, 1810, of N. Y. and Boston, book-
      seller and merchant ; m. ; d. in Boston, 25 Jan., 1885.
ii   Wm. Augustus[6], b. 31 Jan., 1812 ; painter and bookseller in
      Boston ; d. 20 June, 1854. He m. E. Maria Gregg and had :
      1 *E. Maria.*[7]
iii Chas. Peirce,[6] b. 30 Jan., 1814 ; hatter in Rochester, then in
      Philadelphia, afterward gas manufacturer in Havana,

Cuba; d. 1884; m., 1st, Eliz. Cole of Rochester, N. H.;
m., 2nd, Helen Jacobus of N. Y., and had by first marriage:
1 *Isabel.*⁷
2 *Lizzie L.*⁷
3 *Chas. Peirce, jr.*⁷
iv Mary Abby,⁶ b. in Portsmouth, 3 May, 1817; m. Martin Parry
Brooks.
v Elizabeth Peirce,⁶ b. 4 Dec., 1820; m. Isaac Parsons Seavey of
Newburyport and then of Portsmouth.
vi Margaret Fisher,⁶ b. 11 Nov., 1823; m., 1st, Thos. Lane Pickering; m., 2nd, John Y. Thompson, res. in Portsmouth, afterward in Newtonville, Mass. Children:
1 *Grace* (Thompson).
2 *Lizzie Goodwin.*
vii Caroline Ellen,⁶ b. 13 Feb., 1827; m. Frank Miller, b.; res. in
Portsmouth, who d. 19 Nov., 1880. He was a printer, editor and leader in the Temperance Reform.

69a

Dea. Matthias Weeks⁵ (*Noah,*⁴ *Matt.,*³ *Sam.,*²
*Leon.*¹) born 1788, died 1847, farmer, and his wife Bet-
sey (Thing), had born in Gilford
Children:

i Dea. Jonathan T.,⁶ b. 26 Sept., 1813; farmer and merchant
in Gilford, who m., 1st, 26 Sept., 1838, Zoa M. (dau. of
Jona.) James, who d. 5 Apr., 1873. He m., 2nd, 20 Aug.,
1874, Nancy Jay (widow of Rev. Elbridge) Knowles of Dover. He has held the offices of captain, selectman, justice
of the peace, deacon of the church, etc.
ii Lavina Thing,⁶ b. 9 Apr., 1816; m. 7 Dec., 1856, David T.
Bartlett, farmer, of Northwood, who d. 1 Oct., 1869.
Their child was:
1 *Florence* (Bartlett), b. 8 Aug., 1859.
iii Betsey,⁶ b. 12 Oct., 1818; m. 15 Nov. [1843]?, Annis C.
James, farmer; d. 12 Feb., 1882; had eight children:
1 *Emma Orilla* (James), b. 14 Oct., 1844; m. 15 Nov.,
1866, A. H. Lamprey, farmer of Belmont, and had six
children: (1) Eva E., (2) Carleton A., (3) Bessie L.,
(4) Leonard, (5) Sadie.
2 *Lauren Weeks,* b. 19 Sept., 1847; m., 1st, Jennie Ray of
Concord, who d. 21 Mar., 1881; m., 2nd, Sarah Holt and
has four children: (1) Howard, (2) Edna, (3) Mattie,
(4) Nellie.
3 *Anna M.,* b. 10 June, 1849; m. 21 June, 1879, E. S.
George, farmer, in Gilford. Children: (1) Agnes B.,
(2) Florence B.
4 *Leland Morrill,* b. 4 May, 1852; farmer; m. 10 July, 1881,
Lizzie A. Britton; res. Gilford.
5 *Rufus Choate,* b. 5 Nov., 1854; mechanic; m. Nov., 1880,
Mary Ellsworth; res. Laconia.

6 *Ella Lavina*, b. 27 July, 1856; unm.
7 *Frank Annis*, b. 25 Mar., 1859; mechanic; m. 15 Nov., 1884, Adella Folsom of Belmont; res. Laconia; has: (1) Edith C.
8 *Zoah Josephine*, b. 23 Mar., 1860; m. 4 Dec., 1884, E. P. Hadley; res. Belmont.

iv   Mary Ann,[6] b. 21 Sept., 1821; d. 16 Nov., 1828.
v   Emeline Roxana,[6] b. 21 Mar., 1827; m. 13 June, 1849, Ezra Eastman, farmer, who d. 14 May, 1863; a soldier in the 12th N. H. Vols. She d. 22 Oct., 1872. Children:
1 *Sydney Matthias* (Eastman), b. 11 Oct., 1849.
2 *Dan'l Webster*, b. 21 Feb., 1851.
3 *Abbie Maria*, b. 16 Dec., 1852.
4 *Nellie J.*, b. 30 Sept., 1855.
5 *Jay Weeks*, b. 25 Aug., 1858.
6 *Nancy Frances*, b. 23 Jan., 1860.
7 *Emma Weeks*, b. 27 Aug., 1862.

69b

Dea. Asa Weeks[5] (*Noah*,[4] *Matt.*,[3] *Sam.*,[2] *Leon.*[1]) born 1790, died 1862, farmer, and his wife Jemima (Marston), had born in Gilford

Children :

1   Stephen Mead,[6] b. 13 July, 1816; m. 14 May, 1836, Jennie Augusta Clark, and had five children. He became a Free Baptist preacher and retired late in life; res. Milford, Mass. Children:
1 *Charles Stephen*,[7] b. in Pelham 26 June, 1860; pattern maker in Worcester, Mass. He m. in Woonsocket, R. I., 1 Jan., 1879, Lettie Cutler Walker, and had five children: (1) Chas. Eugene,[8] b. in Milford, Mass., 22 Apr., 1880. (2) Emeline Lettie, b. 2 Apr., 1881. (3) Arthur Earl, b. in Worcester, Mass., 3 Oct., 1882. (4) Jessie F., b. 26 July, 1884. (5) Lillie Isabella, b. 19 Aug., 1886.
2 *Henry Elmer*,[7] b. in Grafton, Mass., 20 Apr., 1862; m. in Milford, Mass., 18 Apr., 1885, Nellie Florence Partridge, and had: (1) Elmer Leslie,[8] b. in Milford, Mass., 2 Jan., 1886. (2) Percy Jackson, b. in Milford, 13 Aug., 1887.
3 *Mary Luella*,[7] b. in Milford, Mass., 1864.
4 *Edgar Willard*,[7] b. 4 Aug., 1873.
5 *Ernest Asa*,[7] b. 2 Sept., 1875.

ii   Wm. Burleigh,[6] b. 23 Nov., 1818; m. in Gilford, 21 Sept., 1842, Rhoda O. Davis; d. in Rosita, Col., 1 June, 1879. Children:
1 *Clara E.*,[7] b. 7 Sept., 1844; m. 3 Nov., 1867, Geo. F. Buss of Marlboro, N. H., and was divorced; res. 25 Maple street, Worcester, Mass., and has: (1) Gertrude Inez,[8] (2) Waldo Everett.

2 *Cassius Eugene,*[7] b. 10 Sept., 1845; was a soldier in Battery B, Me. Artillery; d. in Norfolk, Va., 19 Jan., 1873.
3 *Sarah D.,*[7] b. 17 Oct., 1851; res. Willimantic, Conn.; P. O. Box 248.
4 *Frederick Arthur,*[7] b. 9 Dec., 1858; unm.
5 *Bertha Agnes,*[7] b. 2 May, 1862; m. 19 Oct., 1881, Wm. J. Hull of Granby, P. Q.

69c
Dea. Noah Weeks[5] (*Noah,*[4] *Matt.,*[3] *Sam.,*[2] *Leon.*[1])
born 1797, died 1872, farmer, and his wife Mary (Dudley), had born in Gilford
Children :

i   Betsey Maria,[6] b. 11 May, 1821; m., 1st, 17 Aug., 1851, A. S. Ellis; m., 2d, Israel Thompson of Belmont. Child of first marriage:
    1 *F. D.* (Ellis).
ii Chas. Henry,[6] b. 14 Apr., 1823, blacksmith; m. 14 Feb., 1852, Polly Wadley; no children. Res. in Centre Harbor.
iii Alvah T.,[6] b. 18 Aug., 1825; m. 8 Aug., 1848, Celina Blaudin, and had:
    1 *Ellen.*[7]
    2 *Cora.*[7]
    3 *Albert.*[7]
iv Mary Jane,[6] b. 15 July, 1827; m. 28 Feb., 1853, B. F. Norton, and d. 4 Oct., 1854. She had one dau.
v   Lyman M.,[6] b. 27 Mar., 1829; m. 29 Feb., 1852, Mary Ann (dau. of Morrill) Thyng and d. 25 Feb., 1854. She d. 23 Jan., 1854. They had:
    1 *Curtis Thyng,*[7] b. 8 Aug., 1853, a moulder, who m. 9 May, 1878, Georgie A. Moulton, and had: (1) Clarence L.,[8] b. 13 Mar., 1880; (2) Arthur Horace, b. 7 Dec., 1882; (3) Harlan Curtis, b. 11 Apr., 1884; (4) infant, b. 20 Sept., 1887.
vi Eleanor P.,[6] b. 10 June, 1832; m. Albert Rogers.
vii Hannah Adeline,[6] b. 3 July, 1834; d. 28 Apr., 1851.
viii Noah D.,[6] b. 13 Oct., 1836, mechanic; m. 23 Apr., 1871, Emma E. Jewell, æ. 20, of Laconia. Children:
    1 *Frank E. Jewell,*[7] b. 21 July, 1873.
    2 *Charles E.,*[7] b. 9 Dec., 1875.
    3 *Lena M.,*[7] b. 17 Jan., 1878.
    4 *Eva L.,*[7] b. 17 May, 1885.
ix Anna F.,[6] b. 14 Oct., 1838; m. 30 Oct.. 1870, Wm. H. Lamprey, of Gilmanton; mechanic. No children.
x   Hazen Prescott,[6] b. 22 Oct., 1840, farmer; he has been selectman of Gilford, representative to the Legislature and held other offices of responsibility; m. 4 Jan., 1870, Mary S. Roberts, and had:
    1 *Walter S.,*[7] b. 20 July, 1874.
    2 *Bessy E.,*[7] b. 30 June. 1884.
xi Sarah S.,[6] b. 18 Nov., 1842; m. 5 Jan., 1867, Hiram Emerson, and had:
    1 *Oscar* (Emerson).

69d

Josiah Weeks[5] (*Josiah*,[4] *Jed.*,[3] *Jos.*,[2] *Leon.*[1]) born 1812, died ——, and his wife Mary K. (Eastman), had born in Bartlett

Children :

 i Helen Amanda,[6] b. 22 Dec., 1840; m. 5 Mar., 1863, Alfred E. Hamilton, a sea captain ; res. Chebeaque Island, Cumberland Co., Me., and has children :
  1 *Clara Mabel* (Hamilton), b. 9 Dec., 1864.
  2 *Walter Wyman*, b. 16 Sept., 1869.
  3 *Alice Maude*, b. 4 July, 1871.
  4 *Alfred Hale*, b. 8 Mar., 1885.
 ii George W.,[6] b. 29 Mar., 1844 ; m. 6 Oct., 1866, Martha Frye Eastman; is a blacksmith in Conway, and has one child :
  1 *Andrew J.*,[7] b. Conway, 19 Dec., 1868.
 iii Andrew J.,[6] b. 18 Sept., 1846; not m.; d. 20 Dec., 1868.
 iv Clara Susan,[6] b. 5 March, 1849; m. 14 Mar., 1869, David O. (son of David and Mary) Hamilton, a farmer, and had children :
  1 *Charles Andrew* (Hamilton), b. 10 Apr., 1870.
  2 *Addie Frances*, b. 4 Dec., 1872.
  3 *Effie May*, b. 13 May, 1874.
  4 *Geo. Wyman*, b. 25 Aug., 1880.
 v Reuben W.,[6] b. 8 June, 1852; m. 20 Dec., 1879, Lizzie A. (dau. of Wm. and Mehitable C.) Seavey, b. 2 March, 1861; he is a merchant and postmaster, at Intervale, Carroll Co., N. H. ; they had b. in Conway :
  1 *Merle D.*,[7] b. 2 Apr., 1881.
  2 *Blanche I.*,[7] b. 11 Dec., 1882.

69e

Levi Weeks[5] (*Jn.*,[4] *Leon.*,[3] *Jos.*,[2] *Leon.*[1]) born 1773, died 1811, and his first wife Betsey S. (Willey), had born in Brookfield

Children :

 i John,*[6] b. abt. 1806; m.; d. In Dover, N. H. Had a son:
  1 *Willey.*[7]
(103) ii Josiah,[6] b. 24 Aug., 1807; m. in Roxbury, Mass., 11 Apr., 1832, Fannie (dau. of Jacob) Glines of Moultonboro, N. H.; settled, 1833, in Wolfboro, a farmer and blacksmith, where he had four children and d. 19 March, 1888, æ. 72 yrs. and 8 mos.
 iii Amasa[6] (Amos in Probate Records), b. abt. 1810; m. Children :
  1 *Eliza*,[7] m., res. in Taunton, Mass.

---

 * John[6] and Amasa are said to have lived in Haverhill, Mass.

2 *Sarah Jane.*[7]
3 (*Willey?*)[7]

By second wife Dolly (Willey), had:

iv Levi,[6] b. 4 Apr., 1812; d. 14 July, 1883, a farmer at Water Village, Ossipee. He m. 4 July, 1841, Hephzibah Goodwin of Shapleigh, Me., and had six children:

1 *Sarah Jane*,[7] b. 17 Nov., 1842, unm., res. 74 Myrtle St., Boston.
2 *Geo. Marcellus*,[7] b. 26 Mar., 1844; a salesman for a tea house in Chicago; m. Agnes Burnfreid. Has no children.
3 *Jere. Burns*,[7] b. 22 Oct., 1845; m. Lizzie M. Randall of Vt., who was a teacher in N. J.; res. 863 Jackson St., Chicago, Ill., 1887. Children: (1) Laura Eloise,[8] b. 30 May, 1876; (2) Florence Bell, b. 23 Aug., 1880; and two sons d. in infancy.
4 *Mary Ellen*,[7] b. 26 June, 1847; m. Peter B. Hersey, farmer in Tuftonboro.
5 *Laura Etta*,[7] b. Feb. 22, 1850; m. John W. Farrar; res. in Boston.
6 *Levi Brown*,[7] b. abt. 1852; res., unm., on the homestead, Water Village, Ossipee.

70

John Weeks[5] (*Jn.*,[4] *Leon.*,[3] *Jos.*,[2] *Leon.*[1]) born 1778, died 1842, and his wife Abigail (Colomy), had born in Wakefield

Children:

i William,[6] b. 8 Sept., 1809; d. 23 June, 1874; m. Elizabeth —— of Effingham, and had:
1 *Mary E.*,[7] b. in Brookfield, 10 Apr., 1840; m. Nov., 1859, Joseph Smith Wentworth, b. 1831, and had b. in Brookfield: (1) Sherman, b. 2 July, 1860; (2) Lizzie May, b. 14 July, 1862; (3) Olive Emma, b. 8 Sept., 1872; (4) Willie R., b. 11 Aug., 1877.
ii Deborah,[6] b. 29 Aug., 1812; m. 29 Nov., 1831, Garland Allen of Wakefield. Children:
1 *Joseph* (Allen), b. 3 May, 1833; m. Sarah Hubbard and had four children. He was killed, 14 May, 1864, in a battle at Ball's Bluff, Va.
2 *Sarah F.*, b. 1 May, 1835; d. 8 Oct., 1862.
3 *Sam'l*, b. 13 Nov., 1842; m. 1 May, 1872, Emma Cummings of Brookfield and had six children. In Brookfield.
4 *John Wesley*, b. 3 Sept., 1849; d. in Feb., 1864
iii Nathan C.,[6] b. 23 Nov., 1818; m. 31 Jan., 1844, Ann Jane (dau. of Spencer) Wentworth, b. 27 Oct., 1819, res. in Brookfield. Eight children:
1 *Emily Ann*,[7] b. 1845; d. 1849.
2 *John Swett*,[7] b. 24 Oct., 1850; m. 24 Dec., 1885, Ruth Young of No. Wakefield.
3 *Geo. W.*,[7] b. 1852; d. Apr., 1856.
4 *Emily A.*,[7] (2nd), b. 6 Oct., 1854; d. 20 Mar., 1885.

12

5 *Horace,*[7] b. 1856; d. 1866.
6 *Jas. M.,* b. Aug., 1858; d. Apr., 1866.
7 *Asa Taylor,*[7] b. 13 May, 1863.
8 *Lucretia,*[7] b. 13 Mar., 1865.

iv   Louisa,[6] b. 4 Oct., 1821; m. 1842, Edmund B. Tibbets, and had:
1 *Susan A.* (Tibbets), b. 17 June, 1847; d. 16 Dec., 1864.
2 *Isaac,* b. 9 July, 1859; d. 9 Oct., 1869.

v   John Wesley,[6] b. 29 Mar., 1827; m., 1st, 10 Nov., 1850, Nancy E. Quimby of Great Falls; she d. 20 Feb., 1881; he m., 2nd, 9 Dec., 1886, Mrs. Mary E. (wid. of Jn. A.) Merrill of Hampton Falls; res. in Brookfield (P. O. Wakefield). Children by first marriage:
1 *Matthias,*[7] b. 5 May, 1852; d. 4 Jan., 1881.
2 *Ardell,*[7] b. 29 June, 1857; d. 21 Jan., 1864.
3 *Lizzie G.,*[7] b. 22 July, 1859; d. 23 Jan., 1864.
4 *Lyman,*[7] b. 6 Dec., 1864.
5 *Dora,*[7] b. 3 Oct., 1868.

71

Phineas Weeks[5] (*Jn.,*[4] *Leon.,*[3] *Jos.,*[2] *Leon.*[1]) born 1786, died 1859, and his wife Martha (Cotton), had born Children :

i   Martha,[6] b. 20 Jan., 1817; m. 10 Mar., 1846, Joshua Cottle, who had five children and died. The mother and three children live at Wolfboro Junction, West Wakefield. Children:
1 *Martha M.* (Cottle), b. 12 Oct., 1846.
2 *Phineas O.,* b. 11 Sept., 1848.
3 *Joshua O.,* b. 27 Feb., 1851; d. 4 Dec., 1864.
4 *Nancy M.,* b. 8 Jan., 1853; d. 14 Dec., 1864.
5 *Mary L.,* b. 3 Oct., 1857.

ii   Phineas J.,[6] b. 9 June, 1819; m. 25 Apr., 1849, Mercie Dennet Hayes of Tuftonboro; res. in Wakefield, a farmer, and had b. in Wakefield:
1 *Charles Albert,*[7] b. 2 Feb., 1850; farmer in Wakefield.
2 *Lizzie Maria,*[7] b. 5 Mar., 1851; m. 11 June, 1871, Chas. H. Jenness; res. Wakefield; had: (1) Perley Albert[8] (Jenness), b. 26 Feb., 1876.
3 *John Henry,*[7] b. 28 Oct., 1854; m. 25 Dec., 1878, Orra Ella Fernald of Ossipee. He is a farmer in Wakefield, and has: (1) Almon Fernald,[8] b. 16 Aug., 1881.

iii   Salome C.,[6] b. 21 Aug., 1821; m. 30 May, 1849, Nathan J. (son of Nathan) Weeks, who d. 4 June, 1861; she d. 2 July, 1884 (see 72-ii). They had b. in Wakefield:
1 *Catharine Voorhees,*[7] b. 26 Oct., 1851; res., 1886, in Wakefield.
2 *Arethusa Ellen,*[7] 14 June, 1854.

iv   Brackett Marshall,[6] b. 11 Mar., 1824; farmer in Wakefield; m., 1st, 26 Nov., 1862, Elizabeth Almena Cottle of Wakefield, who d. 6 Jan., 1869. He m., 2nd, 14 July, 1872, Matilda Allen.

Child by first wife:
1 *Ella*,[7] b. 23 Feb., 1864; d. 26 Mar., 1880.
Children by second wife:
2 *Susie L.*,[7] b. 27 Sept., 1875.
3 *Wm. G.*[7] b. Sept., 1877.
4 *Lizzie A.*,[7] b. 24 Apr., 1879.
5 *Albert*,[7] b. 7 July, 1880.
6 *Matilda A.*,[7] b. 30 July, 1884.
7 *An infant*,[7] b. 20 Feb., 1887.
v Adeline Eliz.,[6] b. 16 June, 1826; m. Miles Randall; d. 26 Nov., 1864. She had six children and all died.
vi Nancy F.,[6] b. 14 Oct., 1828; d. 30 May, 1864.
vii John Furber,[6] b. 7 Mar., 1835; a farmer in Wakefield; m., 1st, 24 June, 1861, Mary Lang, who d. 4 Dec., 1864; m., 2nd, 29 Nov., 1865, Mrs. Lavinia Fogg (*née* Seward).

72

Nathan Weeks[5] (*Jn.*,[4] *Leon.*,[3] *Jos.*,[2] *Leon.*[1]) born 1788, died 1872, and his wife Sally (Clark), had born in Wolfboro

Children :

i Jacob C.,[6] b. 1820, was dealer in paints, oils, etc., in Brooklyn, N. Y.; m. there 16 Feb., 1847, Mrs. Catharine Bedell, (*née* Voorhees) of Brooklyn, and died 7 Aug., 1856. They had :
1 *Sarah C.*,[7] b. 17 Dec., 1847; m. 12 Sept., 1872, Chas. E. Sanderson, and d. 6 May, 1874, *s. p.*
2 *Albert V.*,[7] b. 8 Feb., 1850; d. 2 June, 1879, unm. He was a prominent member of the Crystal Fount Lodge, I. O. O. F. of Woburn, and died of injuries received at the burning of the Chemical Works near that place. He was bookkeeper for the company.
ii Nathan J.,[6] b. 1822; m. 30 May, 1849, Salome C. (dau. of Phineas) Weeks and d. June, 1861 (see No. 71-iii). She d. 2 July, 1884. Children :
1 *Catharine Voorhees.*[7]
2 *Arethusa Ellen.*[7]
iii Algernon S.,[6] b. 29 Aug., 1824; m., 1st, 30 Oct., 1850, Sarah J. Rogers, b. May, 1828, of Jackson, N. H., who d. 27 July, 1874. He m., 2nd, 30 June, 1878, Mrs. Eliz. Moulton; is a farmer in Wakefield. Children :
1 *Frank S.*[7] b. 31 Aug., 1851; m. 1 Aug., 1883, Isabella M. Roles of Ossipee, where, in 1875, he settled as lawyer.
2 *Nathan Otis*,[7] b. 27 June, 1855, a farmer and lumberman in Wakefield. He m., 1st, 20 Nov., 1875, Abbie M. Lary, who d. 10 Aug., 1882; m., 2nd, 25 Sept., 1883, Florence E. Shorey. Children by first marriage : (1) Ethel M.,[8] b. 4 Sept., 1876; d. 1 Aug., 1882. (2) Eva G., b. 29 Jan., 1878.
3 *Edgar*,[7] b. 3 May, 1859, taught school at sixteen years of age; in 1878 entered Colby University, Waterville, Me.,

remained two years; studied law with his brother, Frank
S. Weeks; in 1884, was Register of Probate for Carroll
Co., N. H.
4 *Walter Irving*,⁷ b. 14 Sept., 1867, entered Wakefield Academy; then at Westbrook Seminary, Deering, Me. In
1886, entered Bowdoin College.
iv Sarah C.,⁶ b. 1826; d. 3 June, 1882, unm.
v Dea. Satchell,⁶ b. 1 Dec., 1828; m. 28 Nov., 1856, Sarah (dau.
of Asa) Dow, b. 1839. He is a farmer and a respected
citizen of Wakefield. Children:
1 *Asa H.*,⁷ b. 28 Apr., 1858.
2 *Sarah D.*,⁷ b. 8 May, 1863.

73

Caleb Weeks⁵ (*Jn.*,⁴ *Leon.*,³ *Jos.*,² *Leon.*¹) born
1793, died 1844, and his wife, Patience (Dudley), had
born in Wakefield

Children:

i   Lucinda,⁶ b. Aug., 1818; d. June, 1842.
ii Alpheus,⁶ b. 4 Nov., 1820; m. 6 May, 1848. Laura A. Page,
of Salem, Mass.; res. in Salem, and at Wolfboro, N. H.
Children:
1 *Alonzo P.*,⁷ b. in Lawrence, Mass., 25 Feb., 1849, educated
at Salem; Cashier of Merchants Bank, Boston. He
m. in Boston, Apr., 1871, Mary Emma Chipman of Salem, and had born in Salem, No. 6 Monroe St.: (1)
Laura Edith,⁸ b. 18 Aug., 1872; (2) Annie Ethel, b. 6
Apr., 1876. (3) Henry A., b. 29 June, 1879.
2 *Rev. Alphonso M.*,⁷ in Salem, Mass., 28 Oct., 1850;
studied at Salem, and at Tilton, N. H., grad. from Coll.
Liberal Arts, Boston Univ., 1877, and at Harvard Divinity School, 1880; ordained, 1881, over the First Unita-
rian church, Chelsea, Mass. In 1882, he took charge of
Unity church, Denver, Colorado, where he died of spinal
meningitis, after thirty hours of illness.
3 *Fred L.*,⁷ b. in Salem, 8 Oct., 1856; res. in Boston, Mass.
iii Clarissa,⁶ b. Aug., 1822; d. March, 1846.
iv Sarah,⁶ b. 6 Jan., 1824; d. Aug., 1847.
v   Dudley,⁶ b. 24 Apr., 1828; d. 17 Sept., 1862.
vi Frances,⁶ b. 12 May, 1832.
vii Gilbert M.,⁶ b. Sept., 1840; m.; d. 16 Dec., 1883.

74

James B. Weeks⁵ (*Jn.*,⁴ *Jn.*,³ *Joshua*,² *Leon.*¹)
born 1784, died 1858, and his wife Betsey (Stanley), had
born in Lancaster

---

* All interested in the history of the Weeks Family are indebted to Frank S.
and his brother Edgar Weeks for valuable records of their branch of the family.

Children :

i   Hon. James Wingate,[6] b. 15 July, 1811; farmer, land surveyor, etc., m., 1st, 30 May, 1842, Martha Willard (dau. of Solomon) Hemenway of Lancaster, who d. 5 Sept., 1853, æ. 35 years. He m., 2nd, Mar., 1859, Mary Eliz. (dau. of Dr. Robert) Burns of Plymouth, who d. 2 Feb., 1878, æ. 52. He has been a man of influence and often in office in Lancaster. Children:

1 *Geo. Hemenway*,[7] b. 18 Mar., 1843.
2 *Sarah Wilder*,[7] b. 16 Aug., 1845; m. Frank Oxnard of Me.; d. 16 Oct., 1870. He d. Apr., 1881.
3 *Jas. Wingate*,[7] b. 27 Apr., 1849.
4 *Clara H.*,[7] b. 13 Oct., 1851; d. May, 1881.

ii   Mary Nye,[6] b. 24 Aug., 1813; m. 1 May, 1851, Richard H. Eastman; d. in Lancaster 5 Nov., 1856; had:
1 *Mary W.* (Eastman).

iii Sarah Stanley,[6] b. 15 Nov., 1815; m. 15 Mar., 1839, Edmund C. Wilder; d. in Colebrook 22 Mar., 1842; had one child that died.

iv Hon. Wm. Dennis,[6] b. 28 Feb., 1818; m. 4 July, 1843, Mary Helen Fowler of Woodstock, Conn., b. 1820; d., after a short illness, from a wound in his hand, in Lancaster, 27 Feb., 1885, æ. 67. He was a farmer, a republican, and for years a faithful and popular officer, deputy collector of Internal Revenue, a judge of probate, etc. He had three children:
1 *Emma F.*,[7] b 1853; m. 1877, Burley Roberts, and had b. in Lancaster: (1) Harry W. (Roberts), b. 1880.
2 *Jn. Wingate*,[7] b. 1860; res. in Jacksonville. Fla.; m., 1885, Martha A. (dau. of Jn. G.) Sinclair. No children.
3 *Wm. Chaney*,[7] b. 1863; res., unm., on the homestead in Lancaster.

v   John,[6] b. 30 June, 1822; m. June, 185–, Ellen Merrill of Buffalo, N. Y., where they live with
1 *James B.*[7]
2 *Anna.*[7]

vi Martha Eliza,[6] b. 10 Dec., 1824; d. in Boston, June, 1872.
vii Persis Fayette,[6] b. 3 Feb., 1831; m. 2 Jan., 1854, Rev. Geo. M. Rice, who d. 20 Sept., 1882. Children:
1 *Laura* (Rice), m. Henry Piper of Dublin and has one child.
2 *Geo. M.*, med. student; res. with his mother in Dublin.
3 *William*, a dentist in Boston.
4 *Mary Weeks*, a teacher in Boston.

75

Noah Weeks[5] (*Wm.*,[4] *Jn.*,[3] *Joshua*,[2] *Leon.*[1]) born 1790, died 1875, farmer, and his wife Charlotte (Quimby), had born in Chester

Children :

   i   Sarah,[6] b. 1818; d. unm., 18 June, 1869.
   ii Noah Haines,[6] b. 1819; res. unm. on the homestead, in
          Chester.
  iii Charlotte,[6] b. 1821; d. unm., 17 June, 1862.
  iv William,[6] b. 1823; m. M. J. Moore of Candia, who d. *s. p.*
         He res. in Chester.
   v George Washington,[6] b. 1826; m. Miss Currier, *s. p.*
  vi Asahel,[6] b. 1829; m. Mary K. Dustin, had four children b.
         in Chester:
        1 *George Frank*,[7] b. 13 Feb., 1863; m. 20 July, 1887, Luna
           L. Holman of Chester.
        2 *Asahel Dana*,[7] b. 8 Sept., 1866.
        3 *Chas. C.*,[7] b. 24 June, 1869; d. 10 Feb., 1887; æ. 18.
        4 *John Alphonso*,[7] b. 24 July, 1872.
 vii Angeline,[6] b. 17 Sept., 1832; res. with Noah H. in Chester, unm.
viii Franklin C.,[6] b. 1835; d. unm., in New York, 28 March,
         1864. He was M.D. (Dart. Coll. 1858), Assistant Supt.
         at the Asylum for Insane, Brattleboro, Vt., four years,
         then at the Manhattan Asylum for the Insane, in N. Y.
         City.

76

Charles Weeks[5] (*Wm.*,[4] *Wm.*,[3] *Joshua*[2], *Leon.*[1]) born 1790, died 1863, of Hopkinton, and his wife Phebe (Henry), had born in Hopkinton

Children :

   i   Sarah A., m. Wm. Howe; d. in Goshen in 1886; and had:
        1 *Ada*, w. of Frank Rowe of Waltham, Mass.
        2 *Frank.*
        3 *Minnie.*[7]
   ii Carleton,[6] m. [1825]? Mary —— and had:
        1 *Anna*,[7] w. of Ai Richards of Boston; had one dau.
        2 *Frank*,[7] unm.
  iii Amanda,[6] w. of Horace Straw of Hopkinton, and had:
        1 *Andrew* (Straw), m. and had one son.
  iv Geo. K.,[6] m., 1st, Melinda Green, who d. *s. p.* He m., 2nd,
        Anna ——.
   v Brackett,[6] d. in the army, unm.
  vi Abbie A.,[6] m. Moses E. Dodge, and had:
        1 *Dr. Henry* (Dodge), of Goffstown, who m. Josephine Holt,
         and has one son.
 vii William,[6] m. Martha Warren of Goffstown, and has :
        1 *Geo W.*[7]
viii Josephine,[6] unm.

77

Jonathan Weeks[6] (*Jona.*,[5] *Jona.*,[4] *Jona.*[3] [*Jn.*,[2] *Leon.*[1]] ?) born 1804, died 1865, and his wife Mary (Dame), had born in Rochester, N. H.,

Children :

i　Not named.
ii　George Locke,[7] b. 19 June, 1825; m. in Lowell, Mass., Re-
　　becca Page, and d. there 23 June, 1855.
iii　Rufus Spalding,[7] b. 14 Sept., 1829; m.; d. in Lowell, Mass.,
　　9 Nov., 1858. He left children.
・iv　Jn. Wesley,[7] b. 24 July, 1832; m.; d. in Lowell, 6 Apr., 1856,
　　s. p.
v　Jonathan,[7] b. in Lowell, Mass., 7 Aug., 1835; d. 23 Aug., 1835.
vi　Ovan Francis,[7] b. in Lowell, 30 Sept., 1837; d. there, 5 May,
　　1843.
vii　Joseph Dame,[7] b. in Lowell, Mass., 3 Dec., 1840; m. in
　　Pittsburg, Pa., 28 Feb., 1871, Martha J. (dau. of S. S.
　　and Sarah M.) Fowler of Pittsburg, Pa., b. there. He is
　　editor of American Manufacturer, a weekly paper, in
　　Pittsburg, Pa. They had :
　　1 *Emma A.*,[8] b. in Pittsburg, 18 Nov., 1875.
viii　Edward Francis Locke,[7] b. 4 Nov., 1842; d. in Lowell, 1
　　Apr., 1860.
ix　Mary Ella,[7] b. 14 Apr., 1849.

78

Joseph H. Weeks[6] (*Jos.*,[5] *Jn.*,[4] *Jn.*,[3] *Sam.*,[2] *Leon.*[1])

and his wife Asenath (Barstow), had
Children :

i　Edwin,[7] b. in Newcastle, Me., 11 Sept., 1820; a mason in
　　Thomaston; m. Sept., 1847, Mary A. Overlook of Waldo-
　　boro, Me.; rem. late to Charlestown, Mass. Children :
　　1 *Alfred D.*,[8] b. 1851; foreman, Farmer office, Augusta,
　　Me.; m. 1873, Jennie Stanley of Augusta, Me., and had :
　　(1) Addie,[9] b. June, 1876.
　　2 *James E.*,[8] b. 1854; m. Sept., 1882, Fannie Wetherbee of
　　Charlestown, Mass., where he is a letter-carrier; has
　　(1) Ralph C.,[9] b. Aug., 1884.
　　3 *Emma F.*,[8] b. [1858]?
ii　Elizabeth,[7] b. 14 Nov., 1826; m. Jan., 1848, Abram Par-
　　tridge; d. in Jefferson, Me., 7 Oct., 1852, æ. 26. She had
　　1 Charley,[8] d. æ. 19.
iii　Emily[7] (twin sister of Elizabeth), b. 14 Nov., 1826; d. æ.
　　12.
iv　Elijah B.,[7] b. 1 July, 1828; of Newcastle, Me.; m. Caroline
　　Hodgkins of Jefferson; and had :
　　1 *Melrose*,[8] a carpenter in Charlestown, Mass.
　　2 *Ida C.*,[8] living, unm., with her parents in Newcastle, Me.
　　3 *A dau.*[8]
v　Martha A.,[7] b. 10 June, 1840; m. abt. 1871, Gardner Cram of
　　Brunswick, Me.; d. 1873, leaving an infant that soon died.

79

Ephraim Weeks[6] (*Thos.*,[5] *Jn.*,[4] *Jn.*,[3] *Sam.*,[2] *Leon.*[1])

born 1786, died 1867, and his wife Abigail (Peaslee), had :

Children :

   i   Sewall,⁷ d. an infant.
   ii   Edward,⁷ m. Ruth Chisam of Alna, Me.
   iii   Susan T.,⁷ m. Stinson (son of Winthrop) Weeks, b. 1813;
       had five children (see No. 47–ix).
   iv   Jerusha.⁷
   v   Sewall,⁷ m. Arletta B. Hall; d. 14 May, 1867.
   vi   Rebecca,⁷ m. Joseph Perkins of Newcastle, Me.
   vii   Abigail,⁷ m. Carleton Hoyt of Augusta, Me.
   viii   Ephraim,⁷ m. Clara A. Smith of Boston.
   ix   Thomas,⁷ m. Ellen Clary of Jefferson, Me.

80

Thomas Weeks⁶ (*Thos.*,⁵ *Jn.*,⁴ *Jn.*,³ *Sam.*,² *Leon.*¹) born 1791, died 1881, and his wife Mary (Otis), had born in Jefferson, Me.,

Children :

   i   Samuel Piper.⁷
   ii   Mary O.⁷
   iii   Ruth T.,⁷ m. Mr. —— Shurtleff.
   iv   Thomas W.⁷
   v   Otis T.,⁷ m. Ellen Weeks of Jefferson.

81

Hon. Joseph Weeks, jr.⁶ (*Thos.*,⁵ *Jn.*,⁴ *Jn.*,³ *Sam.*,² *Leon.*¹) born 1793, died 1870, and his wife Jane (Jackson), had born in Jefferson, Me.,

Children :

   i   Margaret J.,⁷ b. 20 Oct., 1820; m. Dr. Briggs T. Carter of
       Jefferson and had no children.
   ii   Leander,⁷ b. 22 Nov., 1823; m. 17 Jan., 1847, Mary Jane Ross
       of Jefferson; rem. Sept., 1852, to Rockland, Me.; was a
       merchant till 1870. From 1858, he was city treasurer
       twenty-seven years. His children b. in Jefferson were:
       1 *Georgia*,⁸ b. 4 Nov., 1847.
       2 *Alphonso R.*,⁸ b. 26 Sept., 1849; is a dealer in crockery in
       Rockland, Me.
       3 *Jennie M.*,⁸ b. in Rockland, 24 July, 1858.
       4 *Frank L.*,⁸ b. 25 June, 1862, is a clerk with his brother, A.
       R. Weeks.
   iii   Rachel M.,⁷ b. 1 Apr., 1826; m. Wm. J. Bond of Jefferson
       and has no children.
   iv   Angella G.,⁷ b. 14 Apr., 1828; m. Edward G. Meserve, and
       d. *s. p.*
   v   Ruth A.,⁷ m. (as 2nd wife), Edward G. Meserve and had
       three children.

82

Benjamin Weeks[6] (*Thos.,*[5] *Jn.,*[4] *Jn.,*[3] *Sam.,*[2] *Leon.*[1])
born 1795, and his wife Jane (Weeks), had
Children :

  i   Abiel,[7] d. young.
  ii William,[7] m. Lucy Shepard of Jefferson, and had :
     1 *Allen,*[8] d. young.
     2 *Florence,*[8] m. William Carpenter of Pittston, Me., and
       had : (1) Harold W.,[9] b. 1882.
  iii Elbridge S.,[7] m. Mary J. Pillsbury of Jefferson, and had :
     1 *Winnie,*[8] m. and had one child.
     2 *Frank,*[8] m. Ellen ———, had one son, and both died.
     3 *Fannie,*[8] a teacher.
     4 *Nellie*[8].
  iv Hannah J.,[7] m. Joseph Chaney of Whitefield. Had two sons.
  v Winthrop,[7] m. Abby Sproul of Jefferson.
  vi Ruth A.,[7] m. Jn. Dunton of Jefferson and had :
     1 *Ellen* (Dunton), wife of Abiel Avery of Jefferson; with
       one son.
  vii Thomas T.,[7] m. Emeline Wallace of Montville, Me., and had :
     1 *Edith,*[8] w. of Capt. Delano of ship Austria.
     2 *Mabel,*[8] a teacher.
  viii Benj. C.[7]
  ix Abiel N.,[7] m. Carrie Meserve and had twins :
     1 *Benjamin.*[8]
     2 *Abiel.*[8]

83

Hon. George Weeks[6] (*Thos.,*[5] *Jn.,*[4] *Jn.,*[3] *Sam.,*[2]
Leon.[1]) born 1803, died 1879, trader, etc., and his wife
Caroline (Haskell), had born in Jefferson, Me.,
Children :

  i   Roswell.[7]
  ii Hon. George E.,[7] b. 16 Dec., 1837, a lawyer, unm. Edu-
     cated at the Maine State Seminary, etc. ; res. in Augusta,
     Me. ; has represented the city in the Legislature ; in 1880
     was Speaker in the House, in 1884 State Senator.
  iii Susan Frances,[7] b. 9 Sept., 1841 ; m. Capt. R. E. Jones of
     Randolph, Me., and has :
     1 *Carrie P.* (Jones), b. 27 Aug., 1870.
  iv Leslie,[7] b. 16 Oct., 1845 ; dealer in stoves, tin, etc., E.
     Jefferson ; m. Jennie Young.
  v Theodore,[7] b. 14 Sept., 1847 ; farmer in E. Jefferson.
  vi Minerva,[7] m. Briggs C. Farnham, trader, and P. M. in E.
     Jefferson, and has :
     1 *Flora B.* (Farnham), b. 5 Feb., 1876.
  vii Lida R.,[7] b. 5 June, 1856 ; res. in E. Jefferson, Me.

13

84

John Weeks[6] (*Mark*,[5] *Jn.*,[4] *Jn.*,[3] *Sam.*,[2] *Leon.*[1]) born
1789, died 1844, called "John Weeks 3ᵈ of Jefferson,
Me.," and his wife Nancy (Jackson), had born in Jefferson

Children :

  i   Rachel,[7] b. 12 Sept., 1815; m. 2 Feb., 1841, Mellen Linscott;
   res. in Jefferson; had b. there :
   1 *Geo. E.* (Linscott), b. 3 Mar., 1842; m. Sept., 1868, Ellen
    Linscott; is a farmer and teacher in Jefferson.
   2 *Matilda A.*, b. 1 May, 1843; d. 26 Sept., 1857.
   3 *John W.*, b. 7 May, 1848; m. 4 Dec., 1870, Emma Scott; is
    a teacher in Watsonville, Cal.
   4 *Clara B.*, b. 29 Oct., 1854; m. 29 Dec., 1880, Sam'l S.
    Jackson; res. in Jefferson.
  ii   Ambrose C.,[7] b. 30 Nov., 1818; d. æ. 7 yrs.
  iii   Jackson,[7] b. 17 Feb., 1822; m. 27 Aug., 1854, Clara (dau. of
   Jn.) Bird of Rockland, Me., where he is a merchant of
   the firm A. J. Bird & Co; has no children; has aided in
   compiling this work.
  iv   John A.,[7] b. 1 July, 1826; m. Harriet N. (dau. of Joseph G.)
   Weeks (see No. 45-v); is a farmer on the homestead in
   Jefferson; had b. there :
   1 *Alice E.*,[8] b. 14 Apr., 1858; m. L. E. Cudworth; res. in
    Bremen, Me.
   2 *Laura E.*,[8] b. 23 Sept., 1861; unm.
   3 *A. Herbert*,[8] b. 2 Apr., 1868.
   4 *Katie C.*,[8] b. Oct. 7, 1875.
  v   Lysander M.,[7] b. 4 Nov., 1829; m. Oct., 1863, Fannie J. Gordon of Brunswick, Me.; is an architect and builder in
   Brooklyn, N. Y., *s. p.*
  vi   Emily N.,[7] b. 18 Aug., 1833; m. 1867, Henry S. Foster of
   Hallowell, Me.; res. in Lowell, Mass. Child :
   1 *Elmer E.* (Foster), b. 3 Oct., 1868; d. 17 Oct., 1879.

85

Daniel H. Weeks[6] (*Winthrop*,[5] *Jn.*,[4] *Jn.*,[3] *Sam.*,[2]
Leon.[1]) born 1796, died 1882, farmer and mason, and his
wife Margaret S. (Simpson), had born in Jefferson, Me.,
Children :

  i   James Potter,[7] b. 24 Nov., 1819; m. Serena Y. Weeks (dau.
   of Thos.[6] and Hannah) of Jefferson (see No. 46-vi); had :
   1 *Wallace*,[8] m. Edith Church of Augusta.

2 *Maria*,[8] m. Chas. Appleton of Vassalboro; had three children.

ii Martha Jane,[7] b. 3 June, 1821; m. Jn. Nowell of Fairfield, Me., who d. 1862, leaving twin daughters; teacher.
  1 *Bertha* (Nowell).
  2 *Barzie*.

iii Hannah,[7] b. 26 Oct., 1822; d. 15 Dec., 1827.

iv Israel Simpson,[7] b. 3 Sept., 1824; unm.

v Margaret E.,[7] b. 28 May, 1826; m. Dan'l Ramsell who, abt. 1858, was instantly killed in a reservoir, at Waterville, Me. She has since been matron of an asylum in Stockton, Cal. Her children:
  1 *Harriet* (Ramsell), m. A. Philip Blake, real estate broker in San Francisco, Cal.
  2 *Emma*, m., 1st, Jn. King and had: (1) Willie, (2) Eva; m.. 2nd, E. Carpenter of Sharon, Mass.
  3 *Lewellyn*, m. Lizzie Baker of Rockland, Me.; res. in Boston.
  4 *Clara*, m. Jack Crawford, and res. in Santa Rosa, Cal.
  5 *Ida May*, m. Lewis (son of Wm.) Weeks of Jefferson, Me., and went to Santa Rosa, Cal.
  6 *Mary O.*, m. Sabine Thrift of Oakland, now of Petaluma, Cal.

vi Hannah,[7] 2nd, b. 1 Jan., 1828; m. Simon Nowell of Fairfield, Me.; d. 1860. Children:
  1 *Frank* (Nowell),
  2 *Ella*.
  3 *Etta*, m. Chas. Pease of Avon, Me.
  4 *Georgiana*, m. Farley Boynton, merchant, whose mother was Ruth Weeks; res. in Brookline, Mass. (see No. 46-iv).
  5 *William*, a clerk in Boston.

vii Daniel B.,[7] b. 28 Aug., 1829; d. 14 Dec., 1840.

viii Bethania B.,[7] b. 7 Jan., 1831; m. O. P. Howe, who res. in Augusta, Me., and is a photographer and patentee of " Howe's window screws." Children:
  1 *Lizzie* (Howe).
  2 *Emma*.
  3 *An infant son*.

ix Sarah Ann,[7] b. 4 Apr., 1833; res. in Stockton, Cal.

x Mary Octavia,[7] b. in Hallowell, Me., 6 Oct., 1835; d. in Vassalboro, 13 Aug., 1856.

xi Asenath,[7] b. in Hallowell, 1 July, 1836; m. Hiram Potter of Fairfield, Me., and res. there.

xii Barzania B.,[7] b. 5 Feb.. 1838; m., 1st, Chas. Davenport, farmer of Chelsea, Me., who rem. to Kansas and was murdered there. She m., 2nd, Chas. Kenber of Quincy, Ill., and res. there.

xiii David Harlow,[7] b. 21 Jan., 1841; m. Mary McDonald of Boston. Children:
  1 *Wm. H.*[8]
  2 *Sadie.*[8]
  3 *Etta.*[8]
  4 *Dan'l B.*[8]
  5 *James Melville*,[8] b. in Hingham, Mass., 4 Mar., 1885.

86

Myrick L. Weeks[6] (*Daniel,*[5] *Jn.,*[4] *Jn.,*[3] *Sam.,*[2] *Leon.*[1]) born 1813, died ——, farmer, and his wife Harriet (Wallace), had born in Jefferson, Me.,

Children :

i   Luanna,[7] b. 1848; d. 1849.
ii   Geo. F.,[7] b. 1849; unm.; farmer and stock dealer in Jefferson.
iii   Chester W.,[7] b. 1851; unm.; merchant in Kingman, Kingman Co., Kansas.
iv   Annabell,[7] b. 1855; d. 1864.
v   Cora A.,[7] b. 1857.
vi   Hattie A.,[7] b. 1861; d. 1875.
vii   Carrie M.,[7] b. 1863.

87

Mark Weeks[6] (*Chase,*[5] *Cole,*[4] *Jn.,*[3] *Sam.,*[2] *Leon.*[1]) born 1800, died 1851, farmer, and his wife Clarissa (Osgood), had born in Sanbornton

Children :

i   Martha March,[7] b. 4 Oct., 1824; res. in Laconia.
ii   Nancy,[7] b. 2 Sept., 1828; d. 1831.
iii   Chase Cawley,[7] b. 29 May, 1836; m. Nov., 1864, Sarah A. Bickford, of Meredith. He was a teamster in Boston, and dealt in carriages.
iv   Mary,[7] b. Nov., 1838; d. Sept., 1841.
v   Horace,[7] b. 8 Feb., 1841; m. 1 May, 1863, Martha A. Moore, of Candia. In 1876, was travelling agent of Am. Screw and Wire Co.

88

William Brackett Weeks[6] (*Jn.,*[5] *Cole.,*[4] *Jn.,*[3] *Sam.,*[2] *Leon.*[1]) and his first wife, —— (Weeks), had :

Children :

i   Josiah,[7] of Waterford, Me., in 1885; had three children.
ii   Henry Brackett,[7] b., 1833 [d. in Saco, Me.]?
iii   Ellen Elizabeth,[7] d. unm.

Wm. B. Weeks married, second, Sally (dau. of Joseph) Farnham, of Sanbornton, and had

iv   Geo. Washington, b. in Sanbornton, 8 July, 1837; m. 18 Aug., 1856, Eliza E. (dau. of Joseph J.) Farnham and res. in New Hampton; had :
1 *Jas. William,*[8] b. in N. Hampton, 23 Feb., 1864, who lived in Sanbornton, with his grandfather, Farnham.

89

Moses Welch Weeks[6] (*Jos.,*[5] *Cole,*[4] *Jn.,*[3] *Sam.,*[2]
Leon.[1]) born 1792, died 1868, farmer on the homestead in
W. Sanbornton, and his wife Rebecca (Sanborn), had born
in Sanbornton
Children :

i   Sally Morrison,[7] b. 3 Feb., 1814; d. 3 Dec., 1816.
ii   Asa,[7] b. 22 Dec., 1816; m., 1st, 10 May, 1838, Agnes D.
     (dau. of Dan'l) Burleigh, who d. 2 Sept., 1856. He m.,
     2nd, in Minnesota, 31 July, 1861, Angie Clark, who d. He
     grad. (Dart. Coll.) 1846; taught in Hanover and So. Bos-
     ton; studied law, practised in Minneapolis; received pa-
     tents on a rifle and a torpedo, which latter has been
     adopted by the U. S. government. His home, in 1876,
     was in Washington, D. C.
iii Sally,[7] b. 5 Dec., 1818; m. Isaac Aldrich, a machinist; res.
     in Franklin; d. Feb., 1854. Her children were :
     1 *G. W.* (Aldrich), b. May, 1848; d. July, 1849.
     2 *Viola E.,* b. 2 Aug., 1849; m., 1865, Frank Drake, ma-
       chinist, of Lake Village, then of Springfield, Mass.
     3 *Ella L.,* b. 31 Oct., 1851; m. June, 1870, Chas. P. Stone
       of Fitchburg, Mass.
     4 *Chas. F.,* b. 4 Feb., 1854; m. 22 July, 1875, Ella M. Lov-
       ering of Worcester, Mass.; he is a painter in Fitch-
       burg.
iv   Matilda Thayer,[7] b. 20 Jan., 1821; d. 27 Apr., 1822.
v   Eleazer Davis,[7] b. 5 Dec., 1822; m. Laura (dau. of C. S.)
     Piper, who d. 18 May, 1848. He m., 2nd, Nancy S. (dau.
     of Nath'l) Piper, who d. 3 July, 1871, in her 46th year.
     He was a teacher, a selectman, a justice of the peace,
     etc., but has since removed from the homestead in San-
     bornton "to Lake Village, where he has been a leader in
     public affairs." Children :
     1 *Ellen E.,*[8] b. 27 Oct., 1845; m. J. H. Skinner, merchant in
       E. Rochester, then in Stoneham, Mass., and has :. (1)
       Lilian Imogene (Skinner), b. 23 Oct., 1870.   (2) Chas.
       Orin, b. 15 Jan., 1872.   (3) Mabel C., b. 16 Nov., 1873.
     2 *Mary Parker,*[8] b. 24 May, 1857.
vi   Cyrene Tucker,[7] b. 31 July, 1824; m. John F. Parker, shoe
     manufacturer of Stoneham, Mass., who d. 13 Sept., 1867.
     She d. 24 May, 1872. Children :
     1 *Walter S.* (Parker), b. March, d. June, 1847.
     2 *Mary,* b. 28 Dec., 1849; d. 16 Aug., 1852.
     3 *Fred. Leon,* b. Dec., 1854; was, in 1876, clerk in the
       mills at Belmont.
vii Lynthia Mary,[7] b. 3 July, 1826; m. Rufus M. Evans, a car-
     penter; res. in Cambridge, Mass. She d. 6 Apr., 1861. He
     d. 19 Dec., 1875. Children :
     1 *Georgiana A.* (Evans), b. 28 Jan., 1846; d. 8 July, 1847.
     2 *Geo. Bancroft,* a carpenter in San Francisco, Cal.

viii Freeman Lowell,[7] b. 31 May, 1830; a miner in California;
   studied and practised medicine in San Francisco, Cal.; m.
   twice; had no children.
ix Almira Green,[7] b. 30 Oct., 1831; m. in Gilford, May, 1849,
   Francis Jewell Hoyt, a mason in Lake Village, b. in Gilford 13 June, 1826. Children:
   1 *Elvira Salina* (Hoyt), b. Oct., 1851; d. 4 Aug., 1854.
   2 *Herbert Freeman*, b. 28 Nov., 1855; res. in Lake Village.

90

JonathanWeeks[6] (*Jona.*,[5] *Cole*,[4] *Jn.*,[3] *Sam.*,[2] *Leon.*[1])
born 1796, died 1872, and his wife Mahala (Colby), had
born in Sanbornton
Children :

i   Horace,[7] b. 6 Sept., 1823; m. 8 Sept., 1850, Abbie Post (dau.
   of Alex.) Kiff; res. in Waltham, Mass.; expressman between Boston and Waltham. Children:
   1 *Lyman Horace*,[8] b. 21 Aug., 1851; grad. Middletown, Conn.,
   1872; is on the editorial staff of the Boston Post. He
   m., 25 Dec., 1877, Ruba Capliner of Northampton, Mass.
   (of German descent), and has: (1) Marian Leslie,[9] b. in
   Boston, 3 April, 1880.
   2 *Frank Marcus*,[8] b. 1 May, 1853; m. 8 Sept., 1875, L. Annie
   Jennison of Waltham, and had: (1) Marjorie Nelson,[9] b.
   14 Feb., 1879.
   3 *Wilbert Lewis*,[8] b. 14 July, 1859; expressman, with his
   father.
ii Hiram,[7] b. 19 July, 1825; m. 22 Mar., 1849, Caroline M.
   Foster, of Newry, Me., sister of his partner, in the firm
   Foster, Weeks & Co., produce, 65 Clinton St., Boston;
   house in Waltham, Mass. Children:
   1 *Hiram Hazen*,[8] b. in Bedford, Mass., 1 Feb., 1850; is in the
   shoe trade, Boston.
   2 *Herbert Delmont*,[8] b. in W. Cambridge, 19 May, 1853; d.
   æ. 1 yr.
   3 *Delmont Locke*,[8] b. 19 Jan., 1855; m. 16 Oct., 1879, Addie
   M. Randall of Waltham; is of the firm Emerson, Weeks
   & Co., 134 Summer St., Boston; house in Waltham.
   4 *Carrie Belle*,[8] b. 31 July, 1858; d. in East Lexington, 13
   Nov., 1859.
   5 *Estelle Amanda*,[8] b. 11 Aug., 1860; d. 8 Aug., 1862.
iii Lyman,[7] b. at Hill, 25 Jan., 1830; m., 22 Nov., 1854, Sarah
   E. Jones of Searsmont, Me., b. 4 May, 1830. He was
   fourteen years on the police in Waltham; in 1885, officer
   in Charlestown State Prison. His child:
   1 *Geo. Lyman*,[8] b. 12 Sept., 1859, in Waltham; m., 1878,
   Alice Worcester of Waltham.
iv Sarah Ann,[7] b. 9 Feb., 1833; m., 25 Jan., 1856, Bradford C.
   Batchelder, b. in Andover, Mass., 3 July, 1814; a carriage
   maker in Waltham.

v Olive Elizabeth,[7] b. 27 Oct., 1839; m. Jason J. Smith, now
of Boston, a physician. She d. in East Somerville, 13
Mar., 1877. Children:
1 *Winfred Jason* (Smith), b. 1860; d. 1865.
2 *Leonard J.*, b. 11 June, 1867.
3 *Alice Maude*, b. 1873; d. æ. near 4 yrs.
4 *Willie F.*, b. 4 Aug., 1875; d. æ. 1 week.

91

Enoch R. Weeks[6] (*Jn.*,[5] *Benj.*,[4] *Jn.*,[3] *Sam.*,[2] *Leon.*[1])
born 1787, died 1867, farmer, etc., and his wife Sally
(Merrill), had

Children :

i Mary M.,[7] b. 9 Jan., 1815; m. 15 Dec., 1833, Ezra W. Cleasby,
b. 28 Feb., 1809; d. 12 May, 1866. Children:
1 *Sarah W.* (Cleasby), b. 11 Apr., 1837; m. 1 Dec., 1860,
Simon P. Chase.
2 *Hannah W.*, b. 22 Sept., 1838; m. 4 June, 1859, Jona.
Batchelder.
3 *Henry H.*, b. 28 July, 1840; m. 20 Dec., 1862, Abbie H.
Clark, and d. 9 July, 1869.
4 *Enoch W.*, b. 24 Oct., 1842.
5 *Geo. B.*, b. 29 Oct., 1844; m. Jenny Hotchkins.
6 *Albert P.*, b. 24 May, 1847; m. Jenny Parsons.
7 *Mary E.*, b. 4 July, 1850; m. Bertram Locke.
8 *Ellen C.*, b. 18 Oct., 1854; m. James Foster.
(**104**) ii Ira M.,[7] b. 12 May, 1817; m., 1st, 23 Feb., 1843, Elizabeth
A. Bixby, and d. 5 Oct., 1881. She was b. 9 Nov., 1823,
had five children, and d. 16 Nov., 1854. He m., 2nd, 8
Sept., 1855, Mrs. Laura A. Harris, b. 17 Nov., 1832, who
had six children.
iii Hannah,[7] b. 11 Mar., 1819; m. 17 May, 1840, Ferdinand C.
Kezer, and d. 30 May, 1857. She had:
1 *Eliza Ann* (Kezer), b. 3 Jan., 1845; m. 30 June, 1864, Jeremiah Howard.
2 *Fayette A.*, b. 1 May, 1848; m. June, 1874, Laura Pear-
sons.
3 *Mary Cordelia*, b. 5 Oct., 1853; d. 13 Feb., 1855.
iv Albe C.,[7] b. 25 Apr., 1821; m. 1 Mar., 1849, Elizabeth S.
Kelly, and had:
1 *Ella F.*,[8] b. 5 Apr., 1850.
2 *Frank P.*,[8] b. 30 July, 1852; d. Oct., 1852.
3 *Carrie Delia*,[8] b. 26 Mar., 1860.
v Esther,[7] b. 28 Mar., 1823; d. 16 May, 1829, æ. 6 yrs.
vi Tamar M.,[7] b. 29 Apr., 1825; m., 8 Apr., 1849, Albert L.
Bixby, b. 18 June, 1825; res. in Nashua, and has aided in
this work. Children:
1 *Charles A.* (Bixby), b. 27 Apr., 1852.
2 *Cordelia J.*, b. 15 June, 1854; d. 10 June, 1868.
3 *Hannah K.*, b. 28 June, 1858.
4 *Benjamin*, b. 1 July, 1863.

    5 *Sarah Lavinia*, b. 24 Nov., 1868.
vii Sarah A.,[7] b. 2 May, 1827; m. 5 Dec., 1850; Levi C. (s. of
    Levi) Whitcher, who was b. 1820, and d. 16 Feb., 1878.
    1 *Chas. E.* (Whitcher), b. 25 Aug., 1853.
    2 *Edwin A.*, b. 16 Mar., 1856; d. 8 July, 1856.
    3 *Harrie A.*, b. 20 Sept., 1858.
    4 *Edwin C.*, b. 21 Feb., 1860.
viii Esther S.,[7] b. 6 June, 1829; d. 30 June, 1843.
ix Enoch R., jr.,[7] b. in Warren, 13 Apr., 1831; m. 5 Oct.,
    1854, Melissa M. Metcalf, b. 27 July, 1834. In 1872, rem.
    to No. Haverhill; has been often elected by the Demo-
    cratic party to the office of town clerk, treasurer, etc. His
    children, born in Warren, were:
    1 *Frank M.*,[8] b. 3 Oct., 1856; d. 29 May, 1858.
    2 *Herbert*,[8] b. 16 July, 1859; d. 7 Apr., 1865.
    3 *Hattie*,[8] b. 20 Aug., 1862; d. 9 Nov., 1872.
    4 *Sarah Lizzie*,[8] b. 12 Nov., 1864.
    5 *Mary Melissa*,[8] b. 14 Feb., 1867.
    6 *Emma D.*,[8] b. 23 Sept., 1869.
x Cordelia T.,[7] b. 10 June, 1835; d. 2 Aug., 1852.

92

John Weeks[6] (*Jn.*,[5] *Benj.*,[4] *Jn.*,[3] *Sam.*,[2] *Leon.*[1])
born 1789, died 1845, farmer, etc., and his wife Abigail
Currier, had born in Danville, Vt.,
Children :

i   Samuel D.,[7] b. Orford, N. H., 26 Jan., 1812; m. 28 Aug.,
    1838, in Lowell. Mass., Olive Wedgewood, b. 1805, res.
    in Lowell. Children :
    1 *Geo. C.*,[8] b. Lowell, 24 June, 1839, res. unm. in Lowell.
    2 *A son*,[8] b. 12 Jan., 1848; res. in Lowell with a family.
ii   John, jr.,[7] b. 10 Mar., 1813; d. 1831.
iii Wm. W.,[7] b. 28 May, 1815; m. 8 June, 1841, Caroline Law-
    rence, b. 10 Oct., 1827. He is a shoe dealer in Montpelier,
    Vt., *s. p.*
iv Joseph S.H.[7] b. 17 Feb., 1817; m., 1st, Jane Kelsey in 1841;
    she d. and he m., 2nd, Laura Heath. His children were:
    1 *Adele*,[8] b. Danville, Vt.; m. Lewis Partridge, and res. in
    Camden, N. J. with children.
    2 *Harvey Kelsey*,[8] m., 2nd, Kate Eastman of Tilton, N. H.,
    and had: (1) Annie.[9]
    3 *Mabel Clifton*,[8] b. Danville, Vt., 1833; m. Frank Reilly,
    hatter in Jersey City, N. J.
v   Alonzo,[7] b. 22 Apr., 1819; m. in Danville, Vt., 11 Feb., 1841,
    Caroline A. Harris, b. 15 Feb., 1820; res. in Littleton; of
    the firm " Weeks, Whittaker & Miner," " White Moun-
    tain Glove Works;" he has been much in town office in
    Littleton. His children were:
    1 *John A.*,[8] b. 20 Oct., 1845; m. in Kalamazoo, Mich., 1873,
    May Little, and is a shoe dealer; res. Yankton, Dak.,

with three children: (1) John Rockwell,[9] b. 3 Feb., 1876; (2) Fleta May, b. 2 Apr., 1878.

2 *Percy*,[8] b. and d. 1850.

3 *Mabel Ina*,[8] b. 14 May, 1858, to whom we are indebted for valuable records.

John Weeks[6] married, second, Rosina Brown, who had :

vi D. Franklin,[7] b. 4 Apr., 1822; d. Feb., 1823.

vii Julia A.,[7] b. 19 Jan., 1824; m , in Danville, 22 Mar., 1847, William Dole, b. 28 Sept., 1823, and d. in Danville, 1883. Had b. in Danville :

1 *Augusta* (Dole), b. 2 April, 1850; m. Frank Pease, and had two children; res. McIndoe's Falls, Vt.

2 *Minnie Adele*, b. 21 June, 1856.

3 *Katie Calista*, b. 23 Nov., 1859.

viii Charles F.[7] b. 15 May, 1827; m. in Danville, 3 Aug., 1850, Ann Somers, b. 25 Aug., 1827; res. in St. Johnsbury, Vt., and has two children :

1 *Bessie B* ,[8] b. 5 June, 1852.

2 *James S.*,[8] b. 17 May, 1863.

ix Andrew J.,[7] b. 8 Mar., 1829; m. Chastina Heath. He is a tanner in Littleton, and had :

1 *John E.*,[8] m. 1883, Hattie Bergen, and has : (1) Chastina Cordelia.[9]

2 *Nellie M* ,[8] b. abt. 1865.

x Lucinda M.,[7] b. 23 Dec., 1830; d. 1833.

xi Augusta M.,[7] b. 16 Jan , 1834; m. 20 Nov., 1863, Jas. B. Mattocks, b. Jan., 1836, cashier of bank of Danville, Vt. Their children were :

1 *Sam'l* (Mattocks), b. 5 July, 1864, is in a bank in Littleton.

2 *Wm. Dale*, b. 26 July, 1866; clerk in Littleton.

3 *Charles H.*, b. 13 Aug., 1871.

xii Henry Clay,[7] b. 30 Jan., 1844; m. 20 July, 1871, Phebe Weed ; was a shoe dealer in Danville, Vt., d. there 22 Jan., 1872.

92a

Jonathan Weeks[6] (*Jn.*,[5] *Benj.*,[4] *Jn.*,[3] *Sam.*,[2] *Leon.*[1]) born 1794, died 1836, tanner and shoemaker, Lyndon, Vt., and his wife Betsey B. (Huse), had born in Lyndon Children :

i Betsey,[7] b. 24 Oct., 1818; m. 1 Jan., 1840, Ephraim C. Brown of Peacham, Vt.; d. in Lyndonville, Vt., 18 Aug., 1879, æ. 61. Had :

1 *Laura Eugenia* (Brown), b. in Peacham, Vt., 28 March, 1850; res. in Kenosha, Wis., 1886.

ii George Huse,[7] b. 2 June, 1821; m. in Danville, Vt., 21 Feb., 1849, Martha Amelia Mattocks, b. in Danville, 16 Sept., 1828, and had :

1 *George Mattocks*,[8] b. 17 Sept., 1853; d. 3 Jan., 1854.

2 *William Mattocks*,[8] b. 24 Apr., 1855; is on the R.R.

14

3 *Harriet Betsey*,[6] b. 24 Apr., 1860; d. 16 July, 1863.
4 *Caroline Esther*,[6] b. 23 Jan., 1863.
iii John Meigs,[7] b. 8 Nov., 1824; m. Louisa McGaffy; res. in
Lyndon.
iv Benj. Franklin,[7] b. 19 Apr., 1827; m. Mary Goodenough;
res. in Racine, Wis.
v Mary Jane,[7] b. in Lyndon, 25 Dec., 1829; res. unm. in
Kenosha, Wis.
vi Charles Marshall,[7] b. 21 May, 1835; m. Jane Wilmot; res.
62 Walker St., Lowell, Mass.

93

Brainard S. Weeks[6] (*Jn.*,[5] *Benj.*,[4] *Jn.*,[3] *Sam.*,[2]
Leon.[1]) born 1801, died 1875, farmer, and his wife Sarah
M. (Chamberlain), had born in Piermont

Children :

i John Spencer,[7] b. 20 Dec., 1841; m., 1st, in Haverhill, 4 May,
1867, Lettie P. Morrill, b. in Orford, 21 Aug., 1843; d. Lawrence, Mass., 20 Mar., 1872; m., 2nd, in Lebanon, N. H.,
14 July, 1874, Nellie J. Read, b. in Nashua, 29 July, 1845.
He was some years in a Lawrence cotton mill, then printer
in Haverhill, Mass.; in 1876 rem. to a farm in Orford, N.
H., his present home. Had one child by first marriage :
1 *Stephen Morrill*,[8] b. Lawrence, Mass., 16 Dec., 1871; in 1888,
student in Haverhill Academy.
Children by second marriage :
2 *Geo. Edwin*,[8] b. 19 Apr., 1880.
3 *Lettie May*,[8] b. 14 Oct., 1882.
ii Esther Minerva,[7] b. 10 Dec., 1842; m. in Bristol, N. H., 31
July, 1864, Alonzo Webster, b. in Wentworth, 12 Jan.,
1840, farmer and carpenter, in Edenville, Iowa. Children
were :
1 *Lettie May* (Webster), b. 13 Sept., 1867; d. in Edenville,
9 Apr., 1869.
2 *Alphonso*, b. 16 Nov., 1870.
3 *Jn. S.*, b. 20 Sept., 1873.
iii Rhoda Ann,[7] b. 23 Jan , 1844; d. 25 May, 1845.
iv William Chamberlin,[7] b. 12 Mar., 1846; insurance agent; m.
28 May, 1874, in Edenville, Iowa, Ruth Ann Scott, b. in
Ohio, 9 June, 1856, and has children :
1 *Lettie May*,[8] b. in Edenville, 13 Sept., 1867; d. in Edenville,
9 Mar., 1869.
2 *Benj. O.*,[8] b. 28 Jan., 1878.
3 *Charles L.*,[8] b. 7 Mar., 1880.
4 *Nellie May*,[8] b. 6 Mar., 1882.
5 *Edith L.*,[8] b. 17 Mar., 1884.
6 *Cecil E.*,[8] b. 11 Sept., 1886.
v Mary Brown,[7] b. 15 Jan., 1848; m. in State Centre, Iowa,
2 Dec., 1868, Frank Edmunds, b. in Chichester, N. H.,
1842. She d. in Edenville, 6 Feb., 1870. Her infant, b. 17
Nov., 1869, d. the same day.

vi Jasoh Gorham,[7] b. 10 Sept., 1850; d. 27 June, 1851.
vii Charles Asa,[7] b. 13 June, 1860; farmer in Collyer, Kansas; m.
    in Edenville, Iowa, 8 Feb., 1883, Emma F. Love, b. in
    Stoutsville, O., 20 Jan., 1863. Children:
    1 *George Arthur*,[8] b. in Edenville, 25 Nov., 1884; d. in Collyer,
      Kansas, 5 Aug., 1886.
    2 *Kittie Grace*,[8] b. in Collyer, Kansas, 18 Mar., 1886.

94

Samuel P. Weeks[6] (*Nath'l*,[5] *Jn.*,[4] *Matt.*,[3] *Jos.*,[2] *Leon.*[1]) born 1784, died 1829, and his wife Huldah (Knight), had

Children:

i   Josiah Knight,[7] b. 3 Dec., 1808; m. Elsie Monk; had b. in
    Paris, Me.:
    1 *Samuel Dexter*,[8] b. Feb., 1830; m., 1st, Linda M. Rawson;
      2nd, Martha Clark; had: (1) Mary,[9] b. in Paris Hill, Me.,
      where he was postmaster and where he d. Nov., 1874.
    2 *James Freeman*,[8] b. 1831.
    3 *Mary Huldah*,[8] m. Jacob Briggs.
    4 *Clarissa*,[8] d. 1875.
ii Napoleon B.,[7] b. 1 Jan., 1811.
iii Sarah,[7] b. in Buckfield, Me., 26 Dec., 1813; m. Silvester
    Tirell of So. Weymouth, Mass.
iv Nathaniel,[7] b. 3 May, 1815; res. in So. Weymouth, Mass.
v   Clarissa,[7] b. in Paris, Me., 3 Feb., 1819; res. in So. Ran-
    dolph, Mass.
vi Andrew,[7] b. 26 Nov., 1821; res. in So. Rumford, Me.
vii Joshua,[7] b. 28 Nov., 1823.
viii Geo. W.,[7] b. 7 Apr., 1826.

95

Maj. Nathaniel Weeks[6] (*Nath'l*,[5] *Jn.*,[4] *Matt.*,[3] *Sam.*,[2] *Leon.*[1]) born 1796, died 1874, merchant, and his wife Harriet B. (Gilman), had born in Exeter

Children: ·

i   George M.,[7] b. 3 Nov., 1821; d. in Exeter, 8 May, 1888; m.,
    in Exeter, 6 Nov., 1847, Ann Towle, b. in Nottingham 24
    Aug., 1824; had b. in Exeter:
    1 *Nath'l Gilman*,[8] b. 22 June, 1848: m. Elizabeth Austin;
      had: (1) Edward Walker,[9] (2) Earl Dwight, (3) Perley
      Gilman, (4) Annie Carter.
    2 *Mary Long*,[8] b. 26 Dec., 1854, is, in 1888, with her Aunt
      Carter.
ii Augustus Henry,[7] b. 13 Jan., 1824; merchant; m. in Exeter,
    19 Oct., 1853, Martha Augusta (dau. of Lewis W.) Per-
    kins; d. in Exeter 18 July, 1879. Their children were:

1 *Frederick Lewis*,[8] b. 3 Sept., 1854; printer; unm. in Exeter.
2 *Harriet Ida*,[8] b. 23 Oct., 1856; res. in Exeter; unm.
3 *Carrie Belle*,[8] b. 30 May, 1860; unm.
4 *Phil. Carter*,[8] b. 7 May, 1865; clerk in hardware store in Exeter.
5 *Julia Frances*,[8] b. 24 Sept., 1874; res. in Exeter with her mother.
iii Nathaniel,[7] b. 14 May, 1826; grocer in Exeter; m. 9 Nov., 1854, Frances A. (dau. of Benj. and Frances) Prescott of Kensington, b. 9 Sept., 1829, who d. in Exeter 18 Oct., 1885. He d. 1 Nov., 1880. Children b. in Exeter:
1 *Winnie F.*,[8] b. 12 Feb. and d. 26 Oct., 1856.
2 *Fannie Amelia*,[8] b. 25 Aug., 1861; m. 18 Nov., 1885, Henry Augustus Shute, lawyer, of Exeter, b. there 17 Nov., 1837.
3 *Everett P.*,[8] b. 10 Feb., 1865; grocer; res. in Exeter.
4 *Nellie A.*,[8] b. 20 June, 1868; d. 30 Aug., 1869.
iv Charles H.,[7] b. 4 July, 1828; d. 13 Sept., 1830.
v Harriet Frances,[7] b. 15 July, 1833; m. in Exeter, 13 Mar., 1860, Rev. Nathan F. Carter, pastor, in 1887, of Congregational Church, Quechee, Vt., *s p.* In 1888, edited "Sketches of Pastors of Congregational Churches in N. H."
vi Caroline Augusta,[7] b. 21 July, 1840; m., 16 Dec., 1868, John E. Rollins,* b. 12 June, 1839, harness-maker of Concord, in 1887, *s. p.*

96

Timothy Weeks[6] (*Nath'l*,[5] *Jn.*,[4] *Matt.*,[3] *Sam.*,[2] *Leon.*[1]) born 1801, died 1854, and his wife Elizabeth B. (Whitney), had

Children :

i Adaline Eliz.,[7] b. in Northampton, Mass., 2 Oct., 1826; m. 1860, N. W. Frye (as 2nd wife); res. in Everett, Mass.; d. Mar., 1887. They had:
1 *Nathan Wyman* (Frye).
ii Mary Abigail,[7] b. in Granby, Conn., 28 July, 1828; m. in Feb., 1849, Henry Augustus Fielding, and res. in Bozeman, Montana; had:
1 *Fred Augustus* (Fielding), m.; with no children.
iii Harriet Gilman,[7] b. in Sutton, Mass., 25 Sept., 1830; m. 1 July, 1849, Jere. S. Hall, who was killed in battle at Gettysburg, Pa., 2 July, 1863. She is a widow in Lowell, Mass., having:
1 *Albert Henry* (Hall), who m. and res. in N. Y. city with two children: (1) Harriet A. (Hall), b. 12 Mar., 1884; (2) Harry M., b. 2 Apr., 1885.

---

*John E. Rollins[6] (son of John and Elizabeth (Hill) Rollins of Exeter, now of Concord) see Rollins' Genealogy.

iv Augustus Whitney,[7] b. in Worcester, Mass., 5 Feb., 1833, is a merchant in Lowell; m., 25 Mar., 1867, Lauretta Frye, and had:
1 *Lauretta E.*,[8] d. an infant.
v Cynthia Jones,[7] b. 25 Mar., 1836, at Cavendish, Vt.; d. at Perkinsville, Vt., 15 May, 1842.
vi Ellen W.,[7] b. in Perkinsville, Windsor Co., Vt., 2 Oct., 1838; m. in Groton, Mass., 8 Dec., 1862, Rev. Edward P. Tenney,* b. in W. Concord, 29 Sept., 1835, and res. in 1885 in Manchester, Mass., with two children:
1 *Emma Wilson* (Tenney), b. in Lowell, Mass., 6 June, 1873.
2 *Elizabeth Hale*, b. in Ashland, Mass., 7 April, 1876.
vii Emeline Dorcas,[7] b. 13 May, 1841; m. 2 March, 1869, Gen. Lester S. Wilson; res. in Bozeman, Montana, with two children living; one deceased.

97

Gilman Weeks[6]*(Jn. L.*,[5] *Jn.*,[4] *Matt.*,[3] *Sam.*,[2] *Leon.*[1]) born 1813, died 1879, farmer, and his wife Sarah (Fairfield), had born in Tamworth

Children :

i Charles,[7] b. 9 June, 1839; res. 1885, in Denver, Col.; m. and has children.
ii Hannah,[7] b. 11 Oct., 1840; d. in Tamworth, 4 April, 1864.
iii Belinda,[7] b. 20 Mar., 1842; d. 2 Jan., 1868. She m. James Phillips of Swampscott, Mass., and had:
1 *Charles* (Phillips), b. May, 1867.
iv George,[7] b. 10 June, 1843; m.; res. in Lawrence, Mass. Had one son.
v Samuel,[7] b. 3 Oct., 1844; res. in Madison.
vi John,[7] b. 1 June, 1847; d. in Tamworth, 9 Aug., 1866.
vii William,[7] b. 16 Nov., 1851, farmer in Tamworth; m. there 7 Nov., 1881, Mary E. (dau. of Zenas and Martha H.) Blaisdell, b. in Tamworth, 21 June, 1849. Children b. in Tamworth :
1 *Hannah M*,[8] b. 14 Dec., 1883; d. 4 July, 1884.
2 *Bessie M.*,[8] b. 1 April, 1885.
3 *Charles*,[8] b. 12 March, 1887.

98

Joseph Weeks[6] (*Eliph.*,[5] *Sam.*,[4] *Matt.*,[3] *Sam.*,[2] *Leon.*,[1]) born 1796, died 1832, farmer, and his wife Sally (Barker), had born in Cornish, Me.,

Children :

---

*Edw. P. Tenney was son of Rev. A. P. Tenney, for thirty-four years the faithful pastor of the Congregational Church in West Concord, N. H.

i   Nancy,[7] b. 1821; m. Sam'l Lord of Limerick, Me., and had :
    1 *Martha Ellen* (Lord), d. 1878.
    2 *Joseph.*
ii Martha K.,[7] b. 1824; m. Sam'l Fenerson, farmer, res. in Gor-
    ham, Me., *s. p.*
iii Ivory B.,[7] b. 4 June, 1827; farmer; m. 22 June, 1856, Mary
    A. (dau. of Sam'l) Moulton of Parsonsfield, and had b. in
    Cornish, Me. :
    1 *Lauretta,*[8] b. 20 Sept., 1857; d. 24 Oct., 1862.
    2 *Joseph S.,*[8] b. 12 May, 1859.
    3 *Geo. W.,*[8] b. 1 Sept., 1861.
    4 *Effie E.,*[8] b. 19 Jan., 1864.
    5 *Birdie M.,*[8] b. 12 Dec., 1865; d. 29 Aug., 1882.

99

James Holmes Weeks[6] (*Eliph.,*[5] *Sam.,*[4] *Matt.,*[3] *Sam.,*[2] *Leon.*[1]) born 1801, died 1880, and his wife Lois (Ballard), had born in Chatham

Children :

i   Mary A.,[7] b. 12 July, 1838; m. Chas. Howe of Fryeburg,
    Me., and had :
    1 *Chas.* (Howe), b. 1863.
    2 *Mary A.*, b. 1864.
    3 *Willie W.*
ii Charles B.,[7] b. 1839; d. 1863, unm.
iii James M.,[7] b. 30 Nov., 1841; a farmer in Chatham; m. Mary
    S. Osgood, of Fryeburg, Me. Children:
    1 *Nellie O.,*[8] b. 1869.
    2 *Kate P.,*[8] b. 1874.
    3 *Winifred,*[8] b. 1884.
iv Lydia B.,[7] b. 6 July, 1844; d., unm., 1883.
v   Susanna P.,[7] b. 1846; d.
vi Henry,[7] b. 1863; d.
vii Submit Y.,[7] d.

100

Rev. Eliphalet Weeks[6] (*Eliph.,*[5] *Sam.,*[4] *Matt.,*[3] *Sam.,*[2] *Leon.*[1]) born 1803, died 1881, and his wife, Lydia (Ballard), had born in Chatham

Children :

i Frank H.,[7] b. 1830; d.. unm., 1858.
ii Lois A.,[7] b. 1832; m. Jas. Holmes Weeks of Chatham, and
   had (see 102–i):
   1 *Addie M.*, b. 1858; d. 1859.
   2 *Addie M.*, b. 1860.
   3 *Frank H.*, b. 1863.
   4 *Alice J.*, b. 1863; d. 1864.
   5 *Fred G.,*[8] b. 1869.

iii Rev. Joseph P.,[7] b. 1834; res. in Conway; m., 1st, Athalinda
Weeks, who d. 1866; m., 2nd, —— and had:
  1 *Gertrude,*[8] b. 1876.
  2 *Florence,*[8] b. 1878; d. æ. 10 months.
  3 *Clara B.,*[8] b. 1881.
  4 *An infant.*[8]

iv Cordelia L.,[7] b. 1844; m. Joseph Erastus Weeks of Westbrook, Me., a farmer, and had (see No. 102–ii):
  1 *Alice J.,* b. 1864.
  2 *Lilla M.,* b. 1871.
  3 *Maude L.,* b. 1876.
  4 *An infant.*

v J. Dana,[7] b. 1846; farmer in Chatham; m. Abbie S. Heath
of Conway, and d. 1876. Children:
  1 *Jennie M.,*[8] b. 1871.
  2 *A. Dana,*[8] b. 1872.
  3 *Grace B.,*[8] b. 1874.
  4 *Frank H.,*[8] b. 1876; d. 1878.

102*

John Weeks[6] (*Eliph.,*[5] *Sam.,*[4] *Matt.,*[3] *Sam.,*[2] *Leon.*[1])
born 1810, died 1880, farmer, and his wife Mehitable
(Holmes), had born in Parsonsfield, Me.,

Children:

i James Holmes,[7] b. 30 Mar., 1831; m. Lois A. Weeks of
Chatham and had five children b. there (see No. 100–ii).

ii Joseph Erastus,[7] b. 18 July, 1833; farmer in Westbrook,
Me.; m. Cordelia L. (dau. of Eliphalet) Weeks and had
four children (No. 100–iv).

iii Dr. Stephen Holmes,[7] b. in Cornish, Me., 6 Oct., 1835;
M.D., University, Penn., 1864; soon settled in Portland,
Me.; taught anatomy and surgery in the Portland Medical
School. In 1876 was chosen Professor of anatomy in Bow-
doin College and in 1880 was in Europe. In 1881 was
Professor of surgery. He m. Mary A. (dau. of Rev. Paul
C.) Richmond of Fryeburg, Me., and had:
  1 *Marion,*[8] b. 1870.

iv Eliphalet,[7] b. in Limerick, Me., 19 Jan., 1837; d. in childhood.

v Athalinda,[7] b. in Limerick, 10 Aug., 1840; m. Rev. J. P.
Weeks of Conway; d. 1866, *s. p.* (see No. 100–iii).

vi Susan A.,[7] b. 18 Mar., 1843; m., 1st, —— Chase and had:
  1 *Frank B.* (Chase).
She m., 2nd, Wm. Head, a farmer on the homestead,
in Chatham, N. H., and had:
  2 *Perley K.* (Head), b. 1877.
  3 *Mabel,* b. 1882.
  4 *An infant,* d.

---

*Records of 101 not received.

vii Dr. Albion,[7] b. 24 Oct., 1845; m.; res. in Providence, R. I.,
    where he died, 10 Feb., 1887, *s. p.*
viii John,[7] b. in Chatham, N. H., 24 Feb., 1848; d. in childhood.
ix John, 2nd,[7] b. in Chatham 22 Aug., 1856, lost for many
    years. He entered Dartmouth College, left on account
    of ill health, travelled, and has not returned.

103

Josiah Weeks[6] (*Levi,*[5] *Jn.,*[4] *Leon.,*[3] *Jos.,*[2] *Leon.*[1])

born 1808, died 1880, blacksmith, etc., farmer, and his
wife Fannie (Glines), had born in Wolfboro

Children :

i   Edwin Levi,[7] b. 15 Apr. [1836];? d. 22 Dec., 1877, æ 42
     yrs. and 8 mos.; m., in Essex, Mass., 23 Nov., 1859,
     Mary Parker Burnham Arnold of Charlestown, Mass.;* had
     b. in No. Somerville, Mass., children :
     1 *Frank Ludlow,*[8] b. 15 Dec., 1860; d. 14 Sept., 1882, æ. 21.
     2 *Fred. Augustus,*[8] b. 26 Aug., 1862; m. 17 June, 1885, Ce-
       cilia Blanche Conners.
     3 *Edith Mabel,*[8] b. 11 Jan., 1864; m. 1 Aug., 1882, Chas.
       Herbert Boothby; had (1) Edith M.,[9] b. 29 May, 1883;
       d. 4 June, 1883. (2) Carl Herbert, b. 8 Oct., 1884.
     4 *Edgar LeForest,*[8] b. 16 July, 1865.
ii Lydia Jane,[7] b. 29 Aug., 1840; m. in Manchester, 25 Nov.,
     1869, Charles H. Nudd of Wolfboro; res. in Lexington,
     Mass. Child :
     1 *Helena M.* (Nudd).
iii Fannie E.,[7] b. 25 Aug., 1845; m. Sept., 1865, Josiah W.
     Chamberlin; res. in Wolfboro, and has :
     1 *Nellie M.* (Chamberlin).
iv Alvin Jacob,[7] b. 15 Mar., 1847; m., 1st, 14 May, 1880, Au-
     gusta M. Wiggin of Tuftonboro, who d. 22 June, 1882.
     He is a farmer; res. in Wolfboro; m., 2nd, 4 May, 1885,
     Alida M. Hinds, and has :
     1 *Lillie M.,*[8] b. 14 April, 1886.

104

Ira M. Weeks[7] (*Enoch R.,*[6] *Jn.,*[5] *Benj.,*[4] *Jn.,*[3] *Sam.,*[2] *Leon.*[1]) born 1817, died 1881, and his first wife,

Elizabeth A. (Bixby), had born

Children :

i   Sabina E.,[9] b. 1 June, 1844; d. 2 Mar., 1850.
ii Charles Al,[8] b. 29 June, 1846; d. 15 Aug., 1849.
iii Albe Cady,[8] b. 5 Dec., 1848.
iv Abel M.,[8] b. 9 Mar., 1851; m. 29 Nov., 1875, Cora A. Smith.
v George H.,[8] b. 5 Mar., 1853; d. 11 Feb., 1865.

---

* Aug., 1887, Mrs. Edwin L. Weeks res. Evergreen Ave., Somerville, Mass.

By his second wife Laura A. (Harris), he had :

vi   Emma Jane Harris,⁸ b. 20 Sept., 1858.
vii Ettie E.,⁸ b. 21 Feb., 1860; d. 9 Feb., 1865.
viii Henry E.,⁸ b. 26 May, 1862.
ix Charles L.,⁸ b. 15 June, 1864.
x   Kate Cordelia,⁸ b. 15 June, 1872.
xi Fred.,⁵ b. 9 Mar., 1875.

FAMILIES WHOSE CONNECTION IS NOT TRACED.

105

James Weeks⁴ (baptized in 1742, as servant of Jonathan³) (*Jn.*,² *Leon.*¹), supposed to have been his nephew, grandson of John,² was a soldier in the Revolutionary War and removed from Greenland and settled in Cabot, Vt., and had two sons :

i James,⁵ b. 1780; m. in Exeter, 30 Nov., 1800, Eliz. Marsh,
    of Exeter, and res. there.
ii John.⁵

James Weeks⁵ (*Jas.*,⁴ *Jn.*,² *Leon.*¹) born 1780, died 1863, brick mason, and his wife Elizabeth (Marsh), had born in Exeter

Children :

i Elizabeth Ann,⁶ b. Sept., 1801; m. Richard Alley, b. Sand
    wich, 1801, and had children :
    1 *James Wm.* (Alley) ,who d. æ. 20.
    2 *Eliz. Frances*, b. 1821; m. 1854, Henry H. Chesley, b. in
      Durham, 1823, now of Newmarket Junction.
    3 *Ellen Sumner.*
    4 *Richard Frank.*
ii James,⁶* b. 1806; m. 1826, Sarah Place of Lee, who d. July,
    1863. He was a bricklayer and a market man, and had six
    children b. in Exeter. He d. there 8 June, 1888. Children :
    1 *Sarah Elizabeth*,⁷ b. 1829; m. Nathan Langmaid of Exeter,
      and had : (1) Nellie,⁸ who m. Harrison Tilton of Deerfield.

---

* "Jas. Weeks, Jr., and Sarah Sheriff, both of Exeter, m. 5 Feb., 1827." (Exeter Town Records.)

15

2 *Wm. P.*,[7] b. 1831; bricklayer in Exeter; m. and had one child.

3 *James*,[7] b. 1833?; a carpenter in So. Framingham, Mass., who m., 1st, Martha Morrison. Children: (1) Charles E.,[8] (2) James, (3) Benjamin J., m. in Exeter, 1 Nov., 1886, Cora L. (dau. of Weare Little) Folsom, of Newport, Me., and res. So. Framingham, Mass. He m., 2nd, Helen Barker, and had: (4) Almira.

4 *Jeremiah*,[7] b. 1833; [Co. B 3d N. H. Reg.]; m.; d. 23 Mar., 1862.

5 *Carrie Cowles*,[7] b. 1836; m. Jotham Rogers of Scituate, Mass., and lives in Somerville, Mass., with four children.

6 *John W.*,[7] b. 1838; m. 1862, Carrie Colcord of Brentwood. Four children: (1) Florence W.,[8] b. 1862. (2) Albert Jacob, in drug store. (3) Gracie L., b. Feb., 1876. (4) Alice C., b. 1877.

iii   Hannah,[6] b. abt. 1810; m. Jn. Glines of Northfield, and had two daus. in Haverhill, Mass.

iv   Abigail,[6] m., 1st, John (or Abr.) Hall of Boston, and had:
1 *John* (Hall).
2 *A dau.*

v   Lydia Ann,[6] b. 1812 (?); m. Elbridge Cole, painter of Somerville, Mass., and had children:
1 *Ambrose* (Cole).
2 *Edson.*

vi   John S.,[6] b. in Exeter, 5 March, 1813; m. 1837, —— Cole of Boston. Children:
1 *Caroline*,[7] b. 7 June, 1838, in Concord; m. 1862, Jn. W. Morse of Brentwood. Children: (1) Florence W. (Morse), b. 1862. (2) Albert J., in drug store. (3) Carrie L., (4) Alice C.
2 *John E. G.*,[7] b. Concord, 1841; d., unm., in the War.
3 *Abby E.*,[7] b. 1843; m. Alvin H. Miles.
4 *James W. A.*,[7] b. 1845, of Exeter.
5 *Sarah E. P.*,[7] b. 13 Feb., 1848; m. Chas. Lewis Rundlett, machinist of Raymond.

John Weeks[5] (*Jas.*,[4] *Jn.*[2]) born in Cabot, Vt. [bro. of Jas.[5]], a teamster; records not received.

WEEKS FAMILY IN KITTERY, ME.

21 July, 1674, Wm. Weeks [supposed] of Kittery, deposed in Rock Co. Court; he was about 45 years old.

Leonard of Greenland came from Wells, Somerset Co., England.

In 1637, Wm. (son of Jn. and Agnes) Weeks was baptized in Compton Marten (Chew Magna), Somerset Co., Eng.

7 Aug., 1639, his brother Leonard was baptized. The father then lived in a part of the parish called Moreton.

About 1680, we find **107** Joseph and **108** Nicholas Weeks of Kittery, brothers.*

Nicholas Weeks was appraiser of estate of Eph. Crocket in September, 1688; witnessed a will 6 June, 1718. Is named in brother Joseph's will, 19 Nov., 1741.

One Joseph Weeks witness of above will and appraiser of estate [son of Nicholas]?

107

Joseph Weeks² [*Wm.¹*]? brother of Nicholas of Kittery, Me., died 1741.

He was appraiser of estate of John Mograg, 15 Mar., 1705-6. He "owned ye covenant" and had his children baptized 16 Oct., 1715. His wife Mary, at his death, between 19 Nov. and 14 Dec., 1741, was executrix of his will, signed 19 Nov., 1741.

His children were :

i   Nicholas, jr.,³ bapt. 1715; [will signed 1769]? ; m. 1721 (published 30 Sept., 1721), Sarah Rice of Kittery; both owned ye covenant in 1735. Children:

(109)   1 *Nicholas*,⁴ bapt. 1735; m. Rhoda ——.

     2 *John*,⁴ m. Children: (1) Mary,⁵ b. 10 Oct., 1791. (2) Phebe, b. 4 Feb., 1794. (3) Sarah, b. 11 Dec., 1800; m. Stephen (son of Nicholas) Weeks of Kittery, b. 22 Jan., 1801.

ii   Benjamin,³ bapt. 1715; m. Elizabeth ——, who in 1737 joined the church. Children :

     1 *Richard*,⁴ bapt. 1736; in Dec., 1751, witnessed a will.

     2 *Benjamin, jr.*,⁴ bapt. 1736.

     3 *Mary*,⁴ bapt. 1736.

     4 *Moses*,⁴ bapt. 1736.

---

* I find Joseph and Nicholas Weeks, farmers, seem to have been men of influence in the community, and that they were called upon to act as appraisers of property, at the settlement of the estates of different persons, who died in Kittery, and their names are found as witnesses upon wills, etc.

iii Abraham,[3] bapt. 1715; m. Sarah ——, who with her infant
 was bapt. 1730.
iv Judith,[3] m. —— Hutchins; was living in Nov., 1741.
v Martha,[3] m. —— Jones; living in 1741.
vi A dau.[3] [Mehitable]? who m. and had:
 1 *Benjamin Morgeridge*,[4] living in 1741.

108

Nicholas Weeks.[2]

Supposed children :

i Joseph Weeks, jr.,[3] m. Sarah ——, who with him joined the
 church in 1739.   Their infant was bapt. 30 Apr., 1732, and
 in 1734 the following persons were baptized, supposed to
 be their children:
 1 *Josiah*.[4]
 2 *William*.[4]
 3 *Joseph*.[4]
 4 *Edith*.[4]
 5 *Sarah*.[4]
 6 *Susanna*.[4]

109

Nicholas Weeks[5] (*Nich.*,[4] *Nich.*,[3] *Joseph*,[2]) of Kittery, Me., and his wife —— (Hutchins), had born in Kittery

Children :

i Stephen,[6*] b. 22 Jan., 1801; m. Sarah (dau. of Jn.)Weeks of
 Kittery, b. 11 Dec., 1800.   Children:
 1 *Luther*,[7] b. 22 Jan., 1823; d. in Brewer Village, 24 Apr.,
 1844.
 2 *Mark S.*,[7] b. 3 Nov., 1825, ship builder; m. 25 June, 1860,
 Susie H. Covell of Boston, and had: (1) Isadore S.,[8]
 b. 30 July, 1862; d. 14 Sept., 1863.   (2) Carrie E., b. 25
 July, 1863; m. Alfred Small of Bucksport, Me.   (3)
 Grace L., b. 13 May, [1800]?
 3 *Phebe*,[7] b. 14 Sept., 1828; d. 22 Sept., 1859; m. Geo. W.
 Doane, Esq.   Children: (1) Luther W. (Doane), b. 12
 Oct., 1849. (2) Walter W., b. 12 Dec., 1852; a merchant
 in Bangor. (3) Geo. E., b. 19 May, 1855. (4) Clara H.,
 b. 7 Jan., 1859.
 4 *Alice*,[7] b. 2 Oct., 1831; m. Galen J. Brewer, farmer and
 machinist; a grandson of Col. Jn. Brewer, the first
 settler in Brewer village.   Children: (1) Sarah, b. 4
 Jan., 1864. (2) Maud W., b. 20 Jan., 1871.

---

* Each of these four sons of Stephen Weeks has been to sea and been master
of a vessel.

5 *Mary Jane.*[7] b. in Brewer Village, 14 Oct., 1834; m. 3
   July, 1859, Joshua (son of Deacon) Hooper, b. in Cas-
   tine, Me., 15 Jan., 1823. He is a merchant in Bucksport, Me., and has three children: (1) John W., b. 6
   Apr., 1860, a merchant in Georgia. (2) Mary A., b. 10
   Feb., 1862; m. Wm. W. Prescott of Brewer, merchant.
   (3) Phebe J., b. 30 Sept., 1863.
6 *Capt. John H.,*[7] b. 14 Mar., 1839, is an officer on the Me.
   Centre R.R.; m. Corinna Hale, and has: (1) Stella,[8] b.
   17 Apr., 1864.
7 *Charles A.,*[7] b. 25 June, 1841; merchant in Broken Bow,
   Nebraska; m. Mary Kerr, *s. p.*
8 *Martha Ann,*[7] b. 14 Nov., 1846; m. Edward Trafton and
   had: (1) John A., b. 1 May, 1878. (2) Bessie C., b. 13
   May, 1880.

    ii   Nicholas.[6]
    iii Samuel.[6]
(110) iv Charles,[6] b. 1805; m. Abigail Lewis of Waterford, Me., and
        had six children.
    v   Betsey.[6]
    vi Alice.[6]
    vii Mary.[6]

110

Charles Weeks[6] (*Nich.,*[5] *Nich.,*[4] *Nich.,*[3] *Joseph*[2])

born 1805, died 1887, and wife Abigail (Lewis), had
Children :

  i   Augustus,[7] m.; had children:
     1 *Anna.*[8]
     2 *Horace A.*[8]
     3 *Emma C.*[8]
  ii Abbie L.,[7] m., 1st, ——Robinson; 2nd, John F. Stewart. One
      child by first marriage:
     1 *Chas.* (Robinson).
  iii Cornelia.[7]
  iv Hannah.[7]
  v   Wm. L.,[7] m; *s. p.*
  vi Charles E.,[7] m; *s. p.*

APPENDIX.

NOTE I.

DEEDS BY LEONARD WEEKS.

DEED OF LEONARD TO JOSHUA WEEKS, RECORDED 4 SEPT., 1707, PER WM. VAUGHN, RECORDER

To all Chistyan People to whoom this prent Deed may com I Lenard Weekes of Greenland, Belonginge to Portsmouth, in ye Province of New Hanpshere, in New England, Planter, Send Greetinge. Know ye that the said Lenord Weekes, as well for and in consideration of the naturall affectyon and fatherly Love w'h I have & do Bare unto my well belove son, Joshawn Weekes of the same town and Provins abovefaid as allso for other good causes & consideratyons mee hereunto moovings (and in confiderasion yt. hee Paye and Performe what I hereafter order him in this Deed) Have Given, & Granted and by these prefents doe Give, Grant and confirme unto the Above mentyoned Jofhewa Weekes all and Singuler thofe severall Parfells of Land and other moovables hereafter mentyoned, viz. Thirty Acres of Land adjoyning to a Place called Turning Poynte be the same moore or Lefe, and six acres of Salte Marfh adjoining to the Above faid land, be the same more or Lefe, Lying on the Westerly side of William ffurburo I allso Give to him two oxen and two cowes, & the one halfe of my Right in a new Saw Mill Lately Bulte upon Weenecut River. I also give unto him, the Said Joshewa Weekes the one halfe of all my Implements of Husbandry, when they shall be Equally Divided betwene my Son Sam'l Weekes and hee the said Joshewa Weekes. The above Joshewa Weeks, To Have and to hoold an Peaceably to Injoy the one mentyoned Thirty Acres of Land be the Same More or Lefe, w'th all the ffences Timber, trees wood and underwood thereunto belonging And the Six Acres of Salt Marfh be the Same more or Lefe, and the one halfe of my Right to the Said Saw-mill, as also the one halfe of my Implements of Husbandry as above said, To him, the Above mentyoned Joshewa Weekes, his Heirs Exec'rs Adm'rs and Assignes, to his & their owne Propper use, Benefts & Behoofes for ever. Hee the Said Joshewa Weekes To Enter Upon and poffefe the above Mentyoned Premefef, all Imedyatly after my Deaceafe, but not Before, Excepte I Shall See Cause to Lett him to Improve Parte thereof Before. In Consideratyon of the above mentyoned premefes, the Said Joshewa Weekes Shall Paye, or Cause well & Truely to be paid unto his Brother John Weekes, the sum of Ten Pounds in, or As money, to be Paid to him Within three yeares after my Deceafe, as allso to pay to my Son Samewell Weekes In Provifyon Paye as money, Twentie Shillinges a yeare towards the maintenanfe of Elisabeth, my now Wife, for so longe as shee Shall Remaine a Widdow, after my Death, and Consideratyon thereof the said Joshua Weekes Shall Have Hoold and Pofsef the above Mentyoned Premefes ffully and quietly w'th out Any matter of Challinge,

Claime or Demand of Anny of my Heires, Exe'rs Adm'rs or Afsigines or of Anny Monny or other Things therefore to be yelded, Paid, or Done anny otherwaies than the Above mentyoned Payment mentyoned in this Deed wch are to be faithfully an carefully Paid and Don as is above mentyoned & for the confermatyon of all above written, I the Said Lenord Weekes have Hereunto Putt my Hand an affixed my Sele this twenty-third Day of Aprill in this year of our Lord Seventeene Hundred & Six an in the fifth yere of the Reigne of our Soveraigne Lady Anne, by the Grace of God of England, Scotland ffrance and Ireland, Queen, Defender of the ffaith, &c.— Signed by a Mark and acknowledged before Henry Dow, Justice of Peace, the 15 May, 1706.

In the deed, 23 April, 1706, to his son Samuel, Leonard Weeks makes a condition :

" That the Said Saml Weekes Shall Paye . . . for Elizabeth my now wife, after my Decease (So longe as Shee shall continue a Widdo) a Convenyent ffier Room, Warme & Comfortable, for her to liue in and to paye — her Seuen Pounds a Yere, in Provityon paye or Monny . . and allso find her wth wood, brought hoome to her House, Cut, fit and Convenyent for her ffier, and to find her the Milke of two Cowes wch two Cowes are to be found for her, wintered and Somered for her, in the Pasture, or So as She may Have them, &c. The Said Saml Weekes Shall Pay or cause to be paid to my Daughter, Mary Weeks Ten Pounds as Monny wth in one yere after my Decease ; and to my Daughter Margaret Weekes the Som of Ten Pounds as monny wth in two yeares after my Decease.

as allso to my Daughter Sarah Weekes the Som of Ten Pounds as money wth in three years after my Decease &c."

NOTE II.

" Nov. ye 24, 1708,— at Meeting of ye selectmen, pursuant a town order, at last gen'll Town Meeting [in March]. In answare to what Samuel Weickes proposed, at sd. Meeting, for ye exchange of twenty acors of lande, granted by sd. town to his father, Leonard Weekes, deceased &c."

The Selectmen of Portsmouth ordered to "exchange 16 acres on the East of Winnicut River for 20 acres West of it at the request of Samuel, son of Leonard Weeks dec'd. This land had been granted to Leonard Weeks."—A. M. H.

Ten years after this, Sam'l Weeks, eldest son of Leonard, was appointed administrator upon a part of the estate not divided, and Samuel Chapman, commissioner, to "examine claims &c. due from the estate," which were settled according to the law as we learn from the Probate Records.

NOTE III.

THE OLD BRICK HOUSE.

It stands on the Weeks place, a little West of the Parade, in Greenland. It is over 36 feet long, 22 feet wide, and the walls of the lower story are 18 inches thick. The bricks in the front wall are of different colors laid in order so as to appear something like the spots on a checker board. There was a rent in the walls, at each end of the house, supposed to have been made by the great earthquake, in 1755. But the walls are now covered by cement, which covers the rent.

The lower story is 8 feet and 6 inches high. The second story is 8 feet, and the steep pitch of the roof affords ample room for the attic. The windows were originally of small, diamond-shaped glass, set in lead; but have been changed to a later style. The timbers are hard wood,— oaken beams, hewn 12 × 14 inches, and the sleepers of red oak, with bark still on, about 10 inches in diameter.

It is supposed that one object in erecting, at that early period, a house so expensive, was to provide more security from the attacks of the Indians. Some twenty years before this was built, Samuel Haines, jr., a brother to the wife of Leonard Weeks, had erected a garrison house not far from this place. There has been much discussion about the date when this house was built, and the question is not yet positively decided.

About 1873, Enoch H. Clark, an aged citizen of Greenland, said, "The owners of the Brick House, told me, it was built by Leonard Weeks' son. As their father told me, it would be, in 1873, 160 to 170 years old."

Tradition says, that a committee from Newmarket visited Greenland, to examine this house before erecting one of the same pattern for Jeremiah Folsom, on an eminence half a mile south of Newmarket village. It was not quite so large as the Weeks' house, and was taken down after standing about one hundred and sixty years.

The granddaughter of the builder told me that her father, Col. Jeremiah Folsom, was born in that house before the workmen had finished the roof. He was born 25 July, 1719. If Leonard Weeks had built the house, he would probably have given some intimation of it, in describing the property, houses and lands, which he conveyed to his children in 1706; but there is no allusion to it.

The conclusion most probable is that his son, Capt. Sam'l Weeks, who inherited the homestead, finding the old house insufficient to accommodate the stepmother and his two unmarried sisters, together with his own large and growing family, erected this house about the year 1710 or 1712, and that in 1890 it will be about one hundred and eighty years old.

J. C.

NOTE IV.

The settlement of the estate of Joshua Weeks, jr., was an occasion of much trouble between two families.

Old Capt. Joshua Weeks seems to have been a quiet farmer with ten children, who was not often noticed in the Court Records. But his oldest son Joshua, jr., married Sarah the daughter of Richard Jenness, a lawyer, and died soon. Nine days after his death, the widow removed back to Rye, the home of her father, taking (it is to be supposed) her property with her. One year afterward she was appointed administratrix upon the estate of her late husband and showed the appraisers property which they estimated at £411-11s.

But as he had received no title to the house and lands where he lived, and most of the stock on the place came from his father's, only £91-11s. were allowed upon that £411-11s.

Two years and a half after her husband's death, the widow had her father-in-law, Capt. Joshua Weeks, cited to appear in court at Portsmouth, and declare upon oath, if he had not in his possession, some of the goods of his deceased son. He appeared; but found it rather hard to tell what had become of all the old clothes, shoes and stockings, etc., of this son who had gone out from home four years before to set up housekeeping for himself.

I have copied a few specimens of the questions put to the old man.

1. About five suits of clothes. He could not tell, 2½ yrs. after the death of his son, how many suits of clothes he had. He knew nothing of the 8 *pairs of stockings* which he was charged with taking. Knew nothing of the two pairs of *shoes*. As to the two pairs of boots, he remembered "only one pair pretty much worn—nothing of the three pairs of gloves." Of the three *hats*, "he knows only one about half worn." He says he has the bedstead & feather bed; but they were his own "lent to his son." "Of the Blankets & coverlets," he "can't say." "Of the 40 bushels of corn, he says, there were not more than ten which was his own & he took it." "As to the 4 bushels of wheat & 4 bush. barley, he knows nothing." As to the 8 barrels of syder, he knows only *three*, & these were his own." "The oxen, cowes horse & sheep were his own, taken there to winter, his son to have the use of them for looking after them." "There was an old sled, & he took it. The hoes & axes, he knows nothing of—the scythe remains where it was when his son died, & he supposes the meal chest is where it was." "The six cords of wood was about *four* cords, belonging to the intestate and his *brother*," etc., etc.

Nearly three years after the death of her husband the widow remembered enough more of his wearing apparel to have another inventory appraised at £57-2s. which was allowed and paid to her.

She was not satisfied, but the next year brought suit against her father-in-law, for a large amount of damages, and the sturdy old captain, being only a farmer, perplexed with the cares of a large estate and a great family, had a small chance in a contest with the smart young widow, her brother Richard, law student, and the wily old lawyer, her father. They secured a verdict of £160 and costs of court, £3-11s.-6, which the sheriff collected, and she acknowledged at the settlement of the estate.

Twelve years afterward the captain made his will and bequeathed a large amount of property to his other children and grandchildren, and twenty shillings in full to the son of the widow in Rye. After all their contention and legal skill, in extorting £160 from Captain Weeks, it is *probable* that if they had made a peaceable settlement in the beginning they might have fared much better in the end.

WILL OF JOSHUA WEEKS.

The last Will & Testament of Joshua Weeks of Greenland in the Province of New Hampshire, Gentleman, being of sound mind & memory but calling to mind the mortality of my body, do therefore this second day of November anno Domini one thousand seven hundred & fifty two make and ordain this my last Will and Testament, that is to say—Principally and First of all I recommend my soul into the hands of God who gave it and my body to the earth from whence it proceeded to be decently buried by my Executors hereafter named; and as to such worldly Estate as it has pleased God to bless me with, I give, devise and bequeath the same in manner following (viz)

16

Imprimis I will that all my just debts and funeral charges be well
and truly paid equally by my Executors hereafter named.

Item I give and bequeath unto my beloved wife Comfort Weeks the
use and improvement of one third part of all my Real Estate also that
half part of my dwelling house which she shall chuse and also all my
household stuff during her natural life as also the use of my negro
woman named Hannah and the improvement of two cows, six sheep,
one horse my riding chair and pew in the meeting house in Greenland
aforesaid so long as she remains my widow (excepting one bed) and
that my son William Weeks shall maintain the said two cows six sheep
and horse winter & summer during my said wifes widowhood.

Item I give devise and bequeath unto my son John Weeks and to
his heirs and assigns forever one half of my lower flats bounding
against my marsh commonly called and known by the name of Furbors
and Shackfords marsh in Greenland aforesaid I also give devise and
bequeath unto my said son John Weeks his heirs & assigns forever ten
acres of land laying in Greenland aforesaid be it more or less adjoying
the land he now has in his possession running northwardly upon the
road that leads from my said son Johns house to my own untill it comes
to a brook and from said brook to run South till it comes to James Cates
land and so bounding on said Cates land and land belonging to John
Watson till it comes to my said son John Weekes's land that he already has also I give & bequeath unto my said son John Weeks his heirs
and assigns my negro whose nam is Neptune.

Item I give and bequeath unto my grandson Joshua Weeks the son
of my son Joshua Weeks deceased twenty shills lawfull money in full
of his portion in my estate to be paid by my son William Weeks
within two years next after my decease. Item I give and bequeath
unto my daughter Mary the wife of Jonathan Chestley one hundred and
ten pounds old Tenor thirty Pounds thereof to be paid by my son William Weeks immediately after my decease the other eighty Pounds
thereof to be paid by my said son William Weeks within two years
next after my decease.

Item I give and bequeath unto my daughter Martha Hilton the wife
of Winthrop Hilton one hundred and ten pounds old Tenor thirty
pounds thereof to be paid by my son William Weeks immediately after
my decease the other eighty Pounds to be paid by my said son William
Weeks within two years next after my decease.

Item I give and bequeth unto my grandson Joshua Wiggin son of
my said daughter Martha Hilton one three year old heifer to be delivered him immediately after my decease by my son William Weeks.

Item I give and bequeath unto my daughter Comfort, the wife of
Walter Weeks one hundred & ten Pounds, old Tenor Thirty Pounds
thereof to be paid by my son William Weeks immediately after my decease the other eighty Pounds thereof to be paid by my said son William Weeks within two years next after my decease.

Item I give and bequeath unto my two grandsons (viz) George
Marshal and John Marshal sons of my daughter Thankfull the wife of
George Marshal (who is lately deceased) eighty Pounds old Tenor,
equally to be divided between them said George Marshal and John
Marshal when they arrive to the age of twenty-one years to be put to
Intrest by my said son William Weeks within two years next after my
decease and by him be paid to them said George Marshall and John
Marshall with the Intrest thereof when they arrive to the age of
twenty-one years.

Item I give and bequeath unto my two Granddauters Margaret Marshall and Comfort Marshall the daughters of my daughter Thankfull Marshall deceased who was the wife of George Marshall : the fifth part of my household goods to be taken care of by my Executors at my own & my wife's decease and by them to be put to Intrest untill the said Margaret and Comfort arives to the age of eighteen years and then be equally with the Intrest thereof delivered unto them by my Executors.

Item I give and bequeath unto my daughter Smith the wife of Ebenezer Smith one hundred and ten Pounds old Tenor, Thirty Pounds thereof to be paid immediately after my decease by my son John Weeks and the other eighty Pounds thereof to be paid by my said son John Weeks within two years next after my decease. I also give & bequeath unto my said daughter Margaret Smith her heirs and assigns my negro woman named Hannah immediately to receive her at my own and my wife's decease. I also give my daughter Margaret my jonne Jack.

Item I give & bequeath unto my four daughters (viz) Mary Chasley, Martha Hilton, Comfort Weeks and Margaret Smith all my household stuff that is not already or hereafter disposed of equally to be divided between them immediately after my own and my wife's decease.

Item I give & bequeath unto my son William Weeks his heirs and assigns forever all my dwelling house barns and out houses to immediately possessed of at my own and my wife's decease together with all my lands meadows, pastures thatch ground and salt marsh laying in Greenland aforesaid or else where excepting what I have already herein and before disposed of. I also give and bequeath unto my said son William Weeks all my horses sheep swine stock of cattle of every sort and kind excepting what is and shall be otherways disposed of and one bed that he have already recied and all my impliments of husbandry all so my guns sword case and the works of Mr Manton and Dr Mathers' Church History and all my right in a negro man named Cesar, that is not already disposed of the better to enable him to pay my debts and my own and my wife's funeral charges.

Item I give unto my son John Weeks and my son William Weeks all my money bills bonds and notes for payment of money equally to be divided between them . . . And I do hereby constitute and ordain and appoint my said sons John Weeks & William Weeks Executors of this my last Will and Testament.

In witness whereof I the said Joshua Weeks have hereunto set my hand & seal the day and year above written &c

Signed sealed published & declared by the said Joshua Weeks to be his last Will and Testament in the presence of us

James Brackett
Marthy Brackett   Joshua Weeks   (SEAL.)
Richard Young

Be it known unto all men by these presents that whereas I Joshua Weeks of Greenland in the Province of New Hampshire Gent. have made and declared my last Will and Testament in writing bareing date the second day of November Anno Domini one thousand seven hundred and fifty-two I the said Joshua Weeks by this present Codicil do ratify & confirm my said last Will and Testament only by this Codicil do explain my true intent and meaning how & in what manner my household stuffs shall be divided that is given to my four daughters (viz) Mary Chesley Martha Hilton Comfort Weeks and Margaret Smith after the fifth part thereof be taken care of by my executors as mentioned in my said last Will and Testament for my two Grandaughters (viz) Margaret Marshall and Comfort Marshall and that is to say my two Executors that I have appointed shall and are hereby ordered to divide my said household stuff that remains into four equall parts for quantity and quality and my said four daughters to draw lots for them.

I give and bequeath unto Joshua Weeks my grandson, the son of my son William Weeks my upper case and bottles lock and key belonging thereunto : and to my household stuff belongs the Suttle in the corn barn and what therein is, the cask in my cellars are not ment houshold stuff nor anything that in them is . . further I give unto my grandson said Joshua Weeks son of my son William Weeks my trunk that I usually put my cloths in.

In confirmation whereof I do hereunto set my hand and seal the eleventh day of January in the thirtyeth year of his majestys reign Anno Domini 1757

Signed sealed published pronounced & declared by the said Joshua Weeks as part of his last Will and Testament in presence of us the subscribers

Nathanael Goss		
Richd Young	Joshua Weeks	SEAL.
Richd R. Goss		
his mark		

A true copy attest Andrew J. Brown Register

NOTE V.

REV. SAMUEL WEEKS the first settled minister in Parsonsfield, Me., in the midst of his usefulness, was in one night crippled and unfitted for labor in the great and destitute field where he had been located.

In the cold winter weather, he left his home, having been called to solemnize a marriage, in Effingham or Porter. After this ministerial duty, he left the place, intending to visit in Hiram; but a blinding storm arose, and he was unable to find his way through the forest by the spotted trees till night set in, and he had no hope of reaching any human habitation till morning. He well knew that if he ceased to exercise, he would perish, with the cold; and so continued his walk, in a circle, round some trees, through the long night. In the morning his cries for help brought to his aid some persons from a house not far distant from the spot where he passed the night. He was so badly frozen, that parts of his feet were amputated; and the whole nervous system had received a shock from which he never recovered. Though he survived this terrible experience for thirty years, he remained an invalid, confined mostly to his house, seeming to have lost his interest in the world and its affairs, spending his days alone, sitting, with his Bible on his knees, in study and meditation. By the fearful exposure, he endured in that one cold night, his large family were deprived of the care of a fond father, and a large parish was deprived of the services of its pastor.

NOTE VI.

REV. JOSHUA W. WEEKS AND REV. JACOB BAILEY DIED IN BANISHMENT.

If we knew all the circumstances, we should be compelled to admit that the preachers in the Episcopal churches, at the time of the Declaration of Independence, deserved more sympathy and less censure than they have received. Most of them had from childhood been trained up to believe that *theirs* was the only true church and that the king of England was the *head* of the church. They had been accustomed to pray for the king, in the sacred language of the Prayer Book, and to alter it seemed like an alteration of the Holy Bible. Besides, they had been supported by the government, and it seemed ungrateful to rebel against those from whom they had so long received their bread. The government expected that the pastors, dependent upon its bounty, would use all their influence to hold their flocks in subjection to the king of England. There were spies watching these preachers, and if anything was uttered, in sermons, prayers or private conversation, which showed any sympathy for the rebels, it was reported to the rulers. If they felt any desire for the independence of the colonies, they could indulge no hope that these few and poor people of the colonies could ever succeed in a war against the most powerful nation in the world. It is hard for us, at this day, to fully appreciate their trials. It was a gloomy prospect for the poor preacher, with a large family, to be shut out from the parish over which he had been placed, and to be deprived of the small stipend he had received from the government to which he had trusted for support.

They doubtless believed that the government under which they lived was "ordained of God," and that it was a Christian duty for every man to live in subjection " to the higher powers." It was hard for many good men to believe that the political opinions, imported from France, were not inseparably connected with the infidel ideas of Thomas Paine and his associates, that no man owes any allegiance to the King of kings. They dreaded to see the government of England exchanged for the government of a rabble.

NOTE VII.

When the Duke of Kent, a son of George III, and the father of Queen Victoria, was commander of the English forces in Nova Scotia, etc., he visited Annapolis, where Rev. J. Bailey was rector of the church. Among those who came to bid him welcome was a company of lads one of whom attracted his special attention. Upon inquiring his name he learned that it was Charles Percy Bailey, a son of the rector of the little church in the place; and he found it not difficult to persuade the father to allow him to take the youth under his own special care. So Charles P. Bailey was taken to England, placed in the military secretary's office, and subsequently commissioned captain, in (the First Royals) the Duke's own regiment. At the commencement of the war of 1812, this regiment was ordered to Canada, where Capt. C. P. Bailey was killed on the 5th of July, 1814, in the battle of Chippewa. In this battle Capt. John W. Weeks, a cousin of Captain Bailey, belonged to the 11th U. S. Infantry.

General Scott had ordered the attack in Echelon of the 11th in advance. The colonel, Campbell, was killed early in the battle, and Major McNeal was carried out of his place by his unmanageable horse. This threw a great responsibility upon Captain Weeks. He said that notwithstanding the roar of the battle, he heard, at times, a click near his head, and looking up, he saw just above his head, a leaning tree was chipped by the bullets, which led him to say " that means me." He took the feather from his cap which distinguished him from the soldiers, and resumed the duties of his office. The two armies were approaching in the bloody conflict, till within a few rods of each other, when the firing slackened and Weeks saw, under the rising smoke, a column of the enemy advancing toward the right flank of the brigade. He instantly ordered a change of front, and poured volley after volley into the flank of this column, as it came up at quick step, till nearly opposite this regiment, when it faltered. A British captain dashed forward, waving his sword, to lead on his men. At the suggestion of Weeks, Sergeant Clark, standing near raised his gun to his face and instantly that captain fell, and the column broke, the soldiers running for their lives.

In the report by the British officers, only one captain was killed in that battle, and he was captain Chas. P. Bailey, an own cousin of Capt. J. W. Weeks.

NOTE VIII.

A SKETCH OF CAPTAIN JOHN WEEKS.

This communication in the *Coos County Democrat*, by the Hon. James W. Weeks of Lancaster, may interest your readers in Greenland and vicinity. Mrs. Spaulding (Martha Weeks) told me that she was fifteen years old when she rode on horseback from Greenland to Lancaster. Her brother, John Wingate (who was afterwards a member of Congress), a boy of eight, rode on another horse with the baggage, while his father walked. After a journey of eight days they settled on the border of the meadows in Lancaster, where the family has been one of the most prominent and influential for more than one hundred years. G. O.

"Capt. John Weeks was born at Hampton, February 17, 1749. He was descended in the third degree from Leonard Weeks, who was born in Wells, Somersetshire, England, in 1635, came to Portsmouth in 1656. In 1667 he married Mary, daughter, of Deacon Samuel Haines, of Portsmouth. Both families were somewhat notable in England, as they were entitled to, and held armorial bearings. Leonard Weeks was a man of property and influence. He owned real estate in Portsmouth, and several farms in Greenland, which he, late in life, deeded to his several sons. Captain Weeks was the sixth child of Dr. John Weeks of Hampton and Martha (Wingate) Weeks, sister of Hon. Payne Wingate. Dr. Weeks died in 1763, when the subject of this sketch was fourteen years old, leaving what was then considered a large property. Tradition says it was designed that he (John) should follow the profession of his father, and his education was commenced accordingly. But inheriting what seemed to him a fortune, instead of pursuing his studies and graduating at Harvard, as his older brother had done, he chose to make long tramps for game up the Kennebec, and in other directions. In one of these he is said to have visited, in company with two or three others, the Upper Coos region, when he was but sixteen years old. In 1770 he married Deborah, daughter of James Brackett of Greenland. She was an educated lady, and fitted to adorn any station in life. He held a Lieutenant's commission in the Revolutionary army, and his money was freely spent in the cause of his country. In 1787 he came to Lancaster, made his location of land, and returned. In the spring of 1788 he came to Lancaster, with his daughter, Pattie, to keep his house and his son, John Wingate (a boy six years old). They came by the way of Baker's river and the Connecticut, driving their stock. In the fall, Mrs. Weeks and the remainder of the family, accompanied by numerous relatives and friends who were to settle near them, came through the Notch of the White Mountains. She made the journey on horseback, bringing her youngest child, seven months old, in her lap, and James B., a boy three years old, riding behind her.

"The log house Capt. Weeks built stood at the top of the bank about fifty rods easterly of the house occupied by the late Wm. D. Weeks. The farm he then commenced has (except for a brief period) remained in the Weeks family for about one hundred years. Here in his new home the Captain kept open house and entertained "right royally" any who came to the settlement; of course he soon became poor. He was a man of strong, good sense, fair education, of genial presence, and at once took an active part in the affairs of the settlement. In 1788 he was elected by his district, consisting of Lancaster, Northumberland, Stratford, Dartmouth, Cockburn, Colburn and Percy, a delegate to the convention that ratified the Federal constitution, and was one of the fifty-seven who voted in the affirmative against forty-six in the negative. In 1792 he represented the Coos District in the General Court. He represented the district at other times, was often selectman and generally moderator of the town meetings. He was an active, honest man, and always ready to lend a hand to aid anything that would benefit the town. He died suddenly at Wakefield, in 1818, while on his way from Lancaster to Greenland, aged sixty-eight. His wife, who was one of the noble women of her day, died July 5, 1831, aged eighty-two. They had seven children: Martha, Deborah, John Wingate, Elizabeth, James Brackett, Polly Wiggin and Sally Brackett. They all lived to old age, the earliest death being at sixty-six. All the Captain's children were prominent persons in the communities in which they lived. One Martha (Mrs. Spaulding) died at the age of ninety-nine. Sally (Mrs. Bucknam) still lives at the age of ninety-eight. John W. was an officer in the war of 1812, and served with distinction, having been engaged in nearly all the hard fighting on the northern frontier. He was a man of great influence in the northern part of the state, and held most of the offices in the gift of the people, including four years in Congress."

THE BAILEY (OR BAYLEY) FAMILY.
(No. 15–v.)
This family were among the first settlers of Rowley, Mass.

James[1] and Lydia had born in Rowley :

1 *John,*[2] b. 1642.
2 *James.*[2]
3 *Thomas.*[2]
4 *Samuel,*[2] b. 1658.
John[2] (*James*[1]) m. Mary Mighill, and had :
    1 *Nathaniel,*[3] b. 1675.
    2 *Thos.,*[3] b. 1677.
    3 *James,*[3] b. 1680.
    And two daughters.
Nathaniel[3] (*Jn.,*[2] *James*[1]) m. Sarah Clark and had children :
    1 *Joseph,*[4] b. 1701.
    2 *Nathaniel.*[4]
    3 *Josiah,*[4] b. 1705.
    4 *David,*[4] b. 1707.
    5 *Samuel,*[4] b. 1709.
    And two daughters.
David[4] (*Nath'l*[3] *Jn.,*[2] *James*[1]) m. Mary Hodgkins, and had children :
    1 *Rev. Jacob,*[5] b. 1731; he says " I was born—of honest parents,
    who, notwithstanding they were extremely industrious,
    could obtain but a scanty maintenance for themselves &
    their numerous family." He gives us a gloomy picture of
    the farmers' sons, in the vicinity of his home, but confesses
    the generosity of his pastor who kindly encouraged him to
    study, and offered to instruct him, for a year, without com-
    pensation. Tradition says Dr. John Weeks noticed his lit-
    erary talent, and lent him assistance in completing his
    education. When the doctor aided in securing his services
    as principal of the High School in Hampton, it is not prob-
    able that he expected the teacher would marry his daughter
    Sarah Weeks, one of the younger pupils in the school. But
    the marriage took place a year before his death. (See No
    15–v.)
    2 *David,*[5] b. 1735.
    3 *Pierce,*[5] b. 1738.
    4 *Amos,*[5] b. 1740.
    5 *John,*[5] b. 1741.
    6 *Nath'l,*[5] b. 1743.
    7 *Ezekiel,*[5] b. 1748.
(See History of Rowley, p. 438.)

BARTLETT FAMILY.
(No. 16–x.)

Richard, John and three others of the name came to Newbury in 1635.

Richard,[1] a shoemaker, brother to John, died 25 May, 1647. Sons:

  1 *John.*[2]
  2 *Christopher.*[2]
  3 *Samuel,*[2] b. 20 Feb., 1646.
  4 *Richard.*[2]
Richard[2] (*Jn.,*[1] or *Richard*[1]), b. 1621; m. Abigail, who d. 1 Mar., 1687. He d. 1698. Sons:
  1 *Richard,*[3] b. 21 Feb., 1649.
  2 *Thos.*[3]
  3 *Jn.,*[3] b. 1655.
Richard[3] (*Richard,*[2] *Richard*[1]), m. 18 Nov., 1673, Hannah Emery; had sons:
  1 *Richard,*[4] b. 1676.
  2 *John,*[4] b. 1678.
  3 *Sam'l,*[4] b. 1680; d. 1685.
  4 *Daniel.*[4]
  5 *Joseph,*[4] b. 1686.
  6 *Sam'l,*[4] b. 1689.
  7 *Stephen,*[4] b. 21 Apr., 1691.
  8 *Thos.,*[4] b. 1695.
Stephen[4] (*Richard,*[3] *Richard,*[2] *Richard*[1]), m.; res. in Amesbury; had five sons.
  1 *Josiah.*[5]
  2 *Joseph.*[5]
  3 *Reuben.*[5]
Hon. Josiah[5] (*Stephen,*[4] *Richard,*[3] *Richard,*[2] *Richard*[1]), governor of N. H., etc., b. in Amesbury 21 Nov., 1729; settled in Kingston; m. 15 Jan., 1754, Mary Bartlett of Newton, his cousin, who d. 1789. He d. 19 May, 1795. Children:
  1 *Hon. Levi,*[6] b. 1763; res. in Kingston.
  2 *Hon. Josiah,*[6] b. 1768; M.D., settled in Stratham; m. Hannah Weeks; d. *s. p.*
  3 *Hon. Ezra,*[6] b. 1770. Had son, Dr. Josiah Bartlett,[7] b. 1803; m. Hannah E. Weeks Thompson; practised in Stratham; was killed on the railway by an accident in May, 1853. He was a man of worth and greatly missed in the church and by the citizens in the town.

BRACKETT FAMILY.
(No. 15–vi.)

Anthony Brackett[1] is said to have come from Wales, emigrated in 1631 and settled at Strawberry Bank (Ports-

17

mouth), N. H.   In 1640, with nineteen others, he conveyed by deed fifty acres of land to the church wardens of
that place for establishing a church.   He afterward settled
on a farm, partly in Stratham and partly in Greenland,
owned in 1860 by D. Littlefield, and died in 1691.

Children :

    1 *Anthony.*[2] ⎫
    2 *Seth.*[2]   ⎬ They settled in Casco, now Portland.
    3 *Thomas.*[2]   ⎭

Thomas[2] (*Anthony*[1]), m. Mary Milton; they had four children.   On
11 Aug., 1676, he was shot by Indians, and his wife with three children was carried into captivity where she d. soon after.   The children
were redeemed by their grandparents, and brought back to Greenland.

Joshua[3] (*Thos.,*[2] *Anthony*[1]), lived with his grandfather, Anthony; m.
Mary (dau. of Leonard) Weeks of Greenland, and had eight children
baptized in 1712.

    1 *Capt. John,*[4] b. 1700; m. Eliz. Pickering; had: (1) Thomas,[5]
        bapt. 1727. (2) Sam'l. (3) Jn., d. 1800. (4) Geo., b. 1737;
        d. 1825, and left $5000, the income of which is to aid in sup-
        porting public worship in the Cong. Church of Greenland,
        $2600 to the Academy in Hampton, and $2000 to aid in
        founding Brackett Academy in Greenland besides other
        bequests.
    2 *Joshua,*[4] of Portland, Me., in 1741.
    3 *Thomas.*[4]
    4 *Sam'l,*[4] of Newmarket; d. 1767.
    5 *Anthony,*[4] of Portland.
    6 *Mary,*[4] d.
    7 *Abigail.*[4]
    8 *Eleanor,*[4] who m. ——— Folsom, and had six children.
    9 *Capt. or Dea. James,*[4] b. 3 Jan., 1714; m., 1st, 24 May, 1739,
        Martha Cate, and had thirteen children.   He was a farmer
        in Greenland.
    10 *Keziah,*[4] b. 1717; m. H. Clark of Greenland, and had eight
        children.
    11 *Margaret,*[4] d. before 1749.
    12 *Nathaniel,*[4] b. 1721; m. Elizabeth ——— ; res. on the home-
        stead, and d. 1778.

Capt. or Dea. James[4] (*Josh.,*[3] *Thos.,*[2] *Anthony*[1]), farmer of Greenland,
born 1714, died 1803, and his wife Martha (Cate), had b. in Greenland :

    1 *Joseph,*[5] b. 14 July, 1740; m. wid. Mary Nye (dau. Dr. Jn.
        Weeks); a lawyer, and a soldier in the Revolutionary war;
        res. in Lancaster and d. 16 Apr., 1813.   Had four children,
        two of whom married children of Capt. John Weeks.
    2 *Judith,*[5] b. 1742; m. ——— Clark of Stratham, and d. Apr., 1811.
    3 *Ebenezer,*[5] b. Nov., 1743; m. ——— Locke of Epsom, and d. there
        in 1820.
    4 *Martha,*[5] b. Dec., 1745; m. Jn. Parrot; res. in Greenland, and
        d. Dec., 1826.

5 *Mary*,[5] b. Dec., 1747; d. Nov., 1817; m. Tufton Wiggin of Stratham.

6 *Deborah*,[5] b. Dec., 1749; w. of Capt. Ju. Weeks, of Lancaster. (See No. 15-vi.)

7 *Dr. James*,[5] b. Oct., 1751; m. a sister of Adino Nye; res. in Lee, then in Lancaster; d. 1802.

8 *Prudence*,[5] b. May, 1753; m., 1st, Richard Haines; 2nd, —— Sanborn; d. 1843.

9 *Joshua*,[5] b. 29 Mar., 1755; inherited the homestead; m. Alice Pickering; res. in Greenland; d. June, 1817.

10 *Comfort*,[5] b. Feb., 1757; m. —— Neal; res. in New York State.

11 *Hannah*,[5] b. 22 Feb., 1759; m., 1st, S. Craighton; 2nd, J. Calph of Sanbornton.

12 *Benj.*,[5] a merchant in Me.; m.; his dau. m. Dr. Trafton of Berwick.

13 *John*,[5] b. 13 June, 1762; d. March, 1765.

THE BURLEY FAMILY*
(No. 5-i, 5-x)

Descended from **Giles**,[1] of Ipswich in 1648, who died before June, 1668, leaving children :

1 *Andrew.*[2]
2 *James.*[2]
3 *Giles.*[2]

Andrew[2] (*Giles*[1]), b. 1657; m. Mary Conant, and had children :
1 *Rebecca*[4], b. 1683.
2 *Hon. Andrew*,[3] b. June, 1694, who m., 1st, Lydia Pengry; 2nd, Hannah Burnham, and had: (1) Andrew,[4] bapt. 1719. (2) Lydia who m. Sam'l Williams, jr., of Ipswich; etc.

James[2] (*Giles*[1]), b. 1659; m. Rebecca Stacy, and d. in Exeter abt. 1721; had children:
1 *William*,[3] b. in Ipswich, 1693, who was at Newmarket, 1746.
2 *Joseph*,[3] d. in Newmarket, 1761.
3 *Thomas.*[3]
4 *James*,[3] b. in Exeter, 1699.
5 *Josiah.*[3]
6 *Giles*,[3] b. 1703.

William[3] (*Jas.*,[2] *Giles*[1]), had children :
1 *John*,[4] b. in Ipswich, 18 Dec., 1717; d. in Newmarket 1776; m., 1st, Sarah Hall of Newfields; 2nd, Elizabeth Chesley; 3rd, Mehitable Sheafe of Portsmouth; children: (1) Sarah,[5] w. of Gen. Jos. Hill. (2) John, b. 1745; m. Anna Hilton. (3) Elizabeth, w. of Dan'l Hill. (4) Margaret, b. 1770, w. of Geo. Frost of Durham, who had: (a) Wm. P.,[6] and (b) George (Frost).
2 *William*,[4] b. 1721; m. Olive —— and had: (1) Eliz.[5] w. of Nath'l Weeks of Loudon, and d. *s. p.* (See No. 13-vi.)

---

* See Burley Gen., by Chas. Burleigh of Portland, Me.

THE CHAPMAN FAMILY.

It is supposed that between 1630 and 1680, more than twenty persons, named Chapman, came from England to America. Some settled in the Middle States. Rev. F. W. Chapman prepared a genealogy of Robert Chapman of Saybrook, Conn., and descendants, and valuable notes upon the families of William, Edward, John and Rev. Benjamin, all of the same state.

Chas. B. Gerard, Esq., of Anderson, Ind., compiled a genealogy of the family of Ralph Chapman of Duxbury, Mass., and the writer has collected extensive records of the family of

Edward Chapman of Ipswich, Mass., who married, first, 1642, Mary, daughter of Mark Symonds, and had :

Simon² (or Symonds), (*Edward¹*), b. 1643; m. Mary, dau. of John Brewer, and had :
>1 *Edward,*³ b. in Rowley 11 May, 1669.
>2 *John,*³ m. Mercy (dau. of Paul) Wentworth.
>3 *Samuel,*³ b. 28 Oct., 1680, in Ipswich; m. Ester Harris; had six daughters and a son: (1) Samuel,⁴ who is supposed to have joined the church in Scarboro, Me., in Mar., 1730.
>4 *Joseph,*³ b. 1682; m. 5 Feb., 1707, Mary (dau. of Paul) Wentworth of Rowley.
>5 *Stephen,*³ b. 1685.
>*And others.*

Nathaniel² (*Edward¹*) m. 1674, Mary Wilborn.
Mary² (*Edward¹*), w. of John Burney.
Samuel² (*Edward¹*), b. 1654; m. May, 1678, Ruth (dau. of Samuel) Ingalls; rem. to North hill in Hampton, now North Hampton; d. 1722. Had born, in Ipswich, eight children :
>1 *Samuel,*³ b. 12 Feb., 1679; m. 1702, Phebe Balch, and rem. first to Hampton, and abt. 1714 to Greenland; had ten children, and d. Apr., 1742.
>2 *John,*³ m. Mar., 1705, Dorothy Chase, and d. Oct., 1705. His posthumous son was : (1) John,⁴ b. Nov., 1705; m. Huldah Hoyt, had four children, and rem. to Epping. Children : (a) Mary,⁵ b. 1730. (b) John, b. Jan., 1734. (c) Edmund, b. in Kensington, 20 Oct., 1736. (d) Hannah, b. Feb., 1739; m. Cole Weeks of Sanbornton, and had ten children.
>3 *Joseph,*³ b. 1685; d. in Hampton, 1750, unm.
>4 *Ruth,*³ b. 1687; m. ―――― Eaton.
>5 *Edward,*³ d. young.
>6 *Mary,*³ d. in Hampton, 1740, unm., æ. 49.
>7 *Job,*³ b. 1693; m., 1st, Mary Chase; 2nd, Rachel Goss. Had four children by first wife, and four daughters by second

wife; d. Sept., 1763. His son: (1) Samuel,[4] b. 1726, was ancestor of the family in North Hampton.

8 *Edmund*,[3] d. unm. at Hampton, 20 Feb., 1739, æ. 42.

John[2] (*Edward*[1]), m. Sept., 1675, Rebecca Smith and d. 10 Nov., 1677. He left a son:

  1 *John*,[3] b. 7 July, 1676; m. 28 Oct., 1702, Eliz. Davis, and had five children: (1) Martha,[4] b. 1703. (2) Elizabeth. (3) Rebecca, b. 1713. (4) John, b. 2 Jan., 1715. (5) Davis, b. 26 Jan., 1717.

Samuel[3] (*Sam.*[2] *Edw.*[1]), b. 1679, d. 1742, and his wife Phebe, had born in Hampton:

  1 *Paul*[4], b. 4 Nov., 1704; m. Mary (dau. of Sam'l) Weeks of Greenland. Children: (1) Samuel,[5] b. Jan. 1745; m. Betsey ———; res. in Wakefield, and had: (a) Betsey,[6] (b) Lydia. (2) Job, b. 1 Nov., 1747; m. 8 Jan., 1771, Penelope Philbrook and had b. in Greenland: (a) Benjamin, b. 1773; m. S. Wedgewood and d., s. p., June, 1826. (b) Job, d. June, 1822, unm. (c) Eliphalet, b. 1778; m. Peggy Kennison; had nine children; d. 1863. (d) Sam'l, b. 11 May, 1781; m., 1st, Elizabeth Folsom; 2nd, Mary Hoit; had six children, of whom the eldest was the eldest, and d. in Tamworth, Oct., 1857. (e) Mary, w. of Bradbury Jewell. (f) John, m. Mercy Ballard, and d. 1812. (g) Joseph, b. 1791; m., 1st, Huldah Howard; 2nd, Julia Atkinson, and d. Sept., 1869. In 1793 Job rem. to Deerfield, and in 1802, with his seven children, to Tamworth where his twenty-three grandchildren were born.

  2 *Samuel*,[4] b. 1706; m., 1st, ——— York; 2nd, ———; settled in Newmarket. Had: (1) John,[5] b. 1730, of Newmarket. (2) Samuel, b. 1734; m. Mary Barber and d. 1809. (3) Benjamin, b. Jan., 1737; m. Mary Brackett, had: (a) Paul,[6] (b) John, (c) Joseph, and others. (4) Edmund, b. Feb., 1741. (5) Rev. Eliphaz, b. 7 Mar., 1750; m. Hannah Jackman, and had a large family in Bethel, Me. (6) David, b. 7 Dec., 1752; m. Elizabeth Clark of Stratham, and settled in Newmarket. He had five daughters and four sons.

  3 *Penuel*,[4] b. May, 1711; m. Sarah Lebbee; had four children; d. in Raymond, Sept., 1788. Had: (1) Samuel,[5] of Epsom. (2) Tryphena, b. in Exeter, Nov., 1758; m. Jona. Ellsworth, and rem. to Vermont. (3) Sarah, m Aaron Ellsworth. (4) Ruth, 2nd wife of A. Ellsworth, who d. 1818.

  4 *Joseph*,[4] b. 10 June, 1713, of Newmarket and Exeter; m. Mary Winn, and had: (1) Capt. Levi,[5] b. 1754, who went from Epping to Nottingham and had seven children. (2) Smith, b.———; m. 1779, Sarah Foss Burley, and had: (a) Levi.[6] (b) Kate. (c) Nancy, w. of Paul Chapman. (d) Mary, w. of Thos. York. (e) Jas. Burleigh, b. 1784, who m. Hannah Fernald.

THE CHESLEY FAMILY.
(No. 5–iii; 12–iv.)

Philip,[1] of Dover, 1642; Oyster River, 1644; married Elizabeth ———; d. before 1685; had:

1 *Thomas.*[2]
2 *Philip.*[2]

Thomas[2] (*Philip*[1]), b. 1644; m. about 1663, Elizabeth Thines; had eight children; was killed by Indians 15 Nov., 1697.   His children were:

    1 *Thomas*,[3] b. 4 June, 1664; constable at Oyster River, 1696; d. before 1708.   He left a son: (1) Samuel,[4] b. 1691.
    2 *John*,[3] m. Hannah ———.
    3 *George*,[3] m. Deliverance ———; d. early.
    4 *Elizabeth*,[3] m. ——— Davis.
    5 *Joseph*,[3] m. Sarah Smith; d. 1731.
    6 *Sarah*.[3]
    7 *Susanna*,[3] w. of Jn. Smith.
    8 *Mary*.[3]

Philip[2] (*Philip*[1]), b. 1646; d. 1695; m. Sarah ———; had:
    1 *Capt. Samuel*,[3] m. Elizabeth ———; was a good soldier; killed 1707.
    2 *James*,[3] m. Tamson Wentworth; was killed 15 Sept., 1707. His son: (1) James,[4] m. Mehitable Waldron.
    3 *Philip*,[3] had grant of land 1694; was living in 1715.
    4 *Ebenezer*.[3]

Ensign Joseph[3] (*Thos.*,[2] *Philip*[1]), d. 1731, and wife Sarah, had:
    1 *Joseph*.[4]
    2 *Thomas*,[4] who m. Mary Hill; bapt. 17 Feb., 1718–19; d. about 1810.
    3 *James*.[4]

Thomas[4] (*Joseph*,[3] *Thos.*,[2] *Philip*[1]) and wife Mary (Hill), had six or more children, among whom were:
    1 *Thomas*.[5]
    2 *Benjamin*,[5] b. about 1741; m. Deborah (dau. of Miles) Randall. Children: (1) Miles,[6] m. Deborah Furber; settled in New Durham. (2) Benjamin, m. ——— Page; settled in Middleton. (3) Isaac, m. a Griffin; res in Rochester; d. *s. p.* (4) Valentine, went to Maine and was lost. (5) James, m. Sally Reynolds; res. and d. on the homestead in Durham. (6) Elder Israel, m. Betsey Folsom; was a Christian Baptist preacher. (7) Thomas, b. 1792; m. Joanna Folsom; res. in Lee. (8) Abigail, m., 1st, a Clark; 2nd, a Hill. (9) Deborah, m. ——— Stone; rem. to Nova Scotia. (10) Susan, m. her cousin Thomas, son of Joseph Chesley. (11) Polly, m. ——— Woodman; rem. to Maine. (12) Nancy, m. ——— Hart; d. in Durham.

THE CLARKE FAMILY.*
(No. 13–vii.)

The Clarke Family of Greenland descended from **Nathaniel**,[1] of Newbury, Mass., who married in 1663, Eliz-

---

* See Clarke Genealogy, by Geo. K. Clarke, 1885.

abeth (daughter of Henry) Somerby, born in 1646, and had eleven children. Of these

1 *Nath'l*,[2] d. 1690, leaving a son.
2 *Thomas*,[2] d. 1722; had eight children.
3 *Rev. John*,[2] of Exeter (Harv. Coll., 1690); organized the First Cong. Ch. in Exeter; m. in 1694, Elizabeth Woodbridge and had four children: (1) Rev. Ward Clark,[3] b. 1703, grad. Harvard Coll., 1723; in 1725, organized the First Church in Kingston, which he served as pastor eleven years, and to which he left, by will, most of his property. His wife was Mary (dau. of Chas.) Frost of Kittery, Me., who d. in 1735, *s. p.*
4 *Josiah*,[2] of Boston.

Henry[2] (*Nath'l*[1]), b. 1673; m., 1st, in 1695, Elizabeth (dau. of Stephen) Greenleaf of Newbury, and had eleven children b. in Newbury. In Jan., 1723-4, he m., 2nd, Mary Peirce, and about 1727 rem. to Greenland, where he d. in 1749.

Enoch[3] (*Henry*,[2] *Nath'i*[1]), b. 1709, was twice married and had seven children.

Henry, jr.[3] (*Henry*,[2] *Nath'l*[1]), m., 1st, 1738, Keziah Brackett; 2nd, Catherine Bean, and had twelve children.

Joseph[4] (*Enoch*,[3] *Henry*,[2] *Nath'l*[1]), b. Jan., 1731-2; m. Eleanor (dau. of Walter) Weeks; had five children, and d. Dec., 1761. His widow m., 2nd, ——— Mason. Had:
1 *Comfort*,[5] m. 1783, John Weeks of Greenland and rem. to Bartlett, N. H., had ten children. He d. in 1825 of a wound received in being thrown from his horse.

THE EASTMAN FAMILY

So numerous and influential in the history of New Hampshire are said to be descended from

Roger Eastman[1] born in Wales, Eng., in 1611, who came to Salisbury, Mass., where he died in 1694. His sons were:

1 *John*,[2] the first male child in Salisbury, Mass., b. Apr., 1640; d. 1720, æ. 80.
2 *Nathaniel*,[2] b. May, 1643; d. 1709.
3 *Philip*,[2] b. 20 Dec., 1644; settled in Haverhill, Mass.; d.
4 *Thomas*,[2] b. Nov., 1646, of Haverhill.
5 *Timothy*,[2] b. 1648, of Hadley, Mass.; m. Lydia Markham.
6 *Joseph*,[2] b. 8 Jan., 1652, of Hadley.
7 *Benjamin*,[2] b. 1653; had five children.
8 *Sam'l*,[2] b. 20 Nov., 1657; in 1686, m., 1st, Eliz. Severance; settled in Kingston, N. H.; m., 2nd, ——— Shuah; d. 27 Feb., 1725, leaving seven sons, of whom were: (1) Samuel,[3] b. 5 Jan., 1696. (2) Joseph, b. 6 Jan., 1698.

John² (*Roger¹*) had:
1 *Zechariah*,³ b. 1679; son: (1) Jeremiah,⁴ b. 1704; m. 10 Feb.,
   1725, Lydia Brown; had b. in Kensington, Dec. 9, 1732: (*a*)
   Jeremiah,⁵ who, in 1762, settled in Deerfield; was twenty
   years town clerk and a very valuable citizen.
Philip,² (*Roger¹*) had:
1 *Capt. Ebenezer*,³ b. 10 Jan., 1689, who m. 4 Mar., 1710, Sarah
   Peaslee; settled in Concord; d. 1748. He had six sons:
   (1) Lt. Eben.,⁴ b. 1711; had eight children; d. 1778; com-
   manded a company at Bunker Hill. (2) Philip, b. 1713; m.
   A. Bradley; three children. (3) Joseph, b. 1715; d. 1803;
   six children. (4) Nathaniel, b. 1717; had six children. (5)
   Moses, b. 1732; had eleven children; d. 1812. (6) Stilson,
   b. 1738. (7) Ruth, m. ——— Weeks.
Samuel² (*Roger¹*), of Kingston, b. 1657; d. 1725; had:
1 *Samuel*,³ b. 5 Jan., 1696; m., 1st, 1728, Sarah Clough; 2nd,
   Shuah Brown.
2 *Joseph*,³ b. 1698.
3 *Ebenezer*,³ b. 11 June, 1702; m. Mary Sleeper.
4 *Thomas*,³ b. 1703.
5 *Timothy*,³ b. 1706.
6 *Edward*,³ b. 30 Mar., 1708.
7 *Benjamin*,³ b. 13 July, 1710.
Samuel³ (*Sam'l*,² *Roger¹*), b. 1696. Children:
1 *Samuel*,⁴ b. 1729.
2 *William*,⁴ b. 1734.
3 *Ezekiel*,⁴ b. 1736.
4 *Lt. Eben.*,⁴ b. 24 Apr., 1746; m. 13 Nov., 1773, Mary Butler.
5 *Nehemiah*.⁴
Lt. Ebenezer⁴ (*Sam'l*,³ *Sam'l*,² *Roger¹*), b. 24 Apr., 1746, and his
wife Mary (Butler), had:
1 *Abigail*.⁵
2 *Eben., jr.*,⁵ b. 1777; m., 1803, Deborah Chesley.
3 *Stephen*,⁵ b. Dec., 1778.
4 *Samuel*.⁵
5 *Nehemiah*,⁵ b. 1782.
6 *Ira Allen*,⁵ b. 1786; d. at sea.
7 *Wm. B.*,⁵ b. 1795.
And five daughters.

THE FOLSOM FAMILY.

(No. 15–x.)

John Folsom,¹ the father of the family in New England, was the son of Adam Foulsham, and was baptized in
Hingham, Eng., in 1615. On the fourth of Oct., 1636,
he married Mary (dau. of Edward) Gilman. In 1638,
he, with the father and the brothers of his wife, "came from
old Hingham in England, to New Hingham, in Mass."

About twelve or fifteen years afterward he removed to
Exeter, N. H., where he died in 1681. His children were :

1 *Sam'l*,[2] bapt. 1641, who m. Mary Robie of Hampton, and had
    six children. His sons were : (1) Eben,[3] (2) Sam'l, (3) Is-
    rael.
2 *John*,[2] bapt. 1641; m. Abigail (dau. of Abr.) Perkins of
    Hampton, and had nine children, of whom (1) John,[3] (2)
    Abraham, and (3) Jonathan, res. in Exeter; (4) Jeremiah
    settled in Newmarket.
3 *Nathaniel*,[2] m. 1674, Hannah Farrow of Ipswich, and had :
    (1) Samuel,[3] b. 1679. (2) Nathaniel. [(3) Jeremiah and (4)
    Edward]?
4 *Israel*,[2] who had a son : (1) Israel,[3] of Newmarket, d. early.
5 *Lt. Peter*,[2] who m. Susanna Cousins, lived south of the road
    from Exeter to Hampton and had six children. His sons
    were : (1) Peter,[3] (2) John, and (3) Benjamin.
6 *Ephraim*,[2] m. Phaltiel Hall, and lived in Newmarket; was
    killed by the Indians in 1709. He had five daughters and
    two sons : (1) Ephraim,[3] and (2) William, of Newmarket.

Dea. John[2] was a man of property and influence and left much land
to his sons :

1 *John*,[3] the eldest, received a large tract of land in the south-
    west of Exeter, near Kingston.
2 *Jeremiah*,[3] had a tract of land near Lamprey river.
3 *Abraham*,[3] } res. near their father.
4 *Peter*,[3] }
5 *Jonathan*,[3] lived on the homestead.

Jeremiah[3] (*Jn.*,[2] *Jn.*[1]), a wealthy farmer in Newmarket, had eight
children :

1 *Elizabeth*,[4] w. of Walter Bryant, Esq.
2 *Susan*,[4] w. of John Mead.
3 *Sarah*,[4] w. of Jacob Low.
4 *Nathan*.[4]
5 *Col. Jeremiah, jr.*,[4] b. 1719; m. Mary Hersey and had ten chil-
    dren one of whom, (1) Levi,[5] m. Joanna (dau. of Dr. Jn.)
    Weeks and settled in Tamworth.
6 *Col. John*,[4] of Stratham.

Jonathan[3] (*Jn.*,[2] *Jn.*[1]) and his w. Anna (Ladd), had several sons
who were prominent men in the Old French War and in the Revolution :

1 *Lt. Jonathan*,[4] b. 1724.
2 *Gen'l Nathaniel*,[4] b. 1726; d. 1790.
3 *Col. Samuel Folsom*,[4] b. 1732; d. 1790.

(See Folsom Genealogy, by J. Chapman.)

THE FOWLER FAMILY.

(See Fowler Family by M. A. Stickney.)

Philip[1] came from Wiltshire, England, and reached
New England in May, 1634. He settled in Ipswich,

Mass., on land still occupied by one of his descendants. His sons, born in England, were:

    1 *Samuel.*[2]
    2 *Joseph.*[2]
    3 *Thomas.*[2]
Joseph[2] (*Philip*[1]), m. Martha (dau. of Richard) Kimball; he was killed by Indians, near Deerfield, 19 May, 1676; had four children:
    1 *Joseph,*[3] b. [1647].
    2 *Philip,*[3] b. 1648.
    3 *John.*[3]
    4 *Mary.*[3]
Philip[3] (*Jos.,*[2] *Philip*[1]), m. 20 Jan., 1672-3, Elizabeth (dau. of Henry) Herrick of Beverly. He was a leading man in the community and opposed the witchcraft delusion in Salem. He had b. in Ipswich:
    1 *Joseph.*[4]
    2 *John.*[4]
    3 *Benj.*[4]
    4 *Philip,*[4] b. 1691.
His daughters were:
    5 *Eliz.*[4]
    6 *Mary.*[4]
    7 *Martha.*[4]
Philip[4] (*Philip,*[3] *Jos.,*[2] *Philip*[1]) m. in Ipswich, July, 1716, Susanna Jacob, and was a tanner in Ipswich. In 1743, he rem. to Newmarket, N. H., where he had purchased " 236 acres, with two houses & barns thereon." In 1760 Josiah Hilton sued him for fifty-six acres of this land and commenced an expensive lawsuit which was continued eighteen years till 1778, when the property which had been taken from their father was restored to the heirs of Philip Fowler, who had sixteen children. (1) Symonds,[5] b. 1734, third son of Philip and Susanna Fowler, m. Hannah Weeks (see No. 7-vii).

THE FRENCH FAMILIES.

Edward[1] of Ipswich, 1636; married Ann ——— ; removed to Salisbury in 1652; died Dec., 1674; left a great estate. Children:

Joseph[2] (*Edw.*[1]), b. in England; m. Susanna——who d. Feb., 1688. His children were:
    1 *Joseph,*[3] b. Mar., 1654; m., 1678, Sarah (dau. of Roger) Eastman, and had: (1) Joseph,[4] b. Mar., 1679. (2) Timothy, b. 1681. (3) Simon, b. 1683.
    2 *Simon,*[3] b. Oct., 1657.
    3 *Edward,*[3] b. 1667; m. Oct., 1695, Mary Winsley, and had: (1) Elisha, b. 1696.

4 *John.*[3]
5 *Sam'l.*[3]

John,[2] (*Edw.*[1]) of Ipswich; m., 1659, Mary Noyes, and rem. to Salisbury. Children:

    1 *John,*[3] b. 1660.
    2 *Edward,*[3] b. July, 1672.
    3 *Nicholas,*[3] d. young.
    4 *James,*[3] b. 15 Aug., 1679.
    5 *Timothy,*[3] b. Aug., 1681; m. Mary—— and had: (1) Josiah,[4]
        b. 1713, who was father of Timothy of Loudon.
    6 *John*[3] (by 2nd wife), b. June, 1686.

Samuel,[2] (*Edw.*[1]) m. June, 1664, Abigail Brown and had sons:

    1 *Samuel,*[3] b. Mar., 1672.
    2 *Henry,*[3] b. 1673.
    3 *Nath'l,*[3] b. Dec., 1678.

Nathaniel[3] (*Sam'l,*[2] *Edw.*[1]), born 1678, died 1750; m. Sarah ——;
rem. to Kingston, and had sons:

    1 *Samuel,*[4] m. Abigail Godfrey, and res. in E. Kingston, and had
        four children.
    2 *Nath'l, jr.*[4]
    3 *Jonathan.*[4]
    4 *Benjamin,*[4] who lived on the homestead.
    5 *Elizabeth.*[4]
    6 *Sarah.*[4]
    7 *Mary.*[4]

Several descendants of this family went to Gilmanton.

William[1] of Stratham had, in Nov., 1708, married Abigail, born 1670 (dau. of Andrew Wiggin, sen.), and her parents gave them one hundred and ten acres of land in Stratham. In 1721, William French and John Sinkler were selectmen.

In June, 1746, William and Abigail French, in a deed, name three of their sons:

    1 *Thomas.*[2]
    2 *Bradstreet.*[2]
    3 *William, jr.*[2]

They are supposed to have had daughters:

    4 *Hannah.*[2]
    5 *Mary.*[2]

And probably other children.

Thomas[2] (*Wm.*[1]) married Eleanor —— and had born in Stratham:

    1 *Thomas,*[2] b. 14 March, 1739.
    2 *Mehitable,*[3] b. 1741; m. Moses Clarke of Stratham.

They had other children, whose names are not recorded.

Thomas[3] (*Thos.,*[2] *Wm.*[1]) b. 14 Mar., 1739; m. Anna (dau. of Abr.) Tilton; d. 21 Oct., 1775; had b. in Stratham, six children:

    1 *Thomas,*[4] b. Mar., 1765.
    2 *Anna,*[4] b. Mar., 1767.

3 *Abraham*,[4] b. 21 Oct., 1768; m. 1796, Hannah Lane.
4 *Daniel T.*,[4] b. 21 Aug., 1771; m. —— Tuck of Brentwood.
5 *Levi*,[4] b. 9 Oct., 1773; m. —— Neal; res. in Lee.
6 *Mark*,[4] b. 27 June, 1775; m. —— Locke of Epsom, d. *s. p.*
About 1781, his widow, Anna, m. Nath'l Avery, and had other children.

THE FROST FAMILY

Descended from **Nicholas Frost**,[1] born in Tiverton, Eng., in 1589, who settled in Kittery, at Sturgeon's Creek in 1636, and died 20 July, 1663, aged 74. His sons were:

1 *Maj. Charles*,[2] b. 20 July, 1631; an active and useful officer in the Indian wars; a representative of the town in the Legislature; was waylaid and killed by the Indians, on the 4 July, 1697, leaving a wid. Mary and two minor sons: (1) Charles,[3] m. Sarah, and had a dau. (a) Mary,[4] w. of Rev. Ward Clark of Kingston. (2) John.
2 *John.*[2]
3 *Nicholas*,[2] who d. *s. p.*
Hon. John[3] (*Chas.*,[2] *Nicholas*[1]), b. Kittery, 1 Mar., 1682; m. Mary (sister of Sir Wm.) Pepperrell and settled in New Castle, and d. 1732, æ. 51. He had seventeen children of whom
   1 *Joseph*[4] (9th ch.), b. 1717; m. Margarette Cotton, and had eleven children. He was a merchant in New Castle where he d. in 1768, æ. 50.
   2 *Hon. Geo.*[4] (11th ch.), b. 26 Apr., 1720; res. New Castle, was Councillor, Delegate, Judge, etc.; m., 2nd, Mrs. Margaret Smith, dau. of Capt. Joshua Weeks of Greenland; rem. to Durham, where he d. 26 June, 1796. Their ch. (1) George[5] who m. Margaret Burley. (2) Mary, w. of Jere. Mead of Newmarket. (3) Martha, w. of Henry Mellen. (4) John, b. 1776, m. —— Salter of Portsmouth and d. *s. p.* in 1847.

THE HAINES FAMILY OF N. H.
(No. 1–ii, 10–i.)

Dea. **Samuel Haines**[1], born in England about 1611, came to New England, on the ship "Angel Gabriel," in 1635, and was wrecked at Pemaquid, Me. Aug. 15, about

1638, he returned to England, and married at Dilton, near Westbury, in Wiltshire, April 1, 1638, Ellenor Neate. On his return, settled at Dover, N. H. About 1650, he removed to Portsmouth, residing in the parish of Greenland till his death, about 1686. He was a prominent citizen, serving as selectman ten years, from 1653 to 1663; and was, at the organization of the First Congregational Church in Portsmouth, ordained deacon in 1671. His children were:

1 *Mary*,[2] m., abt. 1667, Leonard Weeks, b. in England abt. 1635.
2 *Samuel*,[2] b. 1646; m. 9 Jan., 1672-3, Mary Fifield of Hampton, and d. 1688-89.
3 *Matthias*,[2] b. 1650; m. 28 Dec., 1671, Jane (dau. Anthony) Brackett, and d. 1688-9.

Samuel[2] (*Sam'l*[1]) had children:
1 *Sarah*,[3] b. 6 Oct., 1673, w. of Nath'l Huggins, sen.
2 *Eleanor*,[3] b. 23 Aug., 1675; m. her cousin, Capt. Samuel Weeks; d. 19 Nov. 1736.
3 *Matthias*,[3] b. 7 Mar., 1676-7; m. Mehitable Jenness of Rye, and was Dea. of the Cong. Church in Greenland; d. 9 Apr., 1745.
4 *William*,[3] b. 7 Jan., 1678-9; m. 4 Jan., 1704-5, Mary Lewis of Casco Bay, and d. 1760. He had four sons and four daus.: (1) Sarah V.,[4] b. 1705. (2) Mary, b. 1707. (3) Margaret, b. 1710. (4) Matthias, b. 1713. (5) Wm., b. 1715. (6) David, b. 1717. (7) Eleanor, b. 1719. (8) John, b. 1723.
5 *Mary*,[3] b. 27 Jan., 1685-6, w. of Michael Hicks.
6 *Samuel*,[3] b. 5 July, 1687; m. Mehitable Crosby, and d. 7 Sept., 1750.

Dea. Matthias[3] (*Sam'l*,[2] *Sam'l*[1]) had b. in Greenland:
1 *Samuel*,[4] b. 20 Apr., 1716; m. Sarah Whidden.
2 *Joseph*,[4] m. Mary Berry and had five daus.: (1) Eleanor, (2) Hannah, (3) Lydia. (4) Mehitable, (5) Mary.

Samuel[4] (*Matt.*,[3] *Sam'l*,[2] *Sam'l*[1]) of Greenland and Wakefield, had children:
1 *Joseph*,[5] b. 1745; m. Betsey Holt, and d. Jan. 1828.
2 *Matthias*,[5] b. 3 Jan., 1750; m. Mary Edgerly, and in 1796 settled in Loudon; d. 20 Mar., 1838.
3 *Samuel*,[5] b. 15 Aug., 1752; m. Susanna Goss and d. 1838; had four daughters.

Matthias[5] (*Sam'l*,[4] *Matt.*,[3] *Sam'l*,[2] *Sam'l*[1]) had children:
1 *John*,[6] b. 1772.
2 *Sam'l*,[6] b. 1774.
3 *Matthias*,[6] b. 1775.
4 *Polly*,[6] b. 1779.
5 *Sally*,[6] b. 1783.
6 *Joseph*,[6] b. 13 July, 1784; m 13 Sept., 1806, Martha G. Dwinell of Salem, Mass., and d. 29 Nov., 1828. They had five sons and three daus.

Joseph[6] (*Matt.,*[5] *Sam'l,*[4] *Matt.,*[3] *Sam'l,*[2] *Sam'l*[1]) had b. in Canterbury :

1 *Andrew Mack*[7] (seventh child), b. 1 Jan., 1820, m. 17 Aug. 1842, Angeline E. Woodbury of Lynn, Mass., and in 1839 settled in Galena, Ill. During forty years he has, at much expense, collected records of thousands of the Haines family, in America and England, besides lending aid to many others, in their genealogical researches. It is to be hoped that before long the results of his labors may be published for the benefit of his own family and other families connected with it. (See N. E. Hist. & Gen. Register, XXIII, pp. 148–169—his Pedigree.)

THE HALL FAMILIES OF DOVER.

John[1]* brought from England three sons, Ralph, John and Stephen. Stephen settled in Massachusetts ; perhaps father of the Haverhill family.

Ralph[2] (*Jn.*[1]) b. in England about 1619 ; of Exeter, 1639 ; Dover, 1650 ; returned to Exeter, 1664 ; was lieutenant, lot layer, etc. He m. Mary ———— ; had children :

1 *Phaltiel,*[3] w. of Eph. Folsom.
2 *Joseph,*[3] m. Mary (dau. of Edw.) Hilton ; had : (1) Joseph,[4] who d. 1767. (2) Edward of Newmarket, who m. Mary Wilson and had five daughters : (a) Ann,[5] m., in Exeter, 5 Apr., 1730, Rev. John Moody.
3 *Capt. Kinsley,*[3] m., 1674, Eliz. (dau. of Rev. Sam'l) Dudley.

John[2] (*Jn.*[1]) in England about 1620–21 ; m. Esther (dau. of Philip) Chesley in 1647 ; deacon ; d. in 1693 or 94 ; was a man of many offices and excellent character. Children :

1 *John,*[3] b. about 1649 ; m. 8 Nov., 1671, Abigail (dau. of John) Roberts ; had children : (1) ·John,[4] b. 1673. (2) Thos., and (3) Abigail, b. 1680.
2 *Ralph,*[3] m. Mary (dau. of Philip) Chesley ; had : (1) Hateevil,[4] (2) Nath'l, and perhaps others.

Kinsley[3] (*Ralph,*[2] *Jn.*[1]), of Dover and of Exeter, and wife Eliz. had :

1 *Josiah,*[4] ancestor of Governor Langdon ;·m., 1719, Mrs. H., (widow of John) Light. Six children.
2 *Paul.*[4]
3 *Eliz.*[4]
4 *Mary.*[4]
5 *Mercy,*[4] m. Dudley Hilton, who, in 1710, was taken or killed by the Indians.

---

* There was a John Hall in Kittery, Me., in 1640 and 1650 ; also Peter, Thomas and Eleazer, and a Samuel Hall in Salisbury, Mass.

A John Hall resided on the Neck till 1650. Then Sergeant John Hall resided on the line between Dover and Portsmouth; made will, Aug., 1677; had wife Elizabeth and son Joseph, who died 1685. We know of no connection between the two families.

THE HILTON FAMILY OF NEWMARKET.

Edward Hilton[1], with his brother William, came from England and in 1623 settled at Dover Neck, where he was one of the most influential of the early settlers. In 1652, having received a grant of land at Newfields, a part of Exeter, now called South Newmarket, he had removed to that place, where he died in 1671. He had four sons and two daughters.

> 1 *Edward*,[2] b. 1626; m. Ann (dau. of Sam'l) Dudley, b. Oct., 1641. In 1660, he purchased of the Sagamore of Washucke a large tract of land, and d. in 1699. His children were: (1) Winthrop,[3] (2) Dudley, (3) Joseph. And four daughters.
> 2 *Capt. William*,[2] b. 1632; d. 1690, leaving a son: (1) Richard.[3]
> 3 *Samuel.*[2]
> 4 *Charles*,[2] d. unm.
> Col. Winthrop[3] (*Edw.*[2], *Edw.*[1]) [b. 1671]? m. Ann Wilson. He was a military officer,—in 1706, Judge of Court of Common Pleas; was killed by the Indians, while at work with his men, in June, 1710. He had five daughters and a posthumous son:
> 1 *Col. Winthrop*,[4] b. 21 Dec., 1710; m. Mrs. Martha Wiggin, dau. of Capt. Joshua Weeks of Greenland, and had: (1) Winthrop,[5] jr., b. 1737; d. 11 Jan., 1775; leaving three sons: (a) Andrew,[6] (b) Ichabod, (c) Winthrop. (2) Ichabod, b. 1740, m. Susanna Smith, and d. 1822. (3) Ann, b. 1745, w. of John Burleigh, who d. 1769, leaving (a) Martha, w. of Col. Eben Thompson of Portsmouth.

The descendants of Edward Hilton became quite numerous and influential, and still hold a part of the land he owned. Judge John Kelley of Exeter, married Susan

Hilton, and prepared a valuable genealogy of this family, to which I am much indebted for aid in preparing this sketch.

William Hilton, brother of Edward,[1] came from London to Plymouth in New England, Nov. 11, 1621, and wrote back a glowing account of the condition of the colony and the people. In 1631, he had removed to the settlement of Piscataqua river where his brother Edward lived. He was afterward at Exeter, then in possession of the marshes at Oyster River. In 1645, or soon after, he had removed to Kittery Point. He had a wife and a son William and probably others. In the Historic Genealogic Register, Vol. XXXI, p. 179, John T. Hassam, A.M., of Boston, has given a very learned and interesting genealogy of the family of William Hilton.

THE HOWE FAMILY
(No. 40–iii)

From whom Hon. Nath'l, Hon. John W. and Hon. Timothy O. Howe descended. **John Howe,**[1] of Marlboro, Mass., died 1680. In 1656, John Howe and others of Sudbury, Mass., petitioned for a grant of land in a place eight miles west. In 1660, a section, some six miles square, was incorporated as Marlboro, and lots were assigned to John Howe, jr., Abraham and Samuel Howe.

1 *Thos.*[2] b. 1656; d. 1733; was a prominent man in Marlboro. Jonathan[3] (*Thos.*,[2] *Jn.*[2]), b. 23 Apr., 1687; d. 1738.
Eliakim[4] (*Jona* ,[3] *Thos.*,[2] *Jn.*[1]), b. 1723; was an early settler of Henniker, N. H.; m. 15 Dec., 1747, Matilda, b. 1732; had:
   2 *Otis,*[5] b. 1748.
3 *Rev. Tilly,*[6] (Dart. Coll., 1788); d. 1830; unm.
Otis[5] (*Eliak.*,[4] *Jona.*,[3] *Thos.*,[2] *Jn.*[1]) b. 3 Oct., 1748; m. 5 Nov., 1770, Lucy Goodell of Marlboro, Mass., and in 1781 rem. to Hillsboro, N. H.; had fourteen children. Of these,

1 *Nathan,*[6] rem. to western New York; had: (*a*) Hon. Jn. Waite
Howe[7] of Franklin, Pa.
2 *Solomon*[6] was forty years a preacher; had seven children; d.
in Smyrna, N. Y., 1859.
Hon. Nath'l[6] (*Otis,*[5] *Eliak.,*[4] *Jona.,*[3] *Thos.,*[2] *Jn.*[1]) b. 1776; m. Mary
Chase of Paris, Me.; a lawyer, settled first in Paris, then in Bridgton,
Me.; had seven children; d. in Waterford, Me., Jan., 1829. His eldest son,
1 *Algernon S.,*[7] m. Carrie M. Bradbury of Standish, Me.; had:
(1) Anna M.,[8] d. 1888.
2 *Mary,*[7] a teacher in Bethel and in Norridgewock, Me.; m., in
1840, Rev. Jacob Chapman; d. April, 1869, in Deerfield,
N. H., *s. p.*
3 *Charles T.,*[7] is a farmer in So. Waterford, Me., and has had
four children.
Dr. Timothy[6] (*Otis,*[5] *Eliak.,*[4] *Jona.,*[3] *Thos.,*[2] *Jn.*[1]) m. Betsey Howard; settled in Turner, Me.; had:
1 *Hon. Timothy O.*[7] of Green Bay, Wis.
2 *Rev. Zadoc,*[7] a Universalist preacher.

THE LANE FAMILY OF HAMPTON
(No. 40–iii)

Descended from **William**[1] of Boston, who, in 1651,
married, second, Mary, daughter of Thomas Brewer of
Roxbury. His sons, born in Boston, were:

1 *Samuel,*[2] b. 1651.
2 *John,*[2] b. 1653.
3 *Wm.,*[2] b. 1659.
4 *Ebenezer,*[2] b. 1666.
William[2] (*Wm.*[1]) m. Sarah (dau. of Thos.) Webster; rem. to Hampton, abt. 1686. He d. in Hampton 1749. She d. 1745. His sons were:
1 *John,*[3] b. 1685.
2 *Joshua,*[3] b. 1696.
3 *Sam'l,*[3] b. 1698.
4 *Thomas,*[3] b. 1701.
Dea. Joshua[3] (*Wm.,*[2] *Wm.*[1]) m. 1717, Bathsheba (dau. of Sam'l)
Robie; b. Hampton, Aug., 1696, and had sixteen children, thirteen of
whom lived to marry and have families. He had a farm, and also
worked at the trade of tanner and shoemaker in Hampton, where he
was killed by lightning, 14 June, 1766.
Samuel[4] (*Josh.,*[3] *Wm.,*[2] *Wm.*[1]), b. 6 Oct., 1718; m., 1st, Dec., 1741,
Mary James, and rem. to Stratham, where he became town-clerk;
many years deacon in the church and a very useful citizen. He had
eight children, who lived to adult age and had families. His 2nd wife
was Rachel (Parsons) wid. of Gideon Colcord. His eighth child Jabez,[5]
b. 1760; m. Eunice (dau. of Gideon and Rachel P.) Colcord and res. on

19

the homestead in Stratham. They had nine children, the sixth of whom, Charles, m. Hannah French, and was the father of Mary E. Lane, who m. Jacob Chapman.

(N. E. Hist. Gen. Register, xxvii, p. 176; and Lane Families by Jas. P. Lane.)

THE MARCH FAMILY OF GREENLAND.

Hugh[1] of Newbury married Judith ——; died 12 Dec., 1693, æ. 73.

Children:

1 *Geo.*[2] b. 1646; m., 1672, Mary (dau. of Jn.) Folsom of Exeter.
2 *Hugh*,[2] b. 1656; m. Sarah Moody; had: (1) Henry,[3] b. 1686. (2) Sam'l. (3) Daniel. (4) Trueman, b. 1705. And daughters.
3 *John*,[2] b. 1658.
4 *James*,[2] b. 11 Jan., 1664.

George[2] (*Hugh*[1]), b. 1646, d. 1699, and wife Mary (Folsom) had thirteen children, of whom

1 *John*[3] (2nd child), b. 1676; m. Mary Angia and had (1) Jn.,[4] b. 1702.
2 *Israel*[3] (6th child), b. 4 Apr., 1683; m. Mary (dau. of Joseph) Hall of Greenland; res., 1722, a doctor in Hampton; d. 1729 in Greenland or Portsmouth.
3 *Sergeant Hugh*,[3] was killed 9 Sept., 1695, by the Indians at Pemaquid, Me.

Major John[2] (*Hugh*[1]) m., Mar., 1679, Jemima True, and had:

1 *Joseph*,[3] b. May, 1687.
2 *John*,[3] b. Sept., 1690.
3 *Hugh*,[3] b. 1696.
4 *Mary*,[3].
5 *Abigail*.[3]
6 *Elizabeth*.[3]

Lt. James[2] (*Hugh*[1]) and wife Mary had:

1 *Benj.*,[3] b. Nov., 1690.
2 *Nath'l*,[3] b. 1693.

Dr. Israel March[3] (*Geo.*,[2] *Hugh*[1]), b. 1683, d. 1729, and wife Mary (Hall), had:

1 *Dr. Clement*,[4] b. 1707.
2 *Joseph*,[4] bapt. 1716.
3 *Nath'l*,[4] bapt. 1716.
4 *Paul*,[4] bapt.
5 *Mary*,[4] bapt.
6 *Elizabeth*,[4] bapt.

Dr. Clement March[4] (*Israel*,[3] *Geo.*,[2] *Hugh*,[1]), b. 1707, and his wife had, baptized in Greenland:

1 *Mary*,[5] bapt. 1733.

2 *Martha,*[5] bapt. 1733.
3 *Hannah,*[5] bapt. 1735.
4 *George,*[5] bapt. 1737.
5 *Abigail,*[5] bapt. 1740.
6 *Ann,*[5] bapt. 1743.
7 *Elizabeth,*[5] bapt. 1745.
8 *Thomas,*[5] bapt. 1747.
9 *Sarah,*[5] bapt. 1749.
10 *Clement,*[5] *Jr.*, bapt. 1751.

THE MEAD FAMILY.
(No. 5-x.)

Capt. John Mead,[1] mariner, of Stratham, married Susan (daughter of Jeremiah) Folsom, who was born about 1721, in the "Old brick garrison House'" in Newmarket. They resided in Newmarket, had five daughters and four sons.

Children :

1 *Benjamin,*[2] of Newmarket.
2 *John,*[2] settled in Deerfield.
3 *Levi,*[2] b. 1753; m. Susanna, b. 1767 (dau. of Ichabod) Hilton and had : (1) Levi H.[3] b. 1798; m. Catharine Berry of Pittsfield. (2) Elizabeth F. and others.
Jeremy[2] (*Jn.*[1]) b. 1760; m. Mary (dau. Geo.) Frost of Durham, and d. 1839. He res. on the homestead, in Newmarket. Their daughter
   1 *Margaret Frost,*[3] b. 1794; m., in 1820, Hon. Wm. Plummer, jr., of Epping, who d. Sept., 1854.

THE MOODY FAMILY.

William Moody[1] came from Wales to Ipswich, Mass., as early as 1633, and to Newbury in 1635, was a blacksmith, and the first in New England to shoe oxen. Others say he was a saddler, and from Ipswich in England. He had by wife Sarah :

1 *Joshua,*[2] b. 1632, H. Coll. 1653; ord., Portsmouth, 1671. He was imprisoned by Cranfield for refusing to do what his conscience forbade. He rem. to Boston and d. 1697.

2 *Caleb*,[2] b. 1637; m., 1st, Sarah Pierce; 2nd, Judith Bradbury;
    had children: (1) Daniel,[3] b. 1662. (2) Caleb, b. 1666. (3)
    Thomas, b. 1668. (4) Joshua, b. 1671. (5) **William**, b.
    1673. (6) Samuel, b. 1676; d. 1698.
3 *William*,[2] m., Nov., 1684, M. Sewall, and had (1) Dea. Sam'l,[3]
    b. 1689, who d. 1767, and others.
4 [Rev.] *Samuel*[2] [of York, Me.]? m., 1657, M. Cutting, and d.
    1675. Children: (1) William,[3] b. 1661. (2) Samuel, b.
    1671. (3) Cutting, b. 1674, who m. Judith Little, and had
    (*a*) Joseph,[4] b. 1701.

In 1725 there was a Philip Moody in Kingston, and afterward John Moody,[3] perhaps son of Samuel,[2] who had
sons David,[4] Dudley,[4] Rev. Gilman,[4] and John[4]. Capt.
John Moody[4] (*Jn.*,[3] *Sam'l*[2]), Nov., 1764, removed to Gilmanton, and had sons John, Elisha, David and Peter, and
four daughters. Several of this family were connected with
the Weeks family. (See No. 27–i.)

THE MOORE FAMILY OF STRATHAM.

Col. Jonathan Moore[1] a British officer, of Scotch
ancestry, settled in what is now Stratham and had sons:

1 *William*,[2] prominent among the citizens of **Exeter**, lived about
    two miles north from the village, on the east side of the
    river. He had: (1) Thomas,[3] (2) William, and others.
2 *Jonathan.*
Thomas[3] (*Wm.*,[2] *Jona.*[1]) m. 19 Dec., 1734, Rachel Sinkler and had:
    1 *Thomas*,[4] b. 13 Sept., 1735.
    2 *John*,[4] b. 1739.
    3 *William*,[4] b. 1741.
    4 *Rachel.*[4]
    5 *Agnes.*[4]
    6 *Ann.*[4]
    7 *Elizabeth*,[4] b. 1751.
    8 *John*,[4] b. 1 Jan., 1754.
William[3] (*Wm.*[2] *Jona*)[1] had sons:
    1 *William.*[4]
    2 *Dr. Coffin*,[4] b. 1739, m. in Greenland, 1760, Comfort (dau. of
    Dr. John) Weeks and practised in Georgetown, Me., in

Candia, N. H., etc. ; d. there 30 Oct., 1784, æ. 45, leaving four
sons and three daughters.

3 *Harvey.*[4]
4 *Peter.*[4]

William[4] (*Thos.,*[3] *Wm.,*[2] *Jona.*[1]), b. 1741, d. 1802, and his wife, Mary
(Piper]? had born in Stratham :

1 *Elizabeth,*[5] b. 30 Oct., 1766 ; m., 1st, Jas. Sanborn ; 2nd, Chase
Weeks.
2 *Lydda,*[5] b. 1768.
3 *Thomas,*[5] b. 7 Dec., 1770 ; m. Olive Tucker.
4 *Agnes,*[5] b. Oct., 1772.
5 *Jonathan,*[5] b. 26 May, 1774, in Stratham.

They removed to Sanbornton, and had :

6 *Mark,*[5] b. 1776.
7 *William,*[5] b. 1780.
8 *Mary,*[5] b. 1782.
9 *Rachel,*[5] b. 1787.

Dr. Coffin Moore[4] (*Wm.,*[3] *Wm.,*[2] *Jona.*[1]) b. 1739, d. 1784, and his w.
Comfort (Weeks) had :

1 *Coffin,*[5] who m. a dau. of Gen. E. Bucknam of Lancaster, and
settled, a farmer, in that place. His son (1) Dr. E. B.
Moore[6] practised in Epping many years, whence he removed
to Chelsea, Mass., where he d. in 1874.
2 *Dr. Jacob Bailey*[5] m. Polly Eaton, and settled in Andover,
where he d. early, leaving a son (Jacob B. Moore) who,
with Isaac Hill, edited the N. H. Patriot, and published in
1823 a gazetteer of New Hampshire, a work of great value
written by himself and John Farmer.

THE PERKINS FAMILIES OF HAMPTON.

Abraham[1] and wife Mary, born 1618, came from England and settled in Hampton. He was admitted freeman
in May, 1640. They had thirteen children :

Abraham[2] (*Abraham*[1]), b. 2 Sept., 1639, and was killed by Indians in
1677. He was the first male child born in Hampton, and Mary[2] was his
twin sister. He m. Eliz. Sleeper, and had :

1 *John,*[3] of Epping, the father of (1) Lt. Jonathan,[4] b. 1749, who
m. Eliz. Folsom and was distinguished in the Revolutionary
War.

James[2] (*Abraham*[1]), b. 1647 ; m., 1st, Mary——— ; 2nd, Leah Cox, and
had :

1 *Eliz.*[3] w. of Joseph Philbrook ; d. 1736.
2 *James,*[3] b. 1696 ; m. Sarah Nason ; d. 1755 in Kensington.
3 *Moses,*[3] b. 1698 ; m., 1st, Mary Marston ; 2nd, Hannah Nay ; d.
1765 ; had eleven children : (1) James,[4] b. 1731, of Hampton ; m., 1st, Abigail Knowles ; 2nd, Jane Moulton ; nine
children. (2) Samuel, b. 1733 ; d. in Deerfield, 1827, æ. 94.

(3) Sarah, m., 1755, Isaiah Lane; d. in Hampton Falls. (4) Elizabeth, m., 1760, Josiah Lane. (5) David. (6) Moses. (7) Jonathan. (8) Reuben, b. 1747.

Abigail[2] (*Abraham*[1]), b. 2 Apr., 1655; m., 1675, John Foulsham, then of Hampton.

James[3] (*Jas.*,[2] *Abraham*[1]) and wife Sarah had, b. in Kensington, sixteen children, of whom

    1 *Jonathan*,[4] b. 1733; had nine children; d. in the army in 1776.
    2 *Lydia*,[4] m., in 1755, Caleb (son of Josiah) Brown, and d. 1831.
    3 *Simon*,[4] b. 1745; m., 1769, Abigail Blake.

Isaac Perkins[1] [younger brother of Abraham]? born about 1612, was freeman 18 May, 1642, married Susanna ———, and had with others :

    1 *Isaac*.[2] bapt. 8 Dec., 1639, who was drowned.
    2 *Jacob*,[2] bapt. 24 May, 1640; m. 30 Dec., 1669, Mary Philbrook; had five children : (1) Isaac,[3] b. Dec., 1671. (2) Jacob, b. 1674. (3) Abigail. (4) Mary, b. 1678. (5) Benjamin, b. 12 Aug., 1693.
    3 *Benj.*,[2] b. 17 Feb., 1650.
    4 *Caleb*,[2]* m., 1677, Bethia (dau. of Jas.) Philbrick, and had : (1) Rhoda,[3] w. of Elias Philbrook who had seven children in Greenland. (2) Benjamin, b. 1680; d. in Hampton Falls, 1767.
    5 *Ebenezer*,[2] b. 1659; m. Mary ———; had : (1) Daniel,[3] b. 1685. (2) Jonathan, b. 1691.
    6 *Joseph*,[2] b. 1661.

In 1662 there was a William Perkins in Dover, born 1616, who died in Newmarket, 1732, æ. 116? His great grandson, Thomas, died in Wakefield, 1824, æ. 91.

THE PHILBROOK FAMILY.†
(No. 3–v.)

Thomas Philbrook[1] (or **Philbrick**) came from England about 1630; settled in Watertown, Mass. His children, most of them born in England, were :

---

*Caleb may have been son of Abraham Perkins.
†See Philbrick Genealogy by J. Chapman.

1 *James,*[2] a mariner, m. Ann Roberts; had nine children; lived in Hampton.

2 *John,*[2] in 1639, settled in Hampton; was drowned in 1657, had: (1) John,[3] b. about 1648. (2) Ephraim, b. 1656; and four daughters.

3 *Dea. Thomas,*[2] m. Ann Knapp; had seven children; d. 1700, æ. 76.

4 *Elizabeth.*[2]

5 *Hannah.*[2]

6 *Mary.*[2]

7 *Martha.*[2]

John[3] (*Jn.,*[2] *Thos.*[1]), and his wife Prudence Swaine had, b. in Greenland:

1 *John,*[4] b. 1658.

2 *Susanna,*[4] w. of Joshua Berry.

3 *Elias,*[4] b. 1680.

Elias[4] (*Jn.,*[3] *Jn.,*[2] *Thos.*[1]), m., 1st, Rhoda Perkins; 2nd, Penelope Philbrick; had seven children; d. 1747. His sons were:

1 *Elias,*[5] bapt. 1715.

2 *Caleb,*[5] b. 1705.

3 *Eliphalet.*[5]

4 *John,*[5] bapt. 1715; m. Judith Hardy of Exeter; had four children.

5 *Benjamin,*[5] bapt. 1718. He lived on one line between Greenland and Hampton.

Benjamin[5] (*Elias,*[4] *Jn.,*[3] *Jn.,*[2] *Thos.*[1]) m. Mary ———; had:

1 *Mary,*[6] bapt. 1746; m. Col. John Wingate of Wakefield.

2 *Eliphalet,*[6] bapt. 1748, of Wakefield.

3 *Penelope,*[6] b. 1751; w. of Job Chapman of Greenland, who had seven children that settled, about 1802, in Tamworth, where the father d. in 1837, and the mother in 1838.

PICKERING FAMILIES.

John,[1] of Ipswich, 1634, removed to Salem 1637, and died 1657; married Eliz.——, and had:

1 *John,*[2] b. about 1637; m., 1657, Alice Flint and had: (1) John,[3] b. Sept., 1658, the father of (1) Dea. Timothy,[4] b. Feb., 1702-3, who m. Mary Wingate and had: (a) Hon. Timothy,[5] b. 1745; H. Coll. 1763, where his sons and grandsons graduated.

2 *Jonathan,*[2] b. 1639.

And daughters.

Hon. **John**[1] of Portsmouth, speaker of the assembly, and the king's attorney general for New Hampshire, married Jan., 1665, Mary Stanyan and had eight children of whom :

1 *John*,[2] b. 1666, d. 1688, leaving sons: (1) John,[3] (2) Thomas, (3) Daniel.
2 *Thomas*,[2] a farmer with 500 acres in Newington, on the Great Bay; m. and had four sons and eight daughters: (1) Lt. James[3], b. abt. 1680. (2) Elizabeth, who m. Capt. John Brackett, b. 1700, of Greenland, and had : (*a*) Thos.[4] (Brackett), (*b*) Geo., (*c*) Sam'l, (*d*) John, and others. (3) Mehitable, w. of Lt. Sam'l Weeks of Greenland (No. 8).

From Lt. James descended the Pickering family in Newmarket.

THE ROLLINS FAMILY
(No. 16–ix ; 50–ii)

Descended from **James Rawlins**[2] of Dover, who came from England to Ipswich, Mass., in 1632, and settled at Bloody Point (then a part of Dover, now Newington), where he died in 1691. His sons were :

1 *Ichabod*,[2] who m., 1st, Mary Tibbets and was killed by the Indians; he had : (1) Jeremiah.[3]
2 *Thomas*,[2] of Exeter, b. 1641, m. Rachel Cox, and had: (1) Thomas,[3] of Stratham. (2) Moses, of Stratham; had nine children. (3) Joseph, of Stratham; had nine children. (4) Benjamin of Exeter, b. 1678; had eight children. (5) Aaron, of Newmarket, killed by Indians. (6) Samuel, of Newmarket, b. 1690; had nine children. (7) John, of Exeter, who rem. to Damariscotta, Me.; had fourteen children.
3 *Samuel*,[2] of Bloody Point, m. Rebecca Mors, and d. 1694, leaving : (1) Joseph.[3]
4 *James*,[2] of Dover, m. Deborah Peavey in 1717, and d. 1744, leaving sons: (1) Edward,[3] b. 1718. (2) Ichabod. (3) John.
5 *Joseph*,[2] res. in Newington; m. Sarah ———, and had : (1) Joseph,[3] bapt., 1728. (2) Samuel. (3) Noah.
Jeremiah[3] (*Ichabod*,[2] *James*[1]), m. Eliz. Ham, b. 1681, and res. in a part of Dover, now Somersworth, and d. 1768, leaving an only son :
1 Hon. *Ichabod*,[4] b. 1722; m., 1st, Abigail Wentworth; 2nd, Margaret (Cotton), wid. of Joseph Frost of Newcastle and had eight children.
Thomas[3] (*Thos.*,[2] *James*[1]) had :

1 *Caleb*,[4] of Stratham, who d. about 1785, leaving a widow Ruth; had eleven children.

Hon. Ichabod[4] (*Jere.*,[3] *Ichabod*,[2] *Jas.*[1]) b. 1722, d. 1800, of Rollinsford, and his wife Abigail (Wentworth) had four sons of whom:
    1 *John*,[5] b. 1745.
    2 *Ichabod*.[5]
    3 *James*.[5]
    4 *Daniel*,[5] b. 1759, m. 1789, Martha Weeks and had: (1) Ichabod,[6] (2) Wm. W., (3) Ann W.
(See Rollins Families by John R. Rollins, 1874.)

THE SANBORN FAMILY

Descended from two brothers, John[2] and William,[2] sons of **John**,[1] who married the daughter of Rev. Stephen Batchelder and died in England. His widow with her father and two sons came to America and settled in Hampton.

John[2] (*Jn.*[1]) b. about 1620; came to Hampton in 1638; m., 1st, Mary (dau. of Robert) Tucke; 2nd, widow Margaret Moulton (dau. of Robert Page). He was a useful citizen and held various town offices; d. in 1692. Children:
    1 *John*,[3] b. 1649; m., 1674, Judith Coffin; d. 1723. He had sons: (1) John,[4] b. 1683; m. Mehitable Fifield of Kingston. (2) Enoch, b. 1685; m., 1st, E. Dennet, 2nd, widow Godfrey. (3) Peter, m. A. Shaw; d. 1724. (4) Tristram, b. 1691; m. 1711, Margaret Taylor of Exeter and settled in Kingston; had five sons: (*a*) Peter,[5] b. 1713. (*b*) Abraham. (*c*) Tristram. (*d*) Jethro. (*e*) William, b. 1723; m., 1750, Mary Sleeper.
    2 *Richard*,[3] b. 1655; m., 1678, Ruth Moulton; had: (1) John,[4] m. Sarah Philbrook.
    3 *Joseph*,[3] b. 1656; m. Mary Gove; had: (1) Edward[4] and (2) Abraham.
    4 *Nathaniel*,[3] b. 1666.
    5 *Benj.*,[3] b. 1668.
    6 *Jonathan*,[3] b. 1672; m. Eliz. Sherburn; had eight children; d. 1741. His son (1) Samuel,[4] b. 1694. m. Mrs. Elizabeth Colcord, dau. of Peter Folsom, and res. in Kingston.

John[4] (*Rich.*,[3] *Jn.*,[2] *Jn.*[1]) had children:
    1 *Daniel*,[5] b. 1702; m. Cath. Rollins; had ten children. His sons: (1) Daniel,[6] b. 1731, (2) Thomas, (3) Moses, (4) Aaron, (5) Abijah, b. 1748; settled in Sanbornton.
    2 *Ebenezer*,[5] b. 1712, of Hampton; m. Ruth Sanborn; d. April, 1794. His sons were: (1) John,[6] b. 1736. (2) Josiah, b. 1738. (3) Benj., b. 1746. (4) Wm., b. 1753. (5) Eben, b. 1755; settled in Sanbornton, N. H.

20

3 *Benj.*,[5] of Newmarket.
4 *Richard.*[5]
5 *Elisha.*[5]
6 *John.*[5]
7 *James.*[5]
8 *Hannah*,[5] w. of S. Dudley; and five other daughters.

William[2] (*John*[1]) brother of John,[2] b. about 1622; m. Mary Moulton; settled in Hampton Falls; had five sons; d. Sept., 1692. Children:

  1 *William*,[3] b. 1650; m. Mary Marston; d. 1744; had: (1) John,[4] b. 6 Nov., 1680; m. Ruth Robie.
  2 *Josiah*,[3] had: (1) Wm.[4] b. 1682, father of (*a*) Ezekiel,[5] b. 1706, (*b*) Dan'l, (*c*) Wm., (*d*) Joshua.
  3 *Mephibosheth*,[3] b. 1663; d. 1749.
  4 *Stephen*,[3] b. 1671; m., 1693, Hannah, dau. of James Philbrick; had eleven children; d. 1750.

John[4] (*Wm.*,[3] *Wm.*,[2] *Jn.*[1]) b. 1680; d. 1767; had descendants in Sanbornton. His sons were:

  1 *Jeremiah*,[5] b. Feb., 1703; m. Lydia Dearborn; res. in Hampton. Two sons and five daughters.
  2 *Josiah*,[5] b. 19 Aug., 1707; m. T. Drake; res. in Exeter; had a son (1) Josiah, jr.[6]

THE SCAMMON FAMILY.

(BY R. M. SCAMMON OF STRATHAM, N. H.)

Richard Scammon[1] of Portsmouth, born about 1620, is supposed to have been the father of

  1 *Richard*,[2] m., in 1661, Prudence (dau. of Wm. and niece of Major) Waldron of Dover and had seven children b. [in Dover]? (1) Richard,[3] of Dover, who m. Eliz. Wakeley. (2) William, b. 29 Feb., 1664; and there were four daughters.
  2 *Ann*,[2] second wife of Major Waldron.
  3 *John*,[2] res. in Kittery, Me., and had a daughter: (1) Elizabeth,[2] who m. —— Atkins.
  4 *Elizabeth*,[2] m., 1st, Peter Lidgett; 2nd, Hon. John Saffin of Boston.
  5 *Humphrey*,[2] b. 1640; m. Eliz. (dau. of Dominicus) Jordan, and had b. in Saco, Me., five children: (1) Humphrey,[3] b. 10 May, 1677. (2) Elizabeth, m. Andrew Haley. (3) Mary m. —— Puddington. (4) Rebecca, m. —— Hastings. (5) Samuel, b. abt. 1689.

From this family descended Col. James and Hon. John F. Scammon of Saco, M. C., b. 1845–47, and Hon. Seth Scammon of Scarboro', Me.

William Scammon[3] (*Rich.*,[2] *Rich.*[1]) of Stratham, N. H.; m. Jan., 4, 1721, Rachel Thurber of Rehoboth, Mass., and had:

    1 *Richard*,[4] ⎰   twins,   ⎱ m. Elizabeth Weeks (see No. 8–
    2 *Samuel*,[4] ⎱ b. 17 Nov., 1722. ⎰ iii.)
    3 *James*,[4] b. 10 Nov., 1725.
    4 *Elizabeth*,[4] b. 13 Aug., 1728.
    5 *Barnabas*,[4] b. 27 Apr., 1733.

THE THOMPSON FAMILY.

(BY MARY P. THOMPSON OF DURHAM, N. H.)

Robert Thompson[1] was at Oyster river in 1707; married about 1722, Abigail Emerson; died in 1752. They had a daughter Abigail, who married Col. Timothy Emerson, and four sons

Samuel[2] (*Robert*[1]), bapt. Mar., 1723–4; m. Susannah Reynolds of Durham; d. Mar., 1755, leaving a dau. :
    1 *Hannah*.[3]

Robert[2] (*Robert*[1]), b. 8 July, 1726; m. Susannah, dau. of Jonathan Thompson; d. Jan. 12, 1805. He settled in Lee, where his descendants still live.

Judge Ebenezer[2] (*Robert*[1]), b. 5 Mar., 1737; m. Mary Torr, 22 May, 1758; d. 14 Aug., 1802. He settled on the homestead in Durham. studied medicine with Dr. Joseph Atkinson and became an able practitioner; but was called from his profession to serve his fellow citizens in some of the most important offices of the state. He twice declined a seat in Congress; was for many years judge of the Court of Common Pleas, and for a short time of the Superior Court. He had five children :

    1 *Sarah*,[3] m. James Leighton.
    2 *Ann*,[3] m. Rev. Curtis Coe.
    3 *Mary*,[3] m. Richard Pickering of Newington.
    4 *Col. Ebenezer*,[3] b. 12 July, 1762; d. in Portsmouth, 4 Feb., 1828. He m., 1st, Martha Burleigh; 2nd, Mary (dau. of Wm.) Weeks of Greenland; and 3rd, Elizabeth (dau. of Samuel) Hale of Portsmouth. Children by first wife : (1) John Burleigh,[4] b. 21 Nov., 1786; d. unmarried, 7 Oct., 1810. (2) Anne Hilton, b. 19 Sept., 1789; d. unmarried in 1812. (3) Mary, b. 24 Feb., 1792; m. Hon. Wm. Claggett of Portsmouth; d. 28 Mar., 1865. (4) Martha, b. 12 Dec., 1795; d. 8 May, 1796. Children by second wife : (5) Capt. Ebenezer, b. 5 Feb., 1798; m. Mary (dau. of Benjamin) Thompson; died in the night of 26–27 Jan., 1853. He left two sons : (*a*) Charles A. C.[5] who d. 1868, leaving two daus. and a son Dr. George E.,[6] of Boston. (*b*) Col. William H., of Chicago, who has three sons and one dau. (6) Capt. Jacob W., b. 2

Jan., 1802; m. Artemisia Rindge of Portsmouth; d. 7 July, 1864. He left four children, of whom two were sons (b. in Portsmouth) : (*a*) Jacob H., now one of the editors of the N. Y. Times. (*b*) Isaac R., now of Quincy. Mass. (7) Benjamin, b. 31 March, 1804; m. Lucinda J. Drew of Barrington, where he d. 23 Apr., 1875. He had six children, three of whom were volunteers in the late civil war: (*a*) Geo. W., mortally wounded at Morris Island, S. C., 28 July, 1863, and died the next day, aged 26. (*b*) Josiah, d. without issue, 16 March. 1882. (*c*) Jonathan, died in the soldiers' hospital at Washington, D. C., 30 Dec., 1862, aged 21. (8) Rev. Geo. Weeks, b. 29 Mar., 1807; m. Mary (dau. of Dea. Jno.) Wingate, and now resides in Stratham. *s. p.*

5 *Benjamin* (the youngest), b. Mar. 31, 1765; m. Mary Pickering of Newington; d. Jan. 21, 1838. He resided in Durham, where several of his descendants still live.

(See memoir of Judge Ebenezer Thompson.)

THE WIGGIN FAMILY

Descended from **Capt. Thomas Wiggin**[1] who came in 1631 to New Hampshire, agent for the proprietors of "The Upper Plantation," including Dover and parts of Stratham and Newington and Greenland, and returned to England in 1633. A number of colonists came with him on his second visit to New Hampshire. In 1645 he was deputy governor of Dover. He married Catherine—— had two sons and died about 1667.

Andrew[2] (*Thos.*[1]) b. abt. 1635; m. abt. 1659, Hannah (dau. of Gov. Simon and Ann Dudley) Bradstreet of Andover, Mass. He res. on the Squamscot patent, a tract three miles square lying mostly in what is now Stratham, and d. in 1710. In 1656 he gave the town of Exeter from the south end of his patent a tract of land one mile wide. In 1657 his farm was set off to the town of Hampton and so remained until 1692, when it was re-annexed to Exeter. In 1716, with additions it was incorporated as Stratham. His children were:

1 *Thomas*,[3] b. 5 Mar., 1662; m. Martha Denison of Ipswich; d. early.

2 *Simon*,[3] b. 17 Apr., 1664; m., 1st, ——; 2nd, Catherine (wid. of Robt. Tufton) Mason, and had two daus. and (3) Simon,[4] b. 12 Aug., 1701; d. 11 Aug., 1757; who had seven children.

3 *Hannah*,[3] b. 1666; m. S. Wentworth.

4 *Mary*,[3] b. 1668; m. Capt. Jeremy (son of Moses) Gilman, and

Thomas (Thomas) Wiggin did not m Ann
(Gov' Simon) Bradstreet. Gov' Simon had no
daughter Anna. Some of the older books made
the mistake of giving him a Hannah &
an Anna saying Hannah m Andrew
Wiggin & Anna m Mr. Wiggin. The
Hannah & Anna was the same person; and the Andrew & the Mr. Wiggin was the same person.

A. B. Wiggin, Historian
of the Wiggin Union.

had many descendants, among whom were Col. Samuel and
Col. David Gilman of Tamworth.

5 *Abigail*,[3] b. 1670; m. Wm. French of Stratham, and had children.
6 *Andrew*,[3] b. 6 Jan., 1672; m., 1st, —— ——; 2nd, Rachel Chase
(wid. of Jacob Freeze,) and d. Jan., 1756.
7 *Dorothy*,[3] m. ——Gilman.
8 *Bradstreet*,[3] b. 25 Mar., 1675–6; m. Ann Chase and had four
children of whom (1) Chase,[4] b. Oct., 1699, m. Martha
Weeks.
9 *Sarah*,[3] m. Wm. Moore of Stratham, and had: (1) William,
(2) Mary.
10 *Jonathan*,[3] d. 1738; had five daughters and a son: (1) Sarah,[4]
m. —— Hill. (2) Anna, m. J. Jewett. (3) Mary, m.
—— Perkins. (4) Hannah. (5) Lydia. (6) Andrew.

Thomas[2] (*Thos.*[1]), b. 1640; d. 1700, of [Exeter, then of] Dover; m.,
1st, Ann, dau. of Gov. Bradstreet; 2nd, Sarah (sister of Walter) Bare-
foot. Children:
1 *Catherine*,[3] m., 1st, Robt. Tufton; 2nd, Capt. Simon Wiggin.
2 *Sarah*,[3] w. of Henry Sherburne.
3 *Susanna*,[3] w. of —— Johnson.
4 *Thomas*,[3] of Sandy Point. who d. Mar., 1726–7, and had: (1)
John,[4] who m. —— Kennison and had six children: (*a*)
Elizabeth[5], (*b*) Deborah, (*c*) Sarah, (*d*) Budget, (*e*) Joseph,
(*f*) John. (2) Walter, b. [1701]? m., 1st, Mary (sister of
Andrew) Rawlins; 2nd, Deborah Neal; had eight children.
(3) Henry, of Exeter, had sons (*a*) Joseph, (*b*) Joshua and
(*c*) Nathaniel. (4) Andrew, of Newmarket; m. Eliz. Rawlins, had six children. (5) Tufton. m., 1st, Mary (dau.
of Richard) Calley; 2nd, Sarah Darling; seven children.
(6) Samuel, had eight children. (7) Capt Thomas, m.
Dec., 1719, Sarah Piper and had five sons: (*a*) Thomas of
Epping, (*b*) Andrew, (*c*) Eliphalet, (*d*) Jacob, (*e*) Nathaniel.

Hon. Andrew[3] (*Andrew*,[2] *Thos.*[1]), b. 1672; d. 1756; Judge of Probate
etc.; had:
1 *Hannah*,[4] w. of Josiah Burley.
2 *Martha*,[4] w. of —— Rust.
3 *Abigail*,[4] w. of —— Doe of Newmarket.
4 *Mary*,[4] w. of Theophilus Smith, Esq., of Exeter.
5 *Mercy*,[4] w. of —— Sherburne.
6 *Capt. Jonathan*,[4] b. 1740; m., 1st, 1761, Mary Little and had nine
children of whom (1) Edmund[5] and (2) Wm. H., settled in
Thomaston, Me.

Andrew, Esq.[4] (*Jona.*,[3] *Thos.*,[2] *Thos.*[1]), b. 27 Mar., 1719; m., 1st, Anna
Ross; 2nd, Mehitable Moody; 3rd, Sept., 1751, Mrs. Dorothy Sweat,
b. 1727, and d. 1774. His children were:
1 *Andrew*,[5] b. July, 1752; m., 1st, Mary Brackett of Greenland;
d. Jan., 1836. He m., 2nd, Mary (dau. of Hon. Paine) Wingate, and had: (1) Capt. Caleb,[6] (2) Andrew P.
2 *Dorothy*,[5] w. of Rev. James Miltemore.
3 *Levi*.[5]
4 *Caleb*.[5]
5 *Aaron*.[5]
6 *Mary*.[5]

THE WINGATE FAMILY OF NEW HAMPSHIRE*
(No. 5–vi)

Descended from **John**,[1] a planter at Hilton's Point, in 1658. His homestead on Dover Neck has remained in possession of his descendants to this day. An apple tree, planted by his hand, remained till the great storm in 1845. He married, first, Mary (dau. of Hate-evil) Nutter, and second, about 1676, Sarah (widow of Thos.) Canney, and died Dec., 1687. His children were:

1 *Anne*,[2] b. Feb., 1667.
2 *John*,[2] b. 1670, inherited the homestead, and d. 1715.
3 *Caleb*.[2]
4 *Moses*.[2]
5 *Mary*.[2]
6 *Joshua*.[2] b. 2 Feb., 1679; d. 9 Feb., 1769.
7 *Abigail*,[2] b. about 1685.

Capt. Joshua[2] (*John*[1]) m., at Newbury, 1702, Mary (dau. of Henry) Lunt, b. 1682, and rem. to Hampton and had eleven children:

1 *Rev. Paine*,[3] b. Sept., 1703.
2 *Sarah*,[3] b. 1705; m. 1727, Dr. Edmund Toppan, of Hampton, and d. 1801.
3 *Abigail*[3] ⎱ twins, b. 30 June, 1715.
4 *Anna*[3] ⎰
5 *Martha*,[3] b. 30 Mar., 1718; m. Dr. John Weeks of Greenland.
6 *Love*,[3] b. Apr. 1720; m. Rev. Nath'l Gookin of Hampton.
7 *Elizabeth*.[3]
8 *John*,[3] b. Jan., 1724–5; d. Sept. 4, 1812, unm.
9 *Mary*,[3] m. 1728, Dea. Timothy Pickering of Salem, Mass., had nine children; d. 1784.
10 *Joshua*.[3]
11 *Jane*,[3] m. 1732, Rev. Stephen Chase of Newcastle, and had seven children.

Rev. Paine[3] (*Joshua*,[2] *John*[1]) grad. Harv., 1723. He was ord. 15 June, 1726, pastor of the second church of Amesbury (now Merrimac), Mass., Dec. 12, 1727; he m. Mary Balch of Wenham, Mass., and d. 19 Feb., 1786, having served the same church sixty years. He had twelve children.

Rev. and Hon. Paine Wingate[4] (*Rev. Paine*,[3] *Joshua*,[2] *John*[1]) was the most famous of that family, b. 1739, grad. Harvard 1759; m. his cousin Eunice Pickering; was ord. 1763, over the First Cong. Ch., Hampton Falls, dismissed 1776, and rem. to a farm in Stratham. He was often chosen to the most important offices in the state. He d. 7 Mar., 1838, æ. nearly ninety-nine years.

---

* See Hist. Wingate family, Exeter, 1886.

ADDITIONS.

No. 22-iv, p. 26.

iv Marion (Weeks), b. 28 Feb., 1768; d. in Warren, N. H., 7 Aug., 1846; m. Richard Pillsbury, b. 5 Feb., 1763, was killed in 1800 at raising a barn. Children:
1 *Trustram* (Pillsbury), b. 19 Mar., 1787.
2 *John*, b. 11 Nov., 1788.
3 *Thomas*, b. 23 Mar., 1791.
4 *Daniel*, b. 28 Feb., 1793.
5 *Sally*, b. 5 Mar., 1797; m. Jonathan Clough, 14 Nov., 1816; d. 16 Oct., 1882. Children: (1) Amos (Clough) b. 6 Nov., 1818, a carpenter; m. Mary A. Pillsbury, and d. 14 Sep., 1872, *s. p.* (2) Mary, m. James M. Williams of Warren, farmer. Three children. (3) Eunice, b. 21 Nov. 1826; m 14 Oct., 1848, Joseph Clement, farmer of Warren. One child.
6 *Marian*, b. 12 May, 1799.

No. 22-viii, p. 26.

viii Betsey (Weeks), b. 11 Aug., 1775; d. in Bradford, Vt., 7 Apr., 1851; m. Thomas Pillsbury, farmer, b. 27 Nov., 1771; d. in Jan., 1835. Children:
1 *Joseph* (Pillsbury), b. 25 May, 1795, in Warren, farmer; m. Ruth Merrill of Wentworth, and d. of consumption in Bradford, Vt., 24 May, 1855. She d. in Lyndon, Vt., Feb., 1870. Their only child was (1) Dan Young (Pillsbury) a printer who d. in Bradford, Vt., 1863.
2 *Thomas*, b. 25 Sept., 1797, a farmer; m. Mary Osborn, b. 1799, of Bradford, Vt., and d. there 19 Oct., 1863. She d. 26 Nov., 1875. Children in Warren: (1) Betsey, b. 18 Nov., 1823; m. in 1841, M. Denison Farr of Bradford, farmer, b. 29 Nov., 1819. They have one daughter, a teacher, res. in Bradford, Vt. (2) Esther, b. 18 Nov., 1828; m. Hartwell L. Farr, b. Nov., 1821, farmer; res. in Bradford. Of eight children, only one, a son, is living. (7) Ezra, b. in Bradford, Vt., 3 Nov., 1838; d. 26 Dec. 1878; m. Olive T. Davis, 4 July, 1863, who d. 1865. (8) Hartwell, b. in Newbury, Vt., 29 Jun., 1841; m. Sarah Kelley of Bradford who d. of diphtheria, Jan., 1879. Five children, one living.
3 *Esther P.*, b. 19 Nov., 1799; d. Dec., 1842. She m. Timothy Ladd, farmer of Piermont, N. H., b. 19 Sept., 1786, who d. 12 June, 1870. Child: (1) Emeline, b. 11 May, 1822; m. Jn. Hartwell, farmer of Piermont, N. H., b. 23 Oct., 1817. Four children.
4 *Richard*, b. 3 May, 1803; resided on the homestead in Warren, and died unmarried in 1831.

No. 29-i, p. 36.

To 9 *Albert Gallatin* (Weeks) add his children : (1) Rebecca[7], b. ; d. when a child. (2) Arthur, b. abt. 1850; d. in childhood. (3) Albion Albert, b. in Barnstead, 31 May, 1852, printer; m. in Chicago, 11 Jan., 1888, Teresa E. O'Donnell, b. in South Hampton, Eng., Aug., 1858. Child: a son, b. 9 Nov., 1888.

ERRATA.

On page 15 (No. 12-v) for Mary (Weeks) read Mary (Chapman)·
On page 15 (No. 12-vii) for Joseph Weeks, read Joseph Chapman.
On page 33, first line, for Stafford read Strafford, Vt.
On page 36, 22nd line, for North Hampton read New Hampton.
On page 51 (No. 40-ii) for Brownfield read Bloomfield, Me.

INDEX NO. I.

NAMES OF OTHERS CONNECTED WITH THE WEEKS FAMILY.

(The figures refer to the number of the family; the Roman numerals to the order of names in the family.)

———

INDEX NO. II.

TO CHRISTIAN NAMES OF PERSONS NAMED WEEKS.

(The figures refer to the number of the family, the Roman numerals to the order of names in the family.)

A. Dana, 100, v.
A. Herbert, 84, iv.
Abbie A., 76, vi.
Abbie L., 110, ii.
Abby, 31, ix.
Abby E., 105, vi.
Abel M., 104, iv.
Abiel N., 82, ix.
Abigail, 62a, ii.
Abigail,⁴ 7, vi.
Abi.,⁵ 20, ii; 22, ii; 41, iv.
Abi.,⁶ 18, iv; 42, ii; 58, ii; 105, iv.
Abi., 43, viii.
Abi.,⁷ 62a, ii; 62a, ix; 79, vii.
Abi. M., 31, vi.
Abi. P., 47, vi.
Abraham,³ 107, iii.
Abram,⁵ 34, i.
Abraham W., 68, v.
Adalaide, 46, iv.
Adaline B., 41a, iv.
Adaline E., 71, v; 96, i.
Addie, 78, i.
Adele, 92, iv.
Agnes C., 55a, v.
Albe C., 91, iv; 104, iii.
Albert, 42, i.
Albert, 41b, v; 59c, vii; 71, iv.
Albert G., 29, i.
Albert H., 56, i.
Albert J., 105, ii.
Albert M., 29, i; 64, v.
Albert S., 68, viii.
Albert V., 72, i.
Albion, 67, v; 102, vii.
Alden, 42, i.
Alexander B., 48, ii.
Alfred, 41a, v.
Alfred D., 78, i.

Algernon S., 72, iii.
Alice,⁶ 109, i; 109. vi.
Alice C., 29, i; 105, ii.
Alice E., 84, iv.
Alice H., 41, i.
Alice J., 100, iv.
Almeda, 31, i; 47, viii.
Almira. 105, i.
Almira G., 89, ix.
Almira W., 65, iv.
Almon F., 71, ii.
Alonzo, 92, v.
Alonzo P., 73, ii.
Alpheus, 37, ii.
Alpheus E., 54, iv.
Alphonso M., 73, ii.
Alphonso R., 81, ii.
Alvah, 39a, iv.
Alvah T., 69c, iii.
Alvin J., 103, iv.
Alvira, 67, vii,
Ambrose, 45, iv.
Amanda, 48, i; 76, iii.
Amasa, 69e, iii.
Andrew, 94, vi.
Andrew C., 51, xi.
Andrew J., 33, iii; 69d, iii; 92, ix.
Angeline, 75, vii.
Angella, G., 81, iv.
Ann, 55a, iii.
Ann L., 41, i.
Ann L., 29, i.
Ann P., 57, v.
Ann S., 57, ii.
Anna⁵, 22, iii; 27, xiii.
Anna,⁷ 58, iii; 65, i; 74, v; 76, ii.
Anna,⁸ 110, i.
Anna B., 46, v.
Anna F., 62, ii; 69c, ix.

174   INDEX NO. II.

23

INDEX NO. III.

NAMES OF PLACES, PERSONS, FAMILIES, ETC.

www.ingramcontent.com/pod-product-compliance
Lightning Source LLC
Chambersburg PA
CBHW030825270326
41928CB00007B/897